A Primer on Ethnomethodology

A Primer on Ethnomethodology

Kenneth Leiter

OXFORD UNIVERSITY PRESS
New York   1980   Oxford

Copyright © 1980 by Oxford University Press, Inc.

Library of Congress Cataloging in Publication Data

Leiter, Kenneth
  A primer on ethnomethodology.

  Bibliography: p.
  Includes index.
  1. Sociology—Methodology. I. Title.
HM24.L427   301'.01'8   79-12499
ISBN 0-19-502628-4
ISBN 0-19-502629-2 pbk.

Printed in the United States of America

Preface

Those who have tried to introduce themselves to ethnomethodology via Garfinkel's *Studies in Ethnomethodology* and Cicourel's *Cognitive Sociology* have come away from the experience thinking "there must be an easier way to find out what ethnomethodology is all about." As graduate students, my colleagues and I achieved an interpretation by playing the works of Schutz (1962; 1964), Garfinkel (1967), and Cicourel (1973) off against each other. By interpreting each in light of the other, we produced an interpretation that "passed" for ethnomethodology.

Until the last five years, there has been no easier way. Since then, however, there have appeared several fine efforts to ease the rite of passage. Paul Filmer (1973) and his colleagues at Goldsmiths College, London, have written an excellent text that states the ethnomethodological argument and a critique of contemporary sociology. Mehan and Wood's *Reality of Ethnomethodology* (1975) also persuasively states the ethnomethodological perspective. Roy Turner's (1974) *Ethnomethodology* is an excellent collection of studies using this perspective. On the empirical side of the literature are five works essential for the beginner: *Social Organization of Juvenile Justice* (Cicourel, 1968); *Judging Delinquents* (Emerson, 1969); *Theory and Method in a Study of Argentine Fertility* (Cicourel, 1974); *Language Use and School Performance* (Cicourel et al., 1974); and *Language and Social Reality: The Case of Telling the Convict Code* (Wieder, 1974).

After praising the recent literature, it might seem odd to be offering yet another text. This literature can be roughly divided into texts and studies. Taken by themselves, they seem to have done little to reduce sociologists' anxiety over ethnomethodology, nor have they made it any less mysterious. What is needed is a primer that will serve as a bridge between research and texts. Such a primer would provide the reader with a scheme of interpretation that would explicitly link the perspective with research. That is the aim of this book. The plan of the book is as follows.

The first chapter establishes ethnomethodology as the study of commonsense knowledge. To do this, the three phenomena glossed by the term are defined and their interrelationship described. The three phenomena are: the stock of knowledge at hand, the practices of commonsense reasoning, and the commonsense reality or attitude of everyday life. Ethnomethodology is chiefly the study of how the typifications of the stock of knowledge are brought into play through the use of the practices of commonsense reasoning to create and preserve a sense of social reality. By studying common sense in this manner, ethnomethodologists have rendered their perspective distinctive from, but not competitive with, sociology. Where sociology studies the causes of social action, ethnomethodology is the study of how members of society perceive behavior as social action.

Chapter II presents the case for studying commonsense knowledge. The basic argument is that the social construction of social reality forms the basis for the study of commonsense knowledge. The ethnomethodological version of this concept is presented, along with its implications. The chapter closes with a discussion of the importance of studying commonsense knowledge. The next chapter (III) is a description of the intellectual roots of ethnomethodology. The perspective has two major sources: the phenomenology of Husserl and Schutz and Chomsky's generative transformational grammar. Phenomenology provides the basic topics of study as well as a rationale for studying them. Chomsky's linguistics is the source of the generative model used by ethnomethodologists. In addition, generative transformational grammar provides empirical evidence suggesting the use of interpretive procedures, and is used as a "stalking horse" for criticizing normative approaches to social behavior.

The examination of commonsense knowledge continues in Chapter IV, where the scense of social structure is discussed. The idea of the sense of social structure is one of the most misunderstood in ethnomethodology. It is the manner in which members of society experience and use everyday reality. The sense of social structure refers to the face that members perceive the social world as a naturalistic entity independent of perception. The factual properties of social reality are described and illustrated with examples from the literature. The "use" of the facticity of social reality by sociologists and lay members of society is also described. For ethnomethodologists, the sense of social structure is an ongoing product through the use of methods of observing and reporting on society.

The ongoing nature of the product is the topic of Chapter V. Indexicality and reflexivity are two essential properties of behavior and talk; they resist all attempts to eliminate them. As a result, interpretation of objects and events becomes essential as well. Because indexicality and reflexivity are properties of objects and events, the construction of social reality, along with its factual character, is a continuous production. Indexicality and reflexivity are in addition to the sense of social structure the least understood concepts in ethnomethodology. Some of the misunderstandings are discussed and clarified through research examples.

Chapter VI begins with a description of the problem of social order as formulated from within the ethnomethodological perspective. While ethnomethodologists pursue different topics, they can all be related to the problem of social order. The topics discussed include accounts and accounting practices; the use of rules, motives, and social types as members' methods of understanding behavior; and members' methods of conversational sequencing. A common thread joins these topics together: the study of commonsense knowledge.

I feel it is only appropriate to conclude this preface by acknowledging my intellectual debt to the following people who helped me throughout the writing of this book. Needless to say they are not responsible for its content but I would be remiss if I did not express my thanks.

Don Zimmerman, David Roth, Larry Wieder, Dick Cushman, and David Dickens who read the preliminary drafts, made many helpful suggestions and raised new issues throughout the writing. Howard Daudistil, Bill Sanders, Steve Klineberg, and the Department of Sociology at Rice University who supplied encouragement and funds for typing the manuscript.

Aaron Cicourel, Harold Garfinkel, Don Zimmerman, Larry Wieder, and the late Alfred Schutz whose work forms the bedrock of the ethnomethodological perspective.

As a graduate student I was fortunate to be associated with the following people who influenced my interpretation of ethnomethodology in ways I cannot begin to describe: Hugh Mehan, Melvin Pollner, Bob Boese, Kenneth Jennings, Robert MacKay and Warren and Judy Handel. They too were my teachers.

This book is for my Father and Mother: Jack and Nettie Leiter.

Dallas   K.C.W.L.
April 1979

Contents

A Primer on Ethnomethodology

I

Common Sense:
Sociology and Ethnomethodology

A curious fact becomes apparent if you look at the first paragraph—it may occur in the third paragraph—of reportedly revolutionary treatises back to the pre-Socratics and extending up to at least Freud. You find that they all begin by saying something like this: "About the things I am going to talk about, people think they know but they don't. Furthermore, if you tell them it doesn't change anything. They still walk around like they know although they are walking in a dream world." Darwin begins this way, Freud begins in a similar way. What we are interested in is, what is it that people seem to know and use—

HARVEY SACKS
Purdue Symposium on Ethnomethodology

Sacks' statement is an unusual one for a social scientist to make. At first glance, it seems to imply an across-the-board criticism of scientific theories in general. On closer inspection, however, we see that this is not what he is doing at all. He is highlighting the differences in the approaches of the standard sociological and ethnomethodological viewpoints toward social phenomena. Contrary to the established scientific view represented by Darwin and Freud, ethnomethodology does not begin with the assertion that what people know and use is wrong. Rather, it begins by proposing that we need to study what people know and use, commonsense knowledge, because the use of such knowledge by the members of a society produces the sociological phenomena studied by sociologists.

Ethnomethodology is thus sometimes referred to as the study of commonsense knowledge. This has been taken to mean that, in contrast to sociology, ethnomethodology seeks to prove the validity of common assertions or that ethnomethodology advocates the use of commonsense methods of observation. Both misconceptions are products of thinking of commonsense knowledge as just a set of maxims, social types, and rules of thumb that are vague, contradictory, and self-serving. Commonsense knowledge *is* that, to be sure, but it is also *more* than that. Commonsense knowledge also includes practices of commonsense reasoning and the cognitive style through which we experience the social world as a factual object. The works of Alfred Schutz and Harold Garfinkel provide ethnomethodologists with these additional areas of commonsense knowledge. Out of their works emerges the ethnomethodological definition of commonsense knowledge.

Commonsense Knowledge: Three Phenomena

ALFRED SCHUTZ

Alfred Schutz was a phenomenologist who spent most of his life (when he was not being a banker, lawyer, and economist) constructing a phenomenological basis for sociology. He was a student of Husserl and was engaged in carrying out Husserl's application of phenomenology to the social sciences. Husserl's part in this project is discussed in the next chapter. Schutz reasoned that since social action was based on how people perceived social reality, sociology needed a phenomenological basis to study social reality itself. The major part of Schutz's program was the study of how members of society construct social reality, along with its factual properties. To quote Schutz:

> . . . the answer to the question "What does this social world mean for me the observer?" requires as a prerequisite the answering of the quite different questions "What does the social world mean for the observed actor within this world and what did he mean by his acting within it?" In putting our question thus we no longer

naively accept the social world and its current idealizations as ready-
made and meaningful beyond question but we undertake to study
the process of idealization and formulizing as such, the genesis of
the meaning which social phenomena have for us as well as for
actors, the mechanism of the activity by which human beings understand one another and themselves (Schutz, 1964:7).

The social world to which Schutz refers is the commonsense world
of objects and events which we inhabit during most of our waking
hours. The object of his work, which is also the aim of ethnomethodology in general, is to study the processes of sense making (idealizing and formulizing) that members of society, including sociologists, use to construct the social world and its factual properties (its
sense of being ready-made and independent of perception). Schutz
refers to three phenomena in his discussion of commonsense knowledge: the stock of knowledge at hand, the natural attitude of everyday life (the sense of social structure), and the practices of commonsense reasoning.

The Stock of Knowledge at Hand. The stock of knowledge at
hand consists of recipes, rules of thumb, social types, maxims, and
definitions. Recipes include general ways of going about doing
things. If I want to find a used alto saxophone, there are several
recipes I could use. I could call music stores, put a notice on the
bulletin board of a college music department, or go to (or call)
pawnshops in town. For any project, there are many practical recipes
for carrying it out. Some of these are informed by maxims. For example, the last recipe of finding a saxophone in a pawnshop is informed by the maxim that saxophone players are always pawning
their instruments. Another maxim or rule of thumb would be that
pawnshops do not accept checks. So, before I go to the pawnshop, I
should make sure that I have enough cash to purchase the sax.

The stock of knowledge also consists of social types or idealizations
of people, objects, and events that serve as points of inference and
action. Every occupation, for example, has its stock of types of people. Teachers have types of students: behavior problems, immature
students, mature students, independent workers, average students,

bright students, slow students, and poor students. For each of these social types, there are definitions that are invoked by those who use them.

The stock of knowledge at hand possesses the following six properties. First, the stock of knowledge is socially derived:

> Only a very small part of my knowledge originates within my personal experience. The greater part is socially derived, handed down to me by my friends, my parents, my teachers and teachers of my teachers (Schutz, 1964:13).

Second, the stock of knowledge is socially distributed. That is, what each person knows is different from the next; we are all experts and novices depending on the subject. Third, the social distribution of knowledge *is itself* part of the stock of knowledge at hand. Thus, if one is faced with a problem that lies outside one's expertise, one can call on an expert. Fourth, the stock of knowledge is built upon and expressed in everyday language. Indeed, everyday language is the medium of the stock of knowledge at hand. To quote Schutz: (1962:14):

> The typifying medium *par excellence* by which socially derived knowledge is transmitted is the vocabulary and the syntax of everyday language. The vernacular of everyday life is primarily a language of named things and events and any name includes a typification and generalization referring to the relevant system prevailing in the linguistic in-group which found the named thing significant enough to provide a separate term for it. The pre-scientific vernacular can be interpreted as a treasure house of ready-made preconstituted types and characteristics, all socially derived and carrying along an open horizon of unexplored content (1962:14).

Fifth, the typifications, maxims, rules of thumb, and definitions all have an "open horizon of meaning." In other words, they are potentially equivocal, lending themselves to multiple meanings. The bits and pieces of the stock of knowledge derive their meaning (and acquire different meanings) as they are used in different contexts. This is an important property because much of the contradictory character of the stock of knowledge comes from stripping its contents of their situated meanings (Mehan and Wood, 1975). Sociologists, for example, use the contradictory character of commonsense maxims as a negative aspect. They typically point out that in explaining marriage one can use two quite contradictory maxims: opposites attract, and birds of a feather flock together. What one fails to realize is that the meaning of each maxim is determined by the particular cases to which it applies. Therefore, one can use the first maxim to refer to one couple and the second maxim to refer to another couple without being contradictory.

Sixth, the stock of knowledge is not a neatly and logically ordered storehouse of information and typifications. It is not ordered by formal logic because the specific sense of its elements is context dependent. The stock of knowledge is heterogeneous. The contents of the stock of knowledge vary in their degree of clarity and specificity. To quote Schutz:

> In his daily life the healthy, adult and wide-awake human being (we are not speaking of others) has this knowledge, so to speak, automatically at hand. From heritage and education, from the manifold influences of tradition, habits, his own previous reflection, his store of experiences is built up. It embraces the most heterogeneous kinds of knowledge in a very incoherent and confused state. Clear and distinct experiences are intermingled with vague conjectures; suppositions and prejudices cross well-known evidences; motives, means and ends, as well as causes and effects, are strung together without clear understanding of their real connections. There are everywhere gaps, intermissions, discontinuities . . . the rules we apply are rule of thumb and their validity has never been verified . . . (1964:72–73).

The Natural Attitude of Everyday Life. The second phenomenon glossed by the term *commonsense knowledge* is our knowledge and experience of the social world as a factual environment. Schutz constructed a characterization of the social world as it is encountered by people living in it. He termed his characterization the *natural attitude of everyday life.* All members of society encounter a social world with the following six properties.

First, the world is experienced by people as one that is historically organized prior to their arrival on the scene and as one that will continue to exist when they have left it. The social world is experienced as having a past, present, and future.

> This world existed before our birth, experienced and interpreted by others, our predecessors, as an organized world. Now it is given to our experience and interpretation (Schutz, 1962:7).

Second, people experience the world as an intersubjective world. That is, people reciprocally assume that the social world is not just their private world but is "out there" for all members of society to see.

> The world of everyday life into which we are born is from the outset an intersubjective world. This implies on the one hand that this world is not my private one but common to all of us; on the other hand, that within this world there exist fellow men with whom I am connected by manifold social relationships (Schutz, 1962:218).

Third, people accept the world and its objects as they are given through experience. The world, as a fact, is taken for granted, and although particular doubts are from time to time entertained, they are never global doubts of a solipsistic nature.

> It is characteristic of the natural attitude that it takes the world and its objects for granted until counter proof imposes itself. As long as the once established scheme of reference, the system of our and other people's warranted experiences works, as long as the actions and operations performed under its guidance yield the desired results, we trust these experiences. We are not interested in finding out whether this world really exists or whether it is merely a coherent system of consistent appearances. We have no reason to cast doubt upon our warranted experiences which so we believe give us things as they really are (Schutz, 1962:228).

This taking for granted of one's experiences until further notice has the following consequences for the character of people's knowledge of the social world:

This socialized structure gives this kind of knowledge an objective and anonymous character; it is conceived as being independent of my personal biographical circumstances (Schutz, 1962:75).

It is this characteristic of the natural attitude that defines that aspect of people's sense of social structure described as "experiencing the world as an actual or potentially determinate world for all practical purposes." I am not saying that the world is experienced by people as always determinate; rather, that doubts may and do arise, but are resolved in such a way as to sustain the factual properties of the world (Pollner, 1969; Schutz, 1962). As Gurwitsch (1966:xii) proposes:

Such questions, doubts, corrections, however, always concern details within the world, particular mundane existents, and never the world as such and as a whole.

Fourth, people address the world and its objects pragmatically. People are interested only in those features of the world that are relevant to the project of the moment. The world is a stage that must be mastered and dealt with. It is not just something to be studied merely for the pleasure of study.

The natural attitude of everyday life is treated by ethnomethodologists as a specification of people's sense of social structure. That is, the natural attitude is a description of the structure of the social world as it is encountered and experienced by members of society. The natural attitude is a specification of what ethnomethodologists mean by a factual, determinate world. This facticity is the bedrock upon which the stock of knowledge at hand rests. That is to say, commonsense knowledge in the form of the stock of knowledge at hand is gained by viewing social reality as factual, by assuming the natural attitude of everyday life. The stock of knowledge at hand is applied to "concrete situations." The natural attitude of everyday life is a description of the way people view situations as "concrete"—i.e., factual. In Chapter IV we shall see how the natural attitude forms the basis for what Cicourel (1973) calls the members' "sense of social structure," the major topic of study for ethnomethodology.

Practices of Commonsense Reasoning. The third phenomenon commonsense knowledge refers to is the practices of commonsense reasoning. From the perspective of the wide-awake adult living in the social world, the facticity of that world is taken for granted. While there are disagreements as to what the specific facts are, there is agreement as to the existence of facts. For the scientist working from within Schutz's phenomenological sociology, however, the facticity of social reality is viewed as a product of the members' use of commonsense reasoning. The problem of intersubjectivity is the vehicle whereby Schutz introduces the third phenomenon glossed by the term *commonsense knowledge:* the practices of commonsense reasoning.

Schutz's version of the problem of intersubjectivity is couched in a dilemma of sorts. While social reality is experienced from one's own spatial-temporal niche, one also experiences the social world as a world known in common rather than as a private world. The solution Schutz proposes lies in the use of the practices of commonsense reasoning. Schutz (1962:11–12) suggests that

> Common sense thinking overcomes the difference in individual differences resulting from these factors by two basic idealizations: (1) the idealization of the interchangeability of standpoints: I take it for granted, and assume my fellow man does the same, that if I change places with him so that his "here" becomes mine I will be at the same distance from things and see them with the same typicality that he does. (2) The idealization of the congruency of the system of relevances: Until counter evidence I take it for granted— and assume my fellow man does the same—that the different perspectives originating in our unique biographical situations are irrelevant for the purpose at hand. . . .

Here, Schutz is making two points. First, the problem of intersubjectivity is "solved" through the use of commonsense reasoning; note that he is *not* invoking the existence of common cognitive consensus as a solution. Second, he names two practices of commonsense reasoning that people use to create and sustain the factual character of the social world. In Chapter VI we will examine in detail how

Cicourel (1973) and Garfinkel (1967) expand upon Schutz's initial formulation to provide additional practices and enlarge their significance.

The significance of the practices of commonsense reasoning lies in their relation to the natural attitude and the stock of knowledge at hand. It is through the use of commonsense reasoning that people create and sustain the sense of social reality as a factual environment. The practices of commonsense reasoning are a set of methods for turning our personal experience into experience of an objective reality. These practices are also used to decide when to use selected bits and pieces of the stock of knowledge at hand. The contents of the stock of knowledge do not contain instructions concerning when and how they are to be used. They possess an "open structure" which necessitates decisions of appropriateness by members of society (Cicourel, 1973:48–73). *Appropriateness* means two things. First, it refers to the articulation between a selected piece of the stock of knowledge and the situation. Members of society must decide which pieces of the stock of knowledge to use on a specific occasion. Second, because the meaning of the recipes, maxims, rules, and typifications is context dependent, appropriateness also refers to the construction of meaning. That is to say, people use the practices of commonsense reasoning to decide both the situated use and the meaning of the contents of the stock of knowledge at hand.

HAROLD GARFINKEL

In one of his early papers, Garfinkel (1967:262–283) makes the point that social interaction is a product of commonsense knowledge. To make this point, he (drawing on the work of Schutz) broadens the phenomenon of commonsense knowledge to include the natural attitude and commonsense reasoning. The starting point of Garfinkel's argument is a discussion of scientific rationality. Drawing on the work of Schutz, Garfinkel presents the following scientific rationalities:

1. In arriving at the steps for solving a problem, one must use methods that conform to the rules of formal logic and scientific procedure. In short, the scientist operating within the realm of scientific theory must use rules of formal logic to construct the steps for solving a problem.

2. One must use language that is "semantically clear and distinct." The meanings of terms one uses should be unequivocal. In other words, their meaning should remain stable from one situation to another.

3. The insistence on semantic clarity and distinctness is maintained without pragmatic justification. It is an end in itself rather than a means to an end.

4. The definition of the situation must contain facts that have been confirmed by science. Matters of fact must be factual according to scientific knowledge and procedures. Thus, the scientist must base his actions on facts confirmed by science.

These four scientific rationalities form the basis of formal logic used in scientific theorizing. They belong exclusively to that domain. They are not part of commonsense thinking. This is because they are anchored in the reality of scientific theorizing rather than the natural attitude of everyday life. As a result, they are not part of everyday social interaction. In fact, Garfinkel contends that the use of scientific rationalities as a basis for social interaction would make everyday interaction problematic. Trying to hold other parties engaged in social interaction to the scientific rationalities would produce trouble rather than smooth-flowing interaction.

Garfinkel (1967:33–76) provides an excellent illustration of this point in his paper on the routine grounds of everyday life. He reports a demonstration in which students were instructed to engage someone in a conversation and insist on following the scientific rationality of semantic clarity and distinctness. Below are three examples of the results.

1. On Friday night my husband and I were watching television. My husband remarked that he was tired. I asked, "how are you tired? Physically, mentally or just bored?"

S: I don't know, I guess physically mainly.

E: You mean that your muscles ache or your bones?

S: I guess so. Don't be so technical.
   (after more watching)

S: All these old movies have the same kind of old iron bedstead in them.

E: What do you mean? Do you mean all old movies or some of them or just the ones you've seen?

S: What's the matter with you? You know what I mean.

E: I wish you would be more specific.

S: You know what I mean. Drop dead.

2. The victim waved his hand cheerily.

S: How are you?

E: How am I with regard to what? My health? My finances, my school work, my peace of mind, my . . . ?

S: (Red in the face and suddenly out of control) Look, I was just trying to be polite. Frankly, I don't give a damn how you are.

3. My friend and I were talking about a man whose overbearing attitude annoyed us. My friend expressed his feelings.

S: I'm sick of him.

E: Would you explain what's wrong with you, that you are sick?

S: Are you kidding me? You know what I mean.

E: Please explain your ailment.

S: (He listened to me with a puzzled look). What came over you? We never talk this way do we?
   (Garfinkel, 1967:42–44)

These demonstrations suggest "that the scientific rationalities are neither properties nor sanctionable ideals of choices exercised within the affairs governed by the presuppositions of everyday life" (Garfinkel, 1967:277). Attempts to use scientific rationalities as rules of social interaction are resisted and, most important, *render social interaction problematic*. Scientific rationalities have this effect because they are anchored in the reality of scientific theorizing—not the reality of everyday life. Everyday life has its own commonsense rationalities that form the basis for everyday interaction—which, for this very reason, need to be turned into a topic of respectable sociological study.

Four important policies emerge from Garfinkel's paper. First, commonsense knowledge is not just an inferior version of scientific knowledge. It is substantively different in its rationalities and basic attitudes. Second, commonsense includes the commonsense rationalities and the natural attitudes of everyday life. Third, commonsense knowledge is an important part of social interaction. It does not hinder social interaction; rather, social interaction is produced through the use of commonsense rationalities. Fourth, Garfinkel does not state what these rationalities are. The implication here is that they must be discovered through the study of social interaction.

Ethnomethodology
as Distinctive from Sociology

The basic argument in this chapter is that the distinctive character of ethnomethodology is the result of its approach to commonsense knowledge. Commonsense knowledge is not treated as just a collection of beliefs, sentiments, and rules of thumb. In addition to the stock of knowledge at hand, commonsense knowledge for the ethnomethodologist is the study of the use of the practices of commonsense reasoning to create and sustain the factual character of the social world and to employ the contents of the stock of knowledge in concrete situations, where the concreteness of the situation is a product of their use as well. To see how this approach gives ethnomethodology its distinctive character, we must examine how commonsense knowledge is typically treated in sociology.

COMMON SENSE: THE RESIDUAL CATEGORY

It is my contention that commonsense knowledge forms a residual category for conventional sociology. *Residual categories* are phenomena which fall outside of a theory and consequently are not studied by the theorist. As Parsons (1936:17–18) explains, a theory is like a spotlight that identifies the proper topic of study. The residual categories are the darkness around the illuminated spot. They lie outside the area defined by the spotlight and are not deemed worthy of study. By treating commonsense knowledge as the stock of knowledge at hand, and as inferior to scientific knowledge, sociologists have turned all three phenomena glossed by the term *commonsense knowledge* into a residual category.

The residual status of the stock of knowledge, the natural attitude, and commonsense reasoning shows up in introductory treatises and in the substantive work of sociologists. In introductory texts on sociology, commonsense knowledge is restricted to the stock of knowledge at hand, which is portrayed as inferior to scientific knowledge. Consider the following example from a contemporary textbook, *Sociology Today* (Stark et al., 1973). Under the heading "Sociology and Common Sense," the reader is told that sociology studies people and that students think they know a lot about people through commonsense knowledge. The authors then present the following examples of such knowledge:

> For example, there are some findings from sociological research that might confirm the common-sense notions you already have about the world:
>
> Wife slapping and marital violence occur most commonly among the poor, uneducated and Black.
>
> Children from low income homes are more likely to be delinquents than children from upper income homes.
>
> Revolutions are more likely to occur when living conditions continue to be very bad than when conditions are rapidly improving.
>
> The more religious a person is the more likely he is to give time and money to charitable activities.
>
> New birth control methods have reduced the birthrate in the U.S.
>
> If these statements all seemed like simple common sense to you, you can understand the surprise of many sociologists when research

showed that each of the statements is false! A major problem for sociologists and social science is that common sense so often misleads them (Stark, 1973:6).

Various versions of this point of view can be found in other texts. In Berger's *Invitation to Sociology,* it appears as the "debunking function of sociology" (Berger, 1963:10–12). In the latest edition of Selltiz, Wrightsman, and Cook's *Research Methods in Social Relations* (1976:3–5), it appears as the limitations of commonsense knowledge in relation to scientific research.

Regardless of the variations, descriptions of commonsense knowledge found in introductory textbooks have the following features. First, commonsense knowledge is defined entirely in terms of the stock of knowledge at hand. There is no mention of the natural attitude or of the practices of commonsense reasoning. Second, there is no mention of how the natural attitude is used by both the man in the street and the social scientist. Third, there is the implication that while the man in the street uses commonse knowledge, he would be better off using sociological knowledge grounded in science. Fourth, while these descriptions mention the weaknesses of the stock of knowledge at hand, none of them come to grips with the fact that scientific knowledge has yet to replace the use of commonsense knowledge. I will address this fact in the next chapter.

The residual status of commonsense knowledge is also found in the substantive work of sociologists. It is found, for example, in Merton's (1967:114–138) distinction between manifest and latent functions. Merton proposes that the objective consequences of action are independent of the subjective meanings that prompted them. Manifest functions are those objective consequences recognized and attributed to social action and its consequences by a group. Latent functions are "unintended and unrecognized consequences" (Merton, 1967:114) of social action that go unnoticed by the group but not by the sociologist. Sociological study is focused on latent functions.

With this distinction, Merton has enabled the social scientist to recommend his view of social reality over that of the members of society, who presumably deal only with manifest functions. The distinction between manifest and latent functions turns the members' objectification of the social world into a residual category by proposing that the "objective" consequences that members impute to social phenomena are not the real ones. This has the result of making people's processes of idealization and objectification sociologically uninteresting. As a result, the practices people use to construct social reality and its facticity do not figure in sociological explanation.

The literature on complex organizations offers an excellent example of this point. Merton's distinction has served as a basis for talking about the unanticipated consequences of formal organization. A common theme of analysis is that unanticipated consequences of formal organization create an informal organization with its own rules that cover situations and contingencies not covered by the formal organization. Invoking one set of values (informal organization) to cover the gaps created by the abstract character of the formal rules dodges the larger issues of how members make sense of rules and how they use rules on actual occasions (Zimmerman, 1970:223). By dodging this issue, sociologists are saying that the sense-making activities used by members of society are epiphenomenal.

The sociological distinction between manifest and latent functions does not permit the activity of making sense of the rules to become a topic because it does not matter what the members of an organization think. It is assumed that the meaning of rules is objectively given. Gouldner (1963:386–396), in a paper on the functions of bureaucratic rules, states this basic assumption as he describes the "explicational function of rules":

> Like direct orders, rules specify the obligations of the worker, enjoining him to do particular things in definite ways. Usually rules are given or are believed to be given, more deliberation than orders, and thus the statement of obligations they explicate can be taken to be definitive (389).

What seems to matter most to the sociologist is documenting the *sociological version* of social reality. The distinction between manifest and latent functions permits the sociologist to concentrate on his version of social reality and ignore the member of society's version as well as how that version is constructed.

These examples from introductory texts and substantive research and theory show that common sense is a residual category for contemporary sociology. This residual status is the result of restricting the meaning of common sense to the stock of knowledge—which, in turn, is viewed as inferior to scientific knowledge. The residual status of commonsense knowledge is further created through the use of distinctions such as manifest versus latent functions and formal versus informal organization. With these distinctions, the sociologist views social behavior as the product of following rules without raising the following questions about rules and rule use: How are rules made meaningful? How are rules applied to concrete situations? How do members of society use rules?

These questions are not raised because commonsense knowledge is a residual category for sociologists. The residual status is created by substituting a scientific version of rules for a commonsense version. Conventional sociologists view rules as objective statements with meanings that are clear and precise. When formal rules are not clear and precise, the sociological remedy is not to turn to the study of commonsense rationalities but to invoke another set of rules: informal rules. All of the questions in the previous paragraph focus on the use of commonsense rationalities to invoke rules and decide their applicability. The ethnomethodological study of rules involves the study of how their meanings are constructed by members of society. Ethnomethodologists also study how rules are used by members of society: the reasoning involved in deciding the applicability of a rule. In Chapter VII the research on rule use from the ethnomethodological perspective will be discussed. It will be seen that rules are not the causal agents portrayed by sociologists. Rather, they are used by people as interpretive devices to render behavior understandable.

II

Why Study Commonsense Knowledge?

> If the very basic stuff of human living is that terribly precarious thing we call meaning—something that is a continual task for people as they launch on each mundane or dramatic project of everyday life—then meaning and its constitutive practices must be understood.

Gubrium and Buckholdt (1977:194) are calling for the study of meaning as an essential feature of understanding social behavior. They are also describing one of its features which will be the topic of Chapter V: the continuous construction of meaning. Like Garfinkel, Gubrium and Buckholdt are arguing that the meaning that is essential for the construction of everyday projects is commonsense meaning. Scientific rationalities and definitions of the situation do not produce stable interaction; on the contrary, they make it problematic. It is commensense meanings and the practices of commonsense reasoning that are used by people to construct social interaction. Commonsense knowledge (the stock of knowledge at hand, the practices of commonsense reasoning, and the natural attitude) are used by people to understand social interaction as well. It is routinely acknowledged by sociologists that the common denominator of sociological phenomena is social interaction and social reality. This maxim has been so taken for granted that few sociologists realize that they have provided their own justification for the study of commonsense knowledge.

Ethnomethodologists have their own reasons for studying commonsense knowledge and reasons for why that study is important.

The main rationale for studying commonsense knowledge is the fact that social reality is constituted through meaning and people's meaning-endowing activities. Social reality as social interaction is carried out through the use of commonsense rationalities and the stock of knowledge at hand. Social reality as a factual environment of objects and events is likewise the product of commonsense knowledge. There are four reasons why the study of commonsense knowledge is important. First, the sociological version of the problem of social order depends on commonsense knowledge for its solution. Second, the everyday practice of sociological research rests on the use of commonsense knowledge. Third, social forces that influence social conduct are ultimately rooted in people's use of commonsense knowledge. Fourth, the study of commonsense knowledge is a way of studying macro phenomena where it really counts—the level of everyday life. These four statements form the ethnomethodological rationale for studying commonsense knowledge. They are interrelated in that all four are based on the ethnomethodological conception of social reality as a socially constructed reality.

Alfred Schutz (1962; 1964), as noted in the previous chapter, specified the properties of social reality as it is experienced by the layman and the sociologist. He termed that experience of social reality as a factual order the *natural attitude of everyday life*. Laymen and sociologists view the factual character of social reality as simply there. Social reality is viewed as a naturalistic entity that is independent of perception. Furthermore, laymen and sociologists both propose that social reality, like the physical reality of nature, affects our lives. Ethnomethodologists encounter the following paradox: Every time we try to grasp social reality, we find ourselves tied to people's talk and action. What's the solution? Do we say that the social world is made up entirely of talk, like some enormous crap game held up by hot air? Do we doggedly adopt the perspective of the layman as our own and maintain that social reality is independent of our perception? No; instead of trying to decide the issue by saying that social reality is this way or that, ethnomethodologists bracket it. That is to say, they are indifferent to whether the view of "social reality as something out there" is true or not. They do not try to prove or disprove it. Instead, they focus on *how* people make "social reality as something out there" observable to themselves and others through their talk and actions.

This is what ethnomethodologists mean when they refer to the social construction of social reality. This conception of social reality deals with the process of how people experience the social world as factual. Ethnomethodologists take the view that people's experience of the social world is a social product. The intersubjective properties of social reality are viewed as the product of people's sense-making activities. For the *ethnomethodologist* (not the member of society), social reality is the set of activities and interpretive processes of experiencing and depicting the social as factual. Our focus is on describing the work performed by people to generate and negotiate the sense of the objective reality of society and social forces.

A few words of elaboration are required before proceeding further. It should be noted that when an ethnomethodologist refers to the processes of constructing social reality (commonsense reasoning), he is shifting levels of prediction rather than abandoning them altogether. Prediction in contemporary sociology has taken a positivistic-quantitative bias. Prediction and causal analysis have come to mean measuring the interaction and causal connection among variables. Measurement itself has become synonymous with assigning numbers to variables; analysis consists of performing statistical manipulations on them. This mode of prediction and causal analysis dominates current social science (Cicourel, 1964; Phillips, 1971).

The numbers game is not "the only game in town." The other method of doing prediction and causal analysis is ethnographic description. Here one of the goals is the discovery and description of social processes at the level of face-to-face interaction. One of the persistent problems with the numbers game is that even when dealing with social processes it results in "measurement by fiat" (Cicourel, 1964:28), whereby the researcher's point of view is arbitrarily substituted for that of the participants in the interaction. Bales' (1950) *Interaction Process Analysis* is an example whereby the researcher measures group processes from his own point of view. Those using the IPA code group behavior according to the researcher's categories and meaning structures, not according to the meanings and categories of the group members. As a result, the analysis and meaning of group processes as viewed by the participants do not enter into the analysis. Measurement by fiat does not permit the recovery of the participants' point of view. Thus, our quarrel with quantification is not based on the numbers per se as much as the use of numbers to substitute the researcher's point of view for that of the members of society. Numbers become a method of imposing the researcher's measurement system without studying the measurement systems of members of society.

An excellent example of measurement by fiat is the case of survey research and its similarity to IQ testing. The elusive quality of IQ is usually defined as "whatever IQ tests measure." To find out a person's IQ, one derives a number that is a product of taking a test or several tests. The test score does not recover the reasoning and social knowledge used to take the test. The similarities between IQ scores and attitude scores on surveys is striking. In the first place, the measuring instrument is the same: a multiple-choice or fixed-choice questionnaire. In the second place, in both the IQ test and the attitude survey the answers are not negotiable by the subject because they are precoded by the researcher. The precodings are done from the researcher's theory and the tester's adult notion of a correct answer. In both cases, the perspective of the person taking the test and answering the questionnaire is ignored. In the third place, when the subjects' verbal responses are elicited, the answers are often incomplete because verbatim records are costly. Furthermore, where verbatim responses are recorded, they are then converted into numbers via the application of the researcher's coding categories. As a result, in both surveys and IQ scores we do not know *how* the subject interpreted the questions; we do not know the reasoning and the social knowledge used to produce an answer.

Roth's (1974:143–217) study of what IQ tests measure illustrates the ethnographic approach to the problem of measurement by fiat. Roth found that the scores of IQ tests did not permit him to retrieve what the child knows. The method he used to get a representation of the processes that produced the test score was to readminister the test as an open-ended interview that was recorded by audio and video tape. He took students back over the test item by item, asking them to identify the items and to provide reasons for their answers. The result is an elaborated representation of the child's knowledge and reasoning in the child's terms. Tape-recording the interviews is important because it produces a record of the child using his reasoning and knowledge to negotiate the test during the interview, thus preserving the interactional features of their use. The point is that to describe social process at the interactional level, one has to make a shift in the kind of measurement game played. That shift must be from quantitative to ethnographic description. The construction of social reality takes place at the level of face-to-face interaction. As a result, most ethnomethodological research is carried out using this method.

To engage in ethnographic description is not to abandon prediction or causal analysis. Throughout the ethnomethodological and anthropological literature there are predictions and causal statements. When Garfinkel proposes that the documentary method of interpretation is used to produce a sense of social structure, one could predict, as McHugh (1968) did, that disruption of its use will produce a disruption of the factual sense of the environment. When Cicourel and Kitsuse (1963) show how different social types used by high school counselors produce alternative views and reactions to the same behavior, they are predicting that a change in the reporting procedures in an organization will produce different rates. It should be noted that there is a difference in what is being predicted and studied as a result of the prediction. The predictions that come out of ethnographic description lead to an examination of people's methods of sense making and prediction. That examination consists of describing the use of these sense-making methods rather than mapping them quantitatively.

Sociologists usually resist this by proposing that one cannot predict at the commonsense level. They point to the fact that commonsense prediction is often inaccurate. Sociologists usually cite examples similar to the ones presented in the previous chapter and also point out that people can't predict how groups will vote in an election, when revolutions will occur, or when inflation will increase or decrease. These examples have three things in common. First, they are predictions involving extraordinary as opposed to mundane events. Second, as a result, they ignore the massive amount of prediction of mundane events that people do predict. For example, using their stock of knowledge, the police can predict with practical accuracy whether an assault victim will press charges. Parents and children can predict each other's responses to situations. Professors can predict that within five minutes of the end of a class, students will cue them by closing their books and shuffling in their seats. It could be argued that these examples do not have theoretical accuracy. That would depend on whose theory one is referring to. Furthermore, I would argue that the practical accuracy of these predictions has a more solid impact on people's lives than the theoretical predictions of sociologists.

Third, these examples treat commonsense predictions as if they occur without any attention to accuracy. The accuracy of commonsense predictions is a topic of members of society. They assess each other's predictions, and if they are in error, there are consequences; coaches are often fired for making the wrong prediction in a game. The point is that sociological examples of the inaccuracy of commonsense predictions are distorted with regard to the amount of successful predicting people do and by treating those predictions as having no standards of accuracy. When it comes to predicting mundane events in everyday settings, people *in* those settings do an enormous amount of prediction that has practical accuracy. In contrast, when we look at the predictions of sociologists from *outside* social settings, we see a bad track record. Using role theory, for example, halfway houses for paroled felons should work. However, they have not reduced recidivism and have been written off as failures. This is not to say that sociologists cannot predict. Where sociologists have been successful at predicting, it has been on those occasions when the sociologist has become an insider in the setting and when the predictions apply only to that setting.

This book is about prediction—how people accomplish it. The massive amount of prediction people can do in everyday life raises the question of *how* they do it. Ethnomethodology attempts to answer that question by describing the commonsense methods people use to produce the meaningful (and hence predictable) character of their social world. To describe this process, we must shift away from conventional survey and experimental methods toward ethnographic description coupled with the use of video and audio tape recording. In this manner, we can capture the sequentiality of sense making as well as its practices. Ethnographic methods allow us to recover the descriptive work people do to accomplish the predictability of their society.

Another thing should be noted: To speak of the construction of social reality is not to deny the reality of the social world *as it is experienced by the members of society*. We are not proving or disproving the factual character of the social world. It cannot be done, as Pollner (1970) points out, without prejudging the nature of reality. Nor are we seeking to replace the view of "social reality as something out there" with another view. Ethnomethodology is simply the study of the methods people use to generate and maintain their experience of the social world as a factual object. Thus, rather than denying the reality of the social world as people (and scientists) experience it, ethnomethodology begins with a description of that experience (in Chapter IV) and then describes the methods whereby that experience is created and sustained (in Chapters VI and VII).

These last two points raise an important question concerning the status of conventional social forces like norms, values, roles, statuses, social classes, and institutions. If ethnomethodologists do not attempt to predict meanings and do not attempt to replace people's version of social reality with another, then what becomes of social forces that people (and scientists) recognize? In the first place, ethnomethodologists do not propose that social forces do not exist. However, their *interest* in social forces undergoes an important shift in focus. Rather than trying to establish the "causes" of social behavior, ethnomethodologists ask, How do people come to see forces like norms, values, social classes, and institutions as objectively real and as the cause of behavior? As a result of this shift in focus, the variables of conventional sociology are no longer conceived of by the scientist as causal variables. They become interpretive devices that people use in the practical work of making the social world objectively observable and recognizable. This shift in focus is described in more detail in Chapter VII. Zimmerman and Wieder (1970:221–238) and Wieder (1974) show that rules are interpretive devices people use to give meaning and pattern to social conduct. That is, by viewing behavior as something caused by following rules, people are able to find and depict the meaning and organization in human behavior. "Behavior caused by following a rule" then becomes a commonsense method for making sense of social conduct. Thus, from the ethnomethodological perspective, conventional sociological variables become speech categories and theories that people use to present the reality of the social world to themselves and others (Zimmerman, 1970:233; Wieder, 1974:129–166; Gubrium and Buckholdt, 1977:169).

The phrase *construction of social reality* is sometimes taken to mean that all of the interpretive work is explicit. It is true that ethnomethodologists deal mostly with the explicit practices found in people's talk and actions, but there are implicit practices as well. An example of such an implicit practice is what phenomenologists call "the assumption of the identicality of the object." People do not need to be in continual contact with an object (or a person) to recognize it as the same object in two points in time because they assume it is the same object at time one and at time two. Such an assumption, though implicitly made, is essential for observing the regularities of social life (see Chapter VI), for it provides people with a sense of objective reality. The point is that such "background assumptions" (Garfinkel, 1967) provide a tacit context for constituting the sense of objective reality of objects and events. Ethnomethodologists have concentrated their work in settings where the construction of social reality is explicitly carried out. This is because the process of reality construction is best observed in people's talk of social reality. It is through their description or accounts of social reality that the objective sense of that reality is created and maintained. But talk is not the only medium used; people's actions are also used to convey their sense of objective reality.

Some critics of ethnomethodology (Goldthorpe, 1974:455; Coser,

1975:697 and 1976:34) take the position that the social construction of social reality smacks of solipsism. They propose that by viewing social reality as a constructed product, ethnomethodology is proposing that there is nothing to reality but talk—that reality is created out of whole cloth. The criticism is unfounded and, moreover, untrue. It is unfounded because, as Armstrong (1977:6) points out in his review of critiques of ethnomethodology, the charge is never accompanied by an analysis of precisely how ethnomethodology is solipsistic. It is untrue because, unlike its critics, ethnomethodology does not advocate one version of reality (or theory of truth) over another. It cannot be solipsistic for the basic reason that it is indifferent with regard to which view of reality ("reality as something out there" versus "reality as something in the head of the subject") is the correct one.

Such a statement requires some elaboration. There are at least two (more than two if we count dreams, imagination, and hallucinogenic experiences as realities, as Schutz, 1962:207–259, and Casteneda, 1970, 1971, do) competing theories of reality. One theory proposes that reality is independent of perception and that perception reveals only part of the concrete reality. With this view, a distinction is made between a person's perception of reality and the concrete reality. I refer to this view of reality as "reality as something out there." The other view is that the perceived reality and the concrete reality are identical. With this view, there is no dualism; concrete objects consist of acts of perception. This is the view of "reality as something in the mind of the subject." The former view is the view of social reality as it is experienced by laymen and social scientists. In fact, it is the view advocated by critics of ethnomethodology, as seen in the following statement by Goldthorpe:

> Benson speaks of a "correspondence theory of reality" which he suggests I tend to adopt. I do not know what "correspondence theory of reality" might be but assuming that this is just careless phraseology and what Benson wants to refer to here is a correspondence theory of truth, then he is correct in supposing that I adhere to a theory of this general kind: i.e. one which rests on a distinction between reality and our theories about reality. . . . I would see their

key importance as lying in the basis they provide for public discourse concerned with the formulation of and with the criticism of
(i.e. exposure of error in) what can in the end be only conjectures
about reality (1974:131).

Goldthorpe goes on to propose that it is an empirical fact that there
are social forces that condition social conduct without people being
aware of them. Sociologists, he states, are aware of them; that awareness alone justifies viewing such forces as causes of social conduct.

Goldthorpe tries to make ethnomethodologists do two things.
First, he tries to get them to quantify their position by arguing that
it is only through such a procedure that "real" results can be obtained. Second, he tries to get ethnomethodologists to take a position
on which version of reality is the correct one. He challenges them
to prove that their position is the correct one.

This challenge amounts to asking ethnomethodologists to prove
that the layman's version of social reality as reality "out there" is
false. Ethnomethodology offers no such proof. It is not the aim of
this perspective to prove that people's experience of the objective
reality of the social world is false. Its aim is to study the methods
people use to create and sustain that particular sense of social reality.
Ethnomethodologists are indifferent with regard to what kind of
reality social reality *really is*. When an ethnomethodologist refers to
the construction of social reality, he is not saying that people are
wrong in their experience of society as an objective reality. On the
contrary, he is proposing that they do experience social reality in
that manner, and he seeks to describe the methods whereby that
experience is created and sustained.

The ethnomethodological perspective is not advocating one reality
over another. It certainly isn't suggesting that people adopt the phenomenological alternative as the basis of negotiating their everyday
lives. Ethnomethodology does offer an alternative way of *studying*
social life. Such a view permits the social scientist to see the sense of
objective reality of the social world as a social accomplishment. The
reader may feel that adopting such an analytic stance is tantamount
to adopting a solipsistic position. Ethnomethodologists use the ver-

sion of "reality as identical with perception" as an analytical tool for rendering people's sense-making activities (methods) observable. That is not the same thing as saying that people create the world out of whole cloth, nor is it the same as saying that that is how the social world really is. Rather, it is a method for observing people's sense-making methods.

In summary, ethnomethodology does not adopt a solipsistic position. To do so would be to advocate a particular reality as *the* reality. The ethnomethodological position is essentially one of official neutrality or indifference. Ethnomethodological phenomena consist of the methods people use to create a sense of reality of the social world. If people viewed the social world as a phantom reality—a reality made up entirely of illusions—then we would study the methods people used to create and sustain that version. That is the ethnomethodological bracketing. For the ethnomethodologist, the view of "reality as something out there" and the view of "reality as something in the subject's head" are both social products. As it happens, people experience social reality as "out there." Ethnomethodology offers no corrective, nor does it challenge that perception. Instead, it is the study of how that perspective is produced.

As a result of this position, ethnomethodology is the study of all three phenomena glossed by the term *commonsense knowledge*. That is, the natural attitude of everyday life is a description of people's experience of the social world as a factual object. The practices of commonsense reasoning are the methods that people use to articulate selected bits and pieces of the stock of knowledge with concrete situations. The practices of commonsense reasoning are also used to create the concreteness of the situation (the situation *as real*). Such a study has been branded trivial by critics. Lewis Coser (1975) proposes that the study of commonsense knowledge has no relevance for the real issues of sociology: power, stratification, institutions, and sexism.

The study of commonsense knowledge is not trivial for the following reasons. The sociological version of the problem of social order leaves a class of essential phenomena unstudied: people's use of commonsense reasoning. The problem of social order has been claimed to form the paradigm for contemporary sociology by Parsons (1937), Inkles (1964), and Wilson (1970). The accepted sociological key to the problem consists of the explanation of patterns of behavior that are typical, repetitive, and describable without reference to the subjectivity of the people who produce them. The form of causal analysis that is used to explain these patterns of behavior is to describe the norms, values, attitudes, and perceptions of the actor—which, if followed, would produce the patterns of behavior in question.

The sociological problem of order raises what Cicourel (1973) and Garfinkel (1967) refer to as the problem of relevance. It consists of asking, how does the actor make sense of the situation and decide which rule to use as the basis for his conduct? Unless the problem of relevance is solved, the sociologist has created a judgmental dope. As Garfinkel explains:

> By judgmental dope I refer to the man-in-the-sociologists'-society who produces the stable features of the society by acting in compliance with pre-established and legitimate alternatives that the common culture provides . . . the common feature of these "models of man" is the fact that courses of common sense rationalities of judgment which involve the person's use of common sense knowledge of social structures over the temporal succession of here and now situations are treated as epiphenomenal (1967:68).

Without commonsense rationalities, the sociologist's model of the actor cannot construct a situation. Nor can it make sense of the cultural rules, because the processes whereby that work is accomplished are not part of the sociological model of the actor. Thus, commonsense knowledge is an essential part of the sociologist's version of the problem of social order.

Cicourel (1973:11–41, 51–52) proposes that statuses, roles, norms, and values require recognition and interpretation to make them work. Current sociological formulations, he argues, do not make explicit the interpretive work involved in deciding the meanings of rules and their applicability to situations. It is not explicitly stated how the individual assembles appearances into "concrete situations."

Current formulations do not address the issue of how appropriateness is determined. Take, for example, this statement about status: "An individual carries his social position around in his head so to speak and puts it into action when the appropriate occasion arises" (Davis, 1948:68–69). Cicourel and Davis are raising the issue of how people decide what is appropriate. A sociological rule itself does not tell a person how to decide appropriateness. It does not contain a set of instructions for its use, nor does it contain a list of appropriate situations in which it is to be used. The matter cannot be solved by constructing another set of meta-rules because the same question could be raised about those rules as well. The problem of relevance is essentially the problem of meaning—namely, how does the member of society decide the meaning of a rule and its applicability? The problem of relevance can be solved—apart from ignoring it or solving it by fiat—only by studying how everyday situations are created and the methods used to manage the appropriateness of those situations with rules. As Garfinkel has shown in the previous chapter, one cannot program the model of the actor with scientific rationalities because the result would lead to anomic interaction. Thus, the study of commonsense knowledge is an important part of the sociological problem of social order. Even though that problem, with its assumptions of a common cognitive consensus and the naturalistic view of social phenomena, makes its study impossible within the conventional sociological framework.

The practical research-oriented sociologist may view the problems of relevance and social order as matters that concern only theoretical sociologists. He is mistaken. The problem of relevance touches the research-oriented sociologist as well. Researchers have long been confronted with the practical problem of how to decide the meaning of talk and social conduct objectively. Even with coding categories, the problem of deciding which category a piece of talk or conduct fits into remains. Thus, the problem of relevance is something that researchers experience in a very practical way. The problem of relevance is not that one cannot decide the meaning of talk and observations; rather, the problem is *how* one decides. Cicourel (1964; 1974) shows that the researcher uses both the stock of knowledge and the practices of commonsense reasoning to decide the meaning of his data.

> Interviewer and respondent must engage in interpretive work in deciding whether a response is "appropriate" and whether it can both "satisfy" the interviewer and "project" or communicate particular ideas held by the respondent. Yet this interpretive work is neither part of the demographer's or sociologist's theory nor is it acknowledged as basic for making such methods work and for interpreting the findings (1974:94).

Cicourel (1974) replicated a fertility study in Argentina using survey methods. He also instructed his interviewers to keep ethnographic records of their interviews so that he could document their use of commonsense knowledge to interpret the quantitative data with the ethnographic knowledge of the setting. Then he presented the quantitative data along with their sociological interpretations and showed how those interpretations were rooted in the researchers' ethnographic knowledge of the setting.

The point here is not one of criticism. I am not arguing that sociologists should not use commonsense knowledge. On the contrary, that using commonsense knowledge is an essential part of conducting sociological research. It is used to solve the problem of relevance. Thus, commonsense knowledge is anything but trivial; it is the very stuff of which research findings are constituted. The problem of relevance is not just a theoretical problem; it has practical import as well. The layman and the sociologist—as Gubrium and Buckholdt suggested at the beginning of this chapter—are continually confronted with the everyday task of deciding what talk and conduct mean. The study of commonsense knowledge is the study of how they make those decisions. Ethnomethodologists have taken a practical problem for the sociologist and turned it into a new perspective and research strategy (Wootton, 1975).

Sociologists treat commonsense knowledge as trivial by invoking the macro-micro distinction. They argue that because the study of commonsense knowledge is at the level of face-to-face interaction, it has little to say about the social forces at the macro level which affect people's lives and is therefore not worthy of study. If macro forces are important because they influence social conduct, then the study of commonsense knowledge is quite important.

Ever since Durkheim (1938) first proposed that social facts were "external and constraining," sociologists have been concerned with the causal influence of social structure on social conduct. Through countless correlations and descriptions, the message from conventional sociologists has remained the same. Social forces, norms, values, systems of stratification, systems of power, and social institutions cause the patterning of social conduct. As Goldthorpe states:

> I would regard it as empirically evident that social processes do condition interaction—as for example, in determining in the first place the probabilities of who interacts with whom and at least setting limits to possible outcomes—without it being fully necessary that this conditioning is comprehended fully or at all by the actors involved (1974:132).

The view expressed above is that social reality operates like the forces of nature. Not only is social reality "out there," independent of perception; people do not have to know how it operates in order for it to influence their behavior. Just as people don't have to know how a hurricane is generated for it to affect their conduct, they don't have to know all the intricacies of the class system to be affected by it.

Where does this coercive power of social structure come from? Sociologists propose that it comes from being social. That is, social structures are created out of social interaction and then take on an existence that is independent of interaction and the people who created it. Social structures start out as interaction and then become objective facts for the layman and the sociologist. Therein lies their power to coerce: They are objectively real.

> People (as our subjects) have a sense of social (or power) structure that is "only too real." It is people's sense of the "objective" reality of social structure that makes social structure "work" for them and by the way for social scientists who deal objectively with social structure as well (Gubrium and Buckholdt, 1977:185).

In short, it is the sense of being objectively real that provides social structures with their power to coerce and influence social conduct. Social forces have this power because they are experienced as objective realities that do not go away by wishing—a property of a factual environment that Garfinkel terms "moral requiredness" (see Chapter IV). That experience *is* part of the phenomena glossed by the term *commonsense knowledge:* the natural attitude of everyday life.

When social forces are viewed this way, the study of commonsense knowledge becomes anything but trivial. It becomes the study of the social basis of social forces. Such a study, however, does not seek to predict but to describe the methods whereby social forces are endowed with their facticity and how people experience them as "forces acting upon them." Because ethnomethodology concerns itself with the methods people use to construct social interaction as well as their sense of objective reality, it cannot be regarded as trivial; it is the study of the basis of social structure as it exists for the layman and the social scientist.

By taking this position, it may seem that I have gotten pretty far afield from macro processes and social conduct. Actually, it brings macro processes back to where they really count—people's everyday lives. Ethnomethodologists are interested in social forces at the level of everyday life and take the position that if they cannot be found there, they are found only in the imagination of sociologists. The study of commonsense reasoning leads to the study of the operation—rather than the prediction—of social forces. An example of this is *Educational Decision-Makers*, by Aaron Cicourel and John Kitsuse (1963). This is a study of how student careers (college bound versus non-college bound) are created through the activities and interpretations of students by high school counselors. Cicourel and Kitsuse describe the social types used by the counselors to interpret students' behavior and academic performances. They show the interpretive work of placing students into college-preparatory and non-college-preparatory programs. In addition to counselors' interpretations, there are a number of everyday activities that are viewed as methods for producing student careers: routine counseling, designating and placing students in honors versus regular classes, the existence of two different academic programs, the record-keeping process, the interpretation of records by the counselors, and the confidentiality of the records.

Two kinds of counselors are described: professional counselors and teacher-counselors. The former is a specialist who does nothing but counseling, testing, record keeping, and interpreting of students' conduct using social types based on a clinical model of behavior. The latter has little professional training and counsels students part-time. The teacher-counselor interprets students' conduct using social types based on lay models of student behavior. Clinical models view behavior as symptomatic of psychodynamic processes and lead the counselor using such social types to look for deeper causes of a student's conduct. Social types based on lay models basically provide interpretations of behavior that a layman would offer. The result, according to Cicourel and Kitsuse, is that the same behavior is given different meanings, and there are different methods of dealing with that behavior according to which model is used for the interpretation. This study of educational decision making shows that the social rates of college-bound students are not the product of social class ascription but of people's use of commonsense knowledge: the stock of knowledge at hand and the practices of commonsense reasoning.

It is also a study of macro topic at the level of everyday life. One of the major insights of Max Weber (1947) was that the bureaucratic form of organization is spreading to all of our social institutions. Cicourel and Kitsuse's study is a description of the bureaucratization of the educational institution. Bureaucracy involves the following features: a division of labor, record keeping, a hierarchy governed by impersonal rules and the recruitment and advancement of people according to impersonal criteria. Cicourel and Kitsuse describe the specialization and professionalization of the counselor in terms of a specialized training, job, and—most important—a specialized vocabulary of social types used to interpret students' behavior. Their examination of counselors' interpretations shows how rules are used in organizations and the kinds of discretionary practices that constitute using rules. Weber was not insensitive to the effect of bureaucratization on people's lives. He saw it as efficient but also as threatening.

Cicourel and Kitsuse describe the consequences of the clinical model for the privacy of people's lives in discussing how counselors search for the "deeper causes" of a student's conduct. In short, Cicourel and Kitsuse's study of commonsense knowledge speaks directly to a sociological issue: bureaucratic power.

Educational Decision-Makers is not the only piece of research that deals with sociological issues using the ethnomethodological perspective. There is a growing body of research in the area of law enforcement and deviance that uses the ethnomethodological perspective to touch on issues of power, discretion in rule use, and the recognition of deviance (Bittner, 1967; Cicourel, 1968; Emerson, 1969; Daudistil, Sanders, and Luckenbiel, 1978). Sexism and power in conversations is the topic of a study by West and Zimmerman (1975). An analysis of patterns of topic control, interruptions, and silence in everyday conversations reveals how men accomplish sexual dominance. Studies of educational testing by Roth (1974) and MacKay (1974) offer evidence that challenges the conventional approach of cultural deprivation as an explanation for minority group students' failure on standardized tests. Each of these is a study of people's use of commonsense reasoning. At the same time, these researchers describe macro phenomena at the level of everyday life. The study of commonsense knowledge cannot be dismissed as trivial. It must be examined by sociologists to arrive at a deeper understanding of the phenomena *they* are interested in examining.

From the ethnomethodological perspective, commonsense knowledge is a topic worthy of study. In this chapter, I have described the rationale for studying commonsense knowledge and why that study is not a trivial enterprise. Social reality, unlike the physical reality of nature, is a social product. The social world is experienced by layman and sociologist alike as a factual object that is independent of perception and known in common. That factual character is a product of people's sense-making methods. As such, the study of social reality becomes the study of social meaning. Specifically, it becomes the study of the sense-making methods people use to constitute meaning and a meaningful environment of objects and events.

The study of the social construction of social reality is the study of commonsense knowledge. Commonsense knowledge is a product of the way people experience the social world. That is, commonsense knowledge, in the form of the stock of knowledge at hand, is gained by viewing social reality as factual—by assuming the natural attitude (Schutz, 1962; 1964). The stock of knowledge is applied to "concrete situations." The practices of commonsense reasoning are the methods whereby the stock of knowledge is used and the natural attitude of everyday life sustained.

In addition to offering a rationale for the study of commonsense knowledge, I have attempted to show the importance of such a study. At the theoretical level, the study of commonsense knowledge is essential for solving the problem of relevance. At the level of sociological research, commonsense knowledge is used to decide the meaning of talk and social conduct. Finally, we saw that macro sociological forces are rooted in commonsense knowledge. The coercive power of social facts is based on the perception of social forces as objectively real.

In presenting the case for the study of commonsense knowledge, I have relied upon some hidden resources which form the intellectual roots of ethnomethodology. Before examining the natural attitude of everyday life, the properties of talk and behavior that result in the continuous construction of meaning, and the sense-making methods, the intellectual foundations of the perspective need to be examined. These foundations are important because ethnomethodology owes its particular approach to the contributions of Husserl's phenomenology and Chomsky's generative transformational grammar. These perspectives, and their contributions to the intellectual foundations of ethnomethodology are examined in the next chapter.

III

The Intellectual Roots
of Ethnomethodology

This chapter is an examination of the intellectual roots of ethnomethodology. Many of the basic concepts, arguments providing a rationale for the perspective, and the phenomena of the perspective, have their roots in the phenomenology of Edmund Husserl and Alfred Schutz. The linguistics of J. L. Austin, Ludwig Wittgenstein, and Noam Chomsky form another important intellectual tradition which has contributed much to the perspective. The model of the actor implicit in ethnomethodology owes much to everyday language philosophy, generative transformational grammar, and the ethnography of communication. Accordingly, the chapter is divided into two sections: the phenomenological connection and the linguistic connection.

The Phenomenological Connection

The major intellectual heritage of ethnomethodology is the German-French philosophical school of phenomenology. Within the phenomenological movement, there are two men who have universally influenced ethnomethodology: Edmund Husserl and Alfred Schutz. They are not the only phenomenologists who are important. Aaron Gurwitsch, Maurice Merleau-Ponty, Richard Zaner, and Martin Heidigger have also been influential. But it was Husserl and Schutz who established the intellectual basis that ethnomethodologists still use. They provide the basic assumptions and phenomena of study. For this reason, I have chosen to limit my discussion of the phenomenological roots of ethnomethodology to these two men.

EDMUND HUSSERL

Edmund Husserl is the acknowledged founder of modern phenomenology. In two of his works, *Cartesian Meditations* (1960) and *Phenomenology and the Crisis of Philosophy* (1965), he established the theoretical and empirical foundations of ethnomethodology. He defined the basic phenomena of study common to ethnomethodology and phenomenology: the cognitive work of producing the factual character of the social world. Husserl established the rationale for studying these phenomena as well as the relationship of phenomenology to other social sciences. His version of multiple realities forms the basis of the ethnomethodological disinction between the scientific and commonsense rationalities. It was Husserl who proposed that the natural attitude of everyday life was a social product and described some of the practices people use to produce it. These contributions are discussed in detail below.

Husserl's first contribution to ethnomethodology is his description of the basic phenomena of phenomenological and ethnomethodological inquiry. The layman and the scientist, Husserl states, view the world as factual from the outset. It is this "naive attitude" that forms the central topic for phenomenology. Husserl's purpose is not to destroy this presupposition or to prove it false. Instead, he proposes that the object of phenomenology is to study how the presupposition is created and sustained by laymen and scientists. This is the same goal for ethnomethodology as seen in the works of Garfinkel (1967), Zimmerman and Pollner (1970), and Cicourel (1973). Zimmerman and Pollner (1970:80–82) provide a detailed description of how this assumption is used by laymen and sociologists. Ethnomethodologists, following Husserl, do not seek to prove this presupposition false; rather, they attempt to describe the methods whereby it is created and sustained.

Husserl's second contribution to the foundations of ethnomethodology is his argument on behalf of studying the social production of facticity. Husserl begins by noting that the assumption of facticity forms the basis of all social sciences—including the most rigorous experimental psychology. Psychology deals with cognitive products, for all psychological phenomena are products of perception. Yet psychology has left one cognitive product unstudied—the factual character of the social world and of psychological phenomena. The second line of Husserl's argument is the proposal that although psychology claims to be an objective social science, it has failed to eliminate the subjective or introspective from the scientific enterprise. Subjectivity remains a part of science in spite of attempts by the best thinkers to remove it. Their failure lies in the fact that subjectivity is an essential part of science. The "solution" Husserl offers is to study the phenomena using a framework outside natural science.

> If certain riddles are generally speaking inherent in principle to natural science then it is self evident that the solution of these riddles according to premises and conclusions, in principle, transcends natural sciences (1965:88–89).

The third line of Husserl's argument for the study of commonsense reality is the proposal that there is a fundamental difference between natural and social environments. Husserl states that in contrast to the natural environment, the social world is existential in nature. The objects of the social world possess the following properties. Social objects, unlike natural objects, appear only as perceived objects. They depend on human recognition for their existence. Social reality, in contrast to natural reality, remains in constant flux because of its ambiguity and the open-ended character of social objects. As properties of social objects, the aforementioned make the social world an existential rather than a naturalistic reality.

Although Husserl distinguishes between natural and social reality, and describes how the commonsense reality is used as a resource, he does not see phenomenology *replacing* conventional psychology. Like Garfinkel (1967) and Wieder (1976), Husserl took the position that phenomenology and psychology could exist side by side, with each supplementing the other. Out of Husserl's distinction between natural and social environments emerge two separate phenomena: one observable through the methods of naturalistic science, the other observable through the phenomenological method of bracketing. Just as Garfinkel (1967) does not view ethnomethodology as replacing sociology, Husserl is very clear that phenomenology is not replacing psychology. The two fields can exist side by side.

> . . . a really adequate empirical science of the psychical in its relation to nature can be realized only when psychology is constituted on the base of a systematic phenomenology. . . . Only then will the gigantic experimental work of our times, the plentitude of empirical facts and in some cases very interesting laws that have been gathered bear their rightful fruit as the result of critical evaluation and psychological interpretation (1965:120).

Although Husserl sees psychology with a phenomenological "base," he does not portray that base as a radical alteration of psychology. Instead, he views it as enriching the current findings of psychology by making them more consistent with the cognitive presuppositions.

Husserl's arguments for the study of phenomenology form the basis of the rationale for ethnomethodology. Zimmerman and Pollner (1970:80–82) recommend the study of commonsense reality as a topic. The crux of their recommendation is that both laymen and social scientists view the social world as an ordered, factual domain.

> In terms of the substantive themes brought under examination and the formal properties of the structures examined, professional and lay sociologists are in tacit agreement. For example, while the sociologist and policeman may entertain very different theories of how a person comes to be a juvenile delinquent, and while each may appeal to disparate criteria and evidence for support of their respective versions, they have no trouble in agreeing that there are persons recognizable as juvenile delinquents, and that there are structured ways in which these persons come to be juvenile delinquents . . . professional and lay sociologists are mutually oriented to a common factual domain (1970:81).

It is in this context that ethnomethodology treats the factual character of the social world as a social product. In short, the factual properties of the social world are viewed as a social accomplishment. Elliot (1974:21–26) elaborates on Husserl's proposal that science is embedded in the commonsense reality by describing the commonsense assumptions that make scientific knowledge possible. Filmer et al. (1974:15–35) elaborate upon the existential nature of social reality by comparing the properties of social and natural realities as part of their rationale for studying the production of social reality. Cicourel (1973:11–41) demonstrates how the concepts of roles, norms, and values require interpretive procedures (commonsense reasoning) to work. Finally, there are ethnomethodologists who feel that their perspective is neither a corrective nor a replacement for sociology. That view has its basis in Husserl's work. Garfinkel (1967) even expands Husserl's reasoning by proposing that ethnomethodology cannot be a corrective for sociology for the simple reason that there is no substitute for the use of commonsense knowledge.

Husserl's third contribution to the ethnomethodological perspective is his concept of the natural attitude as one of several realities. Husserl was the first to use the term *natural attitude* to denote commonsense reality. The natural attitude or "naivete" is the acceptance of the facticity of the social world as given and independent of perception. It is simply there, always has been, and always will be in the future. Husserl puts it this way:

> Natural science accepts nature as given, a naivete which is so to speak immortal and repeats itself afresh, for example, at every place in its procedure where natural science has resource to pure and simple experience—and ultimately every method of experimental science leads back precisely to experience (Husserl, 1965:168).

The natural attitude is not only the cornerstone of science, it is the major reality. It is "major" in the sense that other realities (scientific theory, dreams, religious-mystical) are transformations of the natural attitude. The natural attitude forms the starting point for several realities available to an individual.

The two other realities Husserl discusses are the *theoretical attitude* and the *mythical-religious* attitude. Both of these realities are transformations of the natural attitude. By "transformation," Husserl does not mean elimination or that one reality is superior to another. His conception of multiple realities is that while other realities are transformations of the natural attitude, all realities are separate. That is, they are free from invidious comparison, and each reality produces different kinds of truth and has different standards for that constituted truth. Husserl lays the foundation for the idea that the attitude of pure theorizing (the theoretic attitude) cannot be the basis for everyday social interaction (as discussed in the previous chapter) that is found in Schutz (1964) and Garfinkel (1967). The first alteration of the natural attitude that produces the attitude of pure theory is the goal of context-free concepts. This alteration is one of the cornerstones of science; it produces the search for "unconditional truth." This is in direct contrast to the kind of truth produced within the natural attitude. The propositions within the natural attitude are always context-dependent—always conditional. The implication that Schutz (1964:76–88) and Garfinkel (1967:262–283) draw from this position is that the scientific goal of context-free propositions is not (and cannot be) a norm governing everyday social interaction. The second alteration consists of suspending the pragmatic interest of the natural attitude.

> The theoretical attitude, even though it too is a professional attitude, is thoroughly unpractical. Thus it is based on a deliberate *epochē* from practical interests (Husserl, 1965:168).

The scientist in his pursuit of unconditional truth, no longer addresses the world from a pragmatic motive. Everything becomes a topic of study, and man becomes the disinterested spectator and overseer of the world—he becomes a philosopher (Husserl, 1965:172). Truth is pursued for its own sake, independent of mastery of the world. Within the natural attitude, on the other hand, man is oriented toward the world in terms of his pragmatic interests.

The mythical religious attitude is the other reality Husserl describes:

> The world in this case is, of course, one that has a concrete traditional significance for the man in question (let us say a nation) and

is thus mythically apperceived. This sort of mythical-natural attitude embraces from the very first not only men and animals and
other infra-humans and infra-animal beings but also the super-
human (1965:170).

This attitude, like the theoretical attitude, is based on an alteration
of the practical-pragmatic view of the natural attitude. The person
within the mythical-religious attitude attends to the world from a
pragmatic motive governed by the notion that the world is dom-
inated by mythical powers. The practical interests, then, consist of
discovering the direction of that domination as opposed to mastery
of the everyday world.

The formulation of multiple realities that is found in Husserl
and in Schutz (1962; 1964) is quite different from that held by the
sociology of knowledge, as exemplified by Karl Mannheim (1936).
Mannheim holds the view that there are multiple revisions of one
fundamental concrete reality. The Husserl-Brentano-Schutz version, on the other hand, based on a congruence theory of reality,
states that there are a number of cognitive styles, each with its own
definition (or constitutive accent) of what is real. An individual
can slip in and out of these realities throughout the course of a
single day. These realities are not simply multiple versions of a
concrete reality; rather, they are separate cognitive realities. Under
this formulation, Mannheim's version is founded upon a particular
reality—the natural attitude—defined in terms of the concrete versus
perceived object (Pollner, 1970). Husserl's formulation permits the
ethnomethodological study of how the natural attitude is created
and sustained. It is true that both Schutz (1964) and Garfinkel
(1967:262–283) expand on Husserl's formulation by specifying additional properties of the natural and theoretical attitudes. They
carry Husserl's proposal forward by showing how the rationalities
of the attitude of pure theorizing do not create social interaction.
This formulation, in turn, has led ethnomethodologists to study
commonsense practices and reality as phenomena and to study, as
Jennings and Jennings (1974:248–299) have done, the practices
scientists use to bridge the realities of pure theory and the natural

attitude. The very idea that commonsense reality is not a corrupted version of scientific reality, and is therefore a topic worthy of study, owes its source to Husserl's formulation of multiple realities.

Husserl's fourth contribution to ethnomethodology is the idea that the natural attitude is a social product, with the practices of its accomplishment being the topic of study. Husserl saw the goal of phenomenology as nothing less than to describe the very processes whereby the structures of the everyday world are provided with their objective character.

> Genuine theory of knowledge is accordingly possible only as a transcendental-phenomenological theory which . . . has to do exclusively with systematic clarification of the knowledge performance, a clarification in which this must become thoroughly understandable as an intentional performance. Precisely thereby every sort of existent itself, real or ideal, becomes understandable as a product of transcendental subjectivity, a product constituted in just that performance (1965:85).

Husserl regards knowledge as a performance, with phenomenology being concerned with the methods that make up or "constitute" that performance. By "intentional performance" Husserl means that knowledge is based upon the assumption of facticity. As a result, the facticity of an object is created in the very act of knowing it. Husserl's statement finds its way into Garfinkel's formulation of the central "study policy" of ethnomethodology

> in contrast to certain versions of Durkheim that teach that the objective reality of social facts is sociology's fundamental principle, the lesson is taken instead, and used as a study policy that the objective reality of social facts as an ongoing accomplishment of the concerted activities of daily life, with the ordinary, artful ways of that accomplishment being by members known, used and taken for granted is, for members doing sociology, a fundamental phenomenon (Garfinkel, 1967:vii).

Ethnomethodology seeks to uncover the practices whereby the factual character of the social world is produced. This topic has its origins in Husserl's formulation of phenomenology.

The objective is constantly there before me as already finished, a datum of my living continuous objective experience and, even in respect of what is no longer experienced, something I go on accepting habitually. It is a matter of examining this experience itself and uncovering intentionally the manner in which it bestows sense, the manner in which it can occur as experience and become verified as evidence relating to an actual existent with an explicatable essence of its own, which is not my own essence and has no place as a constituent part thereof, though it nevertheless can acquire sense and verification only in my essence (1960:106).

The first sentence is a description of the social world's factual character, which is simply there and taken for granted by members of society. The topic and phenomena of ethnomethodology and phenomenology are found in the next sentence. Phenomenology and ethnomethodology examine the properties of facticity as well as the methods people use to produce them. The natural attitude is a specification of facticity as experienced by people. The methods described in Chapter VI are used to produce these properties, along with the sense (experience) that they are independent of production work. The last phrase, beginning with "the manner in which it can occur as experience and become verified as evidence, etc.," is a statement of the paradox that guides ethnomethodology. People produce the facticity of the social world and experience it as independent of their production. Pollner put it this way:

When mundane inquiry reaches out for the real it is confronted by a paradox: the real is precisely that which is independent of its "grasp," and yet it is available only through some sort of grasping (1970:59).

Ethnomethodology, like phenomenology, studies the methods of grasping, the methods whereby the world is observable as a factual domain.

Husserl not only laid out this program, he described some of the practices which, under further explication by Schutz (1962; 1964), Garfinkel (1967), and Cicourel (1973), become the Et Cetera Assumption and the Reciprocity of Perspective. These two interpretive procedures have their roots in the assumption termed by Husserl "the assumption that things are always accessible again":

> On the Ego side there becomes constituted a consequent habituality of continuing acceptance, which thereupon is part of the constitution of the object as simply existing for the Ego: an object that can always be seized again, be it reiterated producings, with synthetic consciousness of the same objectivity as given again in "categorical intuition," or be it a synthetically appertinent vague consciousness (1960:78).

The focal point of the subsequent elaboration is Husserl's idea of reconstructing the object in retrospect. This idea is contained in the phrase "an object . . . can always be seized again, be it reiterated producings, with synthetic consciousness of the same objectivity as given again in 'categorical intuition.'" Schutz, Garfinkel, and Cicourel turn this process into a method whereby the object and its facticity are created through retrospective review.

The reciprocity of perspectives is described by Schutz (1962; 1964), Garfinkel (1967), and Cicourel (1973) as a method whereby the known-in-common character of the social world is achieved. The method itself and its significance have their basis in Husserl's "Fifth Cartesian Meditation." Husserl's description of the method is as follows:

> I do not apperceive him as having more particularly the spatial modes of appearance that are mine from here; rather, as we find on closer examination, I apperceive him as having spatial modes of appearance like those I would have if I should go over there and be where he is (1960:117).

The status of this method as such is seen by the fact that at the outset of the fifth Cartesian meditation Husserl raises the problem of how the world is perceived as known in common while our perception is from our own particular spatial-temporal niche. The reciprocity of perspectives explicitly becomes a method for producing the known-in-common character of the world in Schutz (1962: 10–12) and Cicourel (1973:85–86). The similarity of Schutz and

Cicourel's formulations to that of Husserl reveals Husserl's influence.

In the works of ethnomethodologists Husserl's (1960) processes for creating facticity become either "interpretive procedures" (Cicourel, 1973) or "members' practices" (Garfinkel, 1967; Garfinkel and Sacks, 1970; Zimmerman and Pollner, 1970). The change in name does not alter their theoretical status as methods used by members of society to produce the factual character of social reality. Furthermore, the nature of their "use" by societal members remains unchanged from Husserl to Cicourel and Garfinkel. The ethnomethodologists propose that the use of interpretive procedures is taken for granted or "seen but unnoticed" (Garfinkel, 1967) by societal members. This notion has its roots in Husserl's conclusion to his "Fifth Cartesian Meditation":

> Daily practical living is naive. It is immersion in the already-given world, whether it be experiencing, or thinking, or valuing, or acting. Meanwhile all these productive intentional functions of experiencing because of which physical things are simply there go on anonymously. The experiencer knows nothing about them, and like-wise nothing about his productive thinking. The numbers, the predictive complexes of affairs, the goods, the ends, the works, present themselves because of the hidden performances; they are built up member by member; they alone are regarded (1960:152–153).

This, it seems to me, is the clearest statement of Husserl's contribution to the intellectual roots of ethnomethodology. Husserl describes the taken-for-granted character of the members' methods. He views the facticity of the social world as the product of these "hidden performances." They remain hidden for the man in the street because his attention is not directed at the performance; rather, it is directed at the product. Husserl's statement stands as a description of what it means to "use" the practices and how they are a "hidden resource" (Zimmerman and Pollner, 1970:80–103).

Finally, Husserl saw ethnomethodology as part of the phenomenological program, although different from "pure" phenomenology. Husserl (1965:91) distinguishes between phenomenology's and psychology's interest in consciousness. Each is interested in consciousness, but from a different orientation:

> This we may express by saying that psychology is concerned with "empirical consciousness," with consciousness from the empirical point of view, as an empirical being in the ensemble of nature whereas phenomenology is concerned with "pure" consciousness, i.e. consciousness from the phenomenological point of view (1965:91).

Like psychology, ethnomethodology is interested in consciousness from an empirical point of view. Ethnomethodology, as Pollner (1970:73n) explains, is concerned with how objects are given to consciousness. With this concern, ethnomethodology belongs in the empirical rather than the pure area. Ethnomethodology is also in the empirical area because it endows its phenomena with facticity. Ethnomethodologists view members' methods as factual (Filmer et al., 1972).

Husserl (1960:131–132) anticipates ethnomethodology's interest in the construction of social reality via language use. In the "Fifth Cartesian Meditation" he proposes that there are different levels of application of the phenomenological perspective. The first level described in *Cartesian Meditations* is the phenomenology of the natural world. The second level is the phenomenology of the social world, which deals with the constitution of social acts:

> Consequently there would come into consideration, as inseparable from and (in a certain sense) correlative to the set of problems indicated, the problem of the constitution of the specifically human surrounding world, a surrounding world of culture for each man and each human community; likewise the problem of the genuine, though restricted, kind of objectivity belonging to such a world (1960:131–132).

Husserl, as I pointed out previously, began to follow through on his recommendation. He briefly discusses the problem of intersubjectivity, but he does not apply the phenomenological approach in the manner described above. That task was taken up by one of Husserl's students, Alfred Schutz.

ALFRED SCHUTZ

Schutz's contribution is notable throughout this text; for he is a constant resource. Schutz's work is the touchstone for much of ethnomethodology. It was Schutz who applied Husserl's phenomenology to the social sciences. In doing so, he gave ethnomethodology its topic of study and the rationale for pursuing it.

Schutz's postulate of subjective interpretation forms the major rationale for the study of people's sense-making methods. At a basic level, Schutz states that the social world and social phenomena are meaningful to members of society. Norms, values, social classes, institutions, complex organizations, and other sociological concepts have meaning for the layman as well as the sociologist. A cell does not use a theory of cellular biology to process information, but people in complex organizations use theories of complex organizations to pattern their conduct and to understand the conduct of others.

With the postulate of subjective interpretation, Schutz reorders the basic concern of the sociologist. Sociologists hold that they are providing their readers with a sociological view of the world. They are concerned with depicting the social world from their point of view. Sociological research and theory answer the question, What does the social world mean to me, the sociologist?. From the standpoint of Schutz's postulate, this amounts to putting the cart before the horse. That is, before we can state what the social world means to us as sociologists, we must examine how it is made meaningful by the layman. The question of how the layman constructs the meaningful character of the social world precedes the scientist's question because the social world exists through the meanings people give to objects and events. Therefore, we must examine the processes whereby the social world is constituted as a meaningful entity:

In putting our questions thus we no longer naively accept the social world and its current idealizations and formulations as ready-made and meaningful beyond question, but we undertake to study the process of idealizing and formalizing as such; the genesis of the meaning which social phenomena have for us as well as for the actors, the mechanism of the activity by which human beings understand each other and themselves (1964:7).

Along with this rationale, Schutz provides the groundwork for ethnomethodology by describing its basic topic: the sense-making practices whereby people understand and create the social world.

Schutz's second contribution is his formulation of how scientific and commonsense reasoning differ. This formulation can be found in Chapter I and in Schutz's paper on commonsense and scientific rationalities (Schutz, 1964:64–88). Garfinkel's argument that scientific rationalities do not and cannot form the basis of everyday social conduct has its basis in the following proposal by Schutz:

> What I wish to emphasize is only that the ideal of rationality is not and cannot be a peculiar feature of everyday thought nor can it therefore be a methodological principle of the interpretation of human active daily life (1964:79).

Schutz's statement refers to the study of social behavior, not to the construction of human conduct. It was Garfinkel (1967:262–284) who took Schutz's formulation of scientific rationalities and applied the argument to social interaction. Scientific rationalities, Garfinkel argues, cannot be the basis for everyday social interaction because they produce anomic interaction. Garfinkel goes on to propose that the disjuncture between theory and data is the result of inputing scientific rationalities, in the form of sociological theories, to the layman, whose behavior is based on commonsense reasoning.

In his paper "Multiple Realities," Schutz (1964:207–259) extends the difference between scientific and commonsense rationalities by proposing that they come from the reality of pure theory, whereas commonsense rationalities are anchored in the natural attitude of everyday life. Like Husserl, Schutz saw scientific theorizing as a cognitive style that constitutes a separate reality. Unlike Husserl, Schutz specifies the differences between the two realities. Within the natural attitude, the social world is perceived from within the world via one's personal situation. The pure theorist, on the other hand, suspends his biography and experiences and views the world from a neutral viewpoint as a detached observer. From within the natural attitude, one addresses the world pragmatically, being concerned only with those aspects of it that facilitate or hinder current projects. The pure theorist, however, does not view the world pragmatically. For the pure theorist, the world is an object of study. The layman viewing the world from within the natural attitude never doubts its facticity. The pure theorist is continually doubting the facticity of the social world. Thus, the natural attitude and the attitude of pure theory constitute separate realities, each with its own rules for defining what is "real" and its own set of rationalities. The recommendation that follows from this distinction is this: The social scientist must program his model of the actor with commonsense rather than scientific rationalities. Furthermore, at the empirical level, the study of these commonsense rationalities forms the topic of ethnomethodological study. They are the folk methods used to make the social world observable and understandable.

Ethnomethodologists have gone on to use this distinction between scientific and commonsense rationalities in several ways. First, it is part of the rationale for studying the process of constructing commonsense reality. Second, the natural attitude is used as a specification of the social world as an objective reality. Third, the notion that the layman uses commonsense rationalities forms the basis for discovering what these rationalities are as well as their situated usage. Fourth, the notion of separate realities carries the recommendation that the study of commonsense rationalities and the construction of social reality must occur in everyday settings rather than as theoretical speculation from an armchair (Filmer et al., 1974). As a result, ethnomethodologists tend to be empirically oriented. Fifth, sociological inquiry is a setting for ethnomethodological research. When Schutz (1964:7) terms the process of sense making "the genesis of the meaning which social phenomena have for us as well as for the actors," he is saying that sociologists use the same basic methods as laymen to construct and simultaneously observe the facticity of the social world. Social phenomena are perceived as factual by sociologists and laymen alike, and in both cases that facticity is viewed as a practical accomplishment.

Schutz's third contribution is in laying the foundation for ethnomethodology's topic of study and the practices of commonsense reasoning. Schutz not only intended the natural attitude to serve as the properties of a factual social world, he also intended it to be problematic. Schutz explicitly establishes contradictory properties that turn the natural attitude into a practical accomplishment. The individual views the social world from his own spatial-temporal niche, yet he experiences the social world as a world known in common with his fellow men. To be able to do both of these things the individual uses the following idealizations which transcend the personal viewpoint and permit the individual to experience the social world as social. Schutz (1962:11–14) describes both the paradox and its solution.

Common-sense thinking overcomes the differences in individual perspectives resulting from these factors by two basic idealizations:

1. The idealization of the interchange ability of standpoints: I take it for granted—and assume my fellow man does the same—that if I change places with him so that his "here" becomes mine, I shall be at the same distance from things and see them with the same typicality that he actually does.

2. The idealization of the congruency of the system of relevances: Until counter-evidence I take it for granted—and assume my fellow man does the same—that the differences in perspectives originating in our unique biographical situation are irrelevant for the purpose at hand of either of us and that he and I, that "we" assume that both of us have selected and interpreted the actually or potentially common objects and their features in an identical manner i.e. one sufficient for all practical purposes.

3. The social origin of knowledge forms the third common-sense construct: People assume that much of one's knowledge is handed down from one generation to another. This social knowledge largely consists of typifications that are assumed to be socially derived and which are context dependent for their specific sense.

4. The social distribution of knowledge forms the fourth common-sense construct. It is the assumption that others have more specialized knowledge. All one has to do is seek out such specialists and use their knowledge or have them use their knowledge when you need it.

These four assumptions—or commonsense idealizations, according to Schutz—enable the member of society to experience the social world as a factual environment of objects. They form the basis of Cicourel's analytical description of the interpretive procedures: interchangeability of standpoints, the et cetera principle, and descriptive vocabularies as indexical expressions. First, Schutz's idealizations and interpretive procedures are methods people use to create and sustain the factual character of the social world. We have already seen that this is the case for Schutz. The following statement establishes Cicourel's interpretive procedures as having the same theoretical status:

> The interpretive procedures prepare and sustain an environment of objects for inference and action vis-a-vis a culture-bound world view and the written and "known in common" surface rules (Cicourel, 1973:52).

Furthermore, for Schutz and Cicourel these methods are promissory. They do not settle the world's facticity once and for all. Because they are commonsense assumptions rather than formal scientific ones they must be continually invoked.

Second, where Cicourel does not directly use Schutz's formulation, he expands it into an interpretive procedure. An example of direct use is seen in Chapter VI. The reciprocity of perspectives is identical to the first two idealizations described by Schutz. The interchangeability of standpoints and the congruency of relevance are identical for Schutz and Cicourel. Cicourel enlarges the congruency of relevance to include the assumption that each speaker will produce behavior and descriptions that will be intelligible. I have enlarged this procedure further by adding the proviso that when differences of interpretation cannot be resolved, personal differences are invoked and used as schemes of interpretation.

Cicourel's expansion of Schutz's formulation is best illustrated by the interpretive procedures, normal forms, the Et Cetera Principle, and Descriptive Vocabularies as Indexical Expressions. Cicourel's method of expansion is to take a description by Schutz and turn it into a method for producing a sense of social structure. For example, Schutz describes the everyday vernacular as "a treasure house of ready-made preconstituted types and characteristics all socially derived and carrying along an open horizon of unexplored content." Cicourel takes the notion of "open horizon of unexplored content" and makes of its logical consequence the filling-in procedures that are termed the Et Cetera Principle and Descriptive Vocabularies as Indexical Expressions. The Et Cetera Principle states, in part, that the speaker assumes the hearer will fill in the unstated but intended meanings of his utterances. In Descriptive Vocabularies as Indexical Expressions, Cicourel takes the open horizon and converts it into the following instruction: Treat the everyday vernacular as requiring a context to decide the meaning of a person's talk; to locate its meaning, simply supply a context. Cicourel is saying that the "open horizon of unexplored content" acts as an instruction, informing the individual to locate the meaning of talk or action by supplying a context. In this way, Cicourel has converted Schutz's property of everyday talk into a method for producing the factual sense of talk and behavior.

Schutz's final contribution to ethnomethodology is his conception of social interaction as an interpretive process. Schutz viewed social interaction as a continual process of interpretation and reinterpretation. Except in the case of the pure "we" relationship, where two people completely share each other's experiences, it is impossible to get inside the other person's mind. As a result, social interaction is interpretive. The meaning of a person's behavior is known through imputing meaning to his gestures, facial expressions, and other cues:

> In all other forms of social relationship (and even in the relationship among consociates as far as the unrevealed aspects of the Other's self are concerned) the fellow man's self can merely be grasped by a "contribution of imagination of hypothetical meaning

presentation" that is, by forming a construct of a typical way of behavior, a typical pattern of underlying motives, of typical attitudes of a personality type, of which the Other and his conduct under scrutiny, both of my observational reach, are just instances or examples (1962:17).

The above statement contains the basic notions of how we go about understanding other people. We impute motives, personality types, behavior types, and attitude types to the other and treat his observed behavior as representing the underlying causes of his action. Motives, attitudes, and personality are not forces inside the individual; rather, they are interpretive devices or aids used to render a person's behavior understandable. This is necessary, for as Schutz explains:

In other words only the actor knows "when his action starts and when it ends," that is, why it will have been performed. It is the span of his projects which determines the unit of his action. His partner has neither knowledge of the project preceding the actor's action nor of the context of a higher unit in which it stands. He knows merely (only) that fragment of the actor's action which has become manifest to him, namely, the performed act observed by him or the past phases of the still ongoing action (1962:24).

The understanding of action involves the use of interpretive procedures as well as the imputation of motives. The latter is, according to Schutz, accomplished through the use of interpretive procedures such as the reciprocity of perspectives and normal forms. In the following passage, Schutz analyzes a very ordinary piece of action, Ego asking Alter, "Where is the ink?" Alter points at a table:

The in-order-to motive of my action is to obtain adequate information which in this particular situation presupposes that the understanding of my in-order-to motive will become the Other's because-motive to perform an action in-order-to furnish me this information—provided he is able and willing to do so, which I assume he is. I anticipate that he understands English, that he knows where the ink is, that he will tell me if he knows, etc. In more general terms I anticipate that he will be guided by the same types of motives by which in the past, according to my stock of knowledge at hand, I myself and others were guided under typically similar circumstances. Our example shows that even the simplest interaction in common life presupposes a series of common-sense constructs—in this case constructs of the Other's anticipated behavior—all of them based on the idealization that the actor's in-order-to motives will become because-motives of his partner and vice versa. We shall call this idealization that of the reciprocity of motives. It is obvious that this idealization depends upon the general thesis of the reciprocity of perspectives (1962:23).

The imputation of motives, according to Schutz, is accomplished through the use of interpretive procedures. The reciprocity of perspectives is the basis of assuming a mutual orientation to imputed motives and for assuming that the motives are reciprocal. In short, the reciprocity of perspectives permits Ego and Alter to sustain the sense that the motives they impute to each other are known in common. Normal forms are used when Schutz writes: "I anticipate that he understands English, that he knows where the ink is, that he will tell me if he knows, etc." This is the assumption that the other understands and that the terms used are part of a common corpus of knowledge. The "etc." at the end of this passage could be taken as an indication that the list is infinite and that we simply let the other fill it in himself. It may be read as referring to the "etc." assumption: Ego assumes Alter can fill in the unstated but intended meanings, which are left unstated to avoid an endless test of definitions. In this manner, Schutz provides the groundwork for linking the three phenomena subsumed under commonsense knowledge between interpretive procedures and social interaction. Interpretive procedures are used to impute typical motives, personalities, attitudes, and so on to the others' observed behavior. They constitute the interpretive process underlying the specific sense that is made of a person's behavior. Ethnomethodologists have taken Schutz's proposals and translated them into studies of how interpretive procedures are used to understand and construct social interaction (Emerson 1969; Cicourel, 1973; Leiter, 1974; Mehan, 1974; Wieder, 1974; Skinner, 1975).

The Linguistic Connection

Modern linguistics forms part of the intellectual roots of ethno-methodology. Linguistics, unlike phenomenology, is a more selective resource. It is not used by all ethnomethodologists. Cicourel and his students use modern linguistics as a resource. Ordinarily language philosophy is important for understanding the work of Harvey Sacks, Emmanuel Schegaloff and their students.

Ethnomethodologists not only use different linguistic traditions, but use them in different ways. At times, linguistic models and research findings are used to recommend the study of ethnomethodological phenomena. Other times, linguistics acts as a "straw man." Finally, ethnomethodologists see some of the findings of their research as contributing to the literature on linguistics. If this introduction is vague, it is because it is difficult to place the contribution of linguistics in one single category. Generalizations regarding the linguistic contribution have too many exceptions when applied to ethnomethodologists in general. The situation is complicated by the fact that the linguistic roots of much ethnomethodology are buried so deep as to make them invisible to even the skilled reader.

One solution to these problems is to describe the influence of linguistics on one man's work rather than attempt to describe how linguistics is used selectively. I have chosen Aaron Cicourel's work (1968; 1973; 1974) for several reasons. First, next to Garfinkel and Schutz, Cicourel is one of the founding fathers of the discipline. Second, the linguistic contribution to the ethnomethodological perspective is most visible in Cicourel's work. Third, Cicourel's use of linguistics is not limited to a theoretical resource. It is that, to be sure, but much more. Cicourel uses linguistic findings to recommend the study of ethnomethodological phenomena. Linguistics research is used as a site for ethnomethodological research. Linguistics is treated by Cicourel as a field where the findings of ethnomethodology make a contribution to existing literature. In short, Cicourel's work is a microcosm of the linguistic connection.

The distinguishing feature of Cicourel's work is its use of generative transformational theory as a theoretical resource. The generative model of language, as expounded by Noam Chomsky, is the underlying model of Cicourel's interpretive procedures and their relation to how people understand each other. Language, according to Chomsky, is creative. That is to say, it is free from control by external stimuli and internal drives (Chomsky, 1965:3–30). The source of this freedom lies in the basic mechanism of language production, or its "deep structure." The deep structure consists of a finite set of propositions (subject-predicate form, grammatical relations, functions, and categories). The elements of the deep structure are manipulated by processes called *transformations* (obligatory and optional additions, deletions, and rearrangements) to produce what we perceive as utterances (surface structure). The generative principle that this model forms is stated thus:

> Consequently, the fundamental property of a language must be its capacity to use its finitely specifiable mechanisms for an unbounded and unpredictable set of contingencies (Chomsky, 1965:30).

Here the important point to note is the existence of a generative model of language. The specifics of the model will come under consideration as we examine Cicourel's criticisms of Chomsky and his use of Chomsky as a "stalking horse" of normative social theory. In the generative model, behavior (language) is produced through the use of a finite set of processes. Cicourel (1973:88) sees his own notion of interpretive procedures as forming a generative model for assigning infinite meaning to the social world.

Linking interpretive procedures and surface rules presumes a generative model in the sense of Chomsky's work on generative or transformational grammar. "The interpretive procedures prepare and sustain an environment of objects for inference and action vis-à-vis a culture-bound world view and the written and commonly known surface rules" (Cicourel, 1973:52).

Chomsky's distinction between surface structure and deep structure is used by Cicourel to call attention to the incomplete nature of the sociological normative model. Normative theory provides descriptions of the rules (surface structure) but tells us nothing about the interpretive work people do to decide their meaning and application in concrete situations. In his paper "Acquisition of Social Structure," Cicourel treats norms as "surface rules" (1973:45–52). "Surface rules," like context-dependent sentences and "rules of the game," have an open structure that results in multiple interpretations. Cicourel views the problem of semantic interpretation of sentences as similar to that of deciding the meaning and applicability of a rule. The meaning of rules and sentences is not obvious and objectively fixed for all occasions. Instead, meaning tends to vary from occasion to occasion so that people must continuously construct the meanings of rules and sentences. Just as deep structure forms the ability to produce surface sentences, interpretive procedures constitute the basic ability to assign meaning and decide the applicability of sentences and rules. Below, Cicourel clearly draws on Chomsky's linguistic model to show how interpretive procedures are a necessary part of competent use of linguistic and social rules:

> The acquisition of language rules is like the acquisition of norms; they both presume interpretive procedures. The child must learn to articulate a general rule or policy (a norm) with a particular event or case said to fall under the general rule (Rawls, 1955). There are no surface rules for instructing the child (or adult) on how the articulation is to be made. Members of society must acquire the competence to assign meaning to their environment so that surface rules and their articulation with particular cases can be made (1973:52).

Cicourel's point is that linguistic and social rules are not self-contained instructions for use. They always require some recognition for their meaning and applicability. Cicourel employs the distinction between deep and surface structure to introduce the notion of interpretive procedures and to relate it to social norms and values. At this point, Cicourel is using linguistic theory to build a case for interpretive procedures. In later papers ("Generative Semantics," "Ethnomethodology," and "Cross Model Communication"), he uses the notion of interpretive procedures and indexicality to criticize generative transformational grammar. A hint of such criticism lies in Cicourel's equating linguistic rules with social norms.

Before Cicourel arrived at this point, however, he used the findings of linguistic research to recommend the study of interpretive procedures. Cicourel uses findings of developmental psycholinguistics to suggest a parallel development of interpretive procedures. He argues that interpretive procedures are part of a person's social competence in performance. The research of Brown and Bellugi (1964) on children's acquisition of syntax is an example of how linguistic research is used to recommend the study of interpretive procedures. Brown and Bellugi found that parents regularly expanded the truncated sentences of their children. For example, "Eve lunch" would be expanded to "Eve's eating lunch" or "Eve wants lunch," or "Eve's had lunch." The question they raise is, How does the mother decide, from among many possible expansions, which one is appropriate? The researchers and parents make their decision based on their use of interpretive procedures to supply a context to the telegraphic sentence spoken by the child.

The mother's expansions involve judgmental work, given the ambiguous nature of the child's talk. They possess features that require judgmental interpretation. As Brown and Bellugi explain:

> What kind of instructions will generate the mother's expansions? The following are approximately correct: "Retain the words in the given word order and add those functions that will result in a well formed simple sentence that is appropriate to the circumstances." These are not instructions that any machine could follow. A machine could act on the instructions only if it were provided with detailed specific instructions for judging appropriateness and no such specifications can at present be written (1964:147).

Appropriateness is not recoverable from the sentence; rather, it is supplied by the hearer. The same issue can be raised with regard to the child's utterance. Many telegraphic sentences are not mere imitations but novel sentences generated by the child's grammatical structures. Children do not imitate; they use items of their lexicon to create new utterances. This suggests, Cicourel (1973:50) notes, that the child must acquire interpretive procedures as well. The fact that children often do not understand *double entendres* suggests that their acquisition of interpretive procedures parallels that of language.

The work of performing linguistic analysis also demonstrates the need for interpretive procedures. In his papers on generative semantics and ethnomethodology, Cicourel refers to the conduct of linguistic research as a site of the study of interpretive procedures. He describes how a linguist elicits ethnographic details from an informant when establishing the syntactic rules for a foreign language. The ethnographic details form a context for understanding both the language and the syntactic rules. However, when the formalized properties of the grammar are presented, the ethnographic details used to derive it are not part of the formal analysis: "Yet the ethnographic details were always necessary elements for generating and interpreting the syntactic rules though not part of the linguistic description" (Cicourel, 1973:82). Interpretive procedures are the methods whereby contexts of ethnographic particulars are employed to determine the meaning and existence of rules and sentences. Interpretive procedures are essential elements for discovering linguistic and social rules. The linguist and the layman face very similar situations: making sense of equivocal sentences. They must use interpretive procedures to recognize the rules that could fit the sentence and give it meaning. The linguist and the layman invoke rules as a method of achieving a bounded meaning for talk or behavior.

Cicourel uses linguistics in part as a "stalking horse" against normative theory. Just as Garfinkel used Parson's work to show the inadequacies of normative theory, Cicourel uses Chomsky's generative transformational grammar in the same manner. He is critical of Chomsky, but his criticism is directed at the rule-governed nature of the model and how it creates a judgmental "dope." Cicourel repeatedly criticizes Chomsky's notion that the semantic content of talk is governed by the rules of syntax. Generative transformational grammar stresses the rule-governed nature of the formal properties of language. Meaning is located primarily in syntactical rules. Cicourel criticizes this by first pointing out that while syntax plays a part in constructing meaning, it is not the central element used by adults and children. To make sense of an utterance, the person must go beyond syntax and linguistic markers. To confine oneself to these elements of linguistic theory is to become a judgmental dope.

Teachers use question-commands like "Can you close the door?" to order students to do tasks. These question-commands have all the linguistic markings of a question. If the student relies upon the linguistic markings to determine the semantic content and his own response, he will reply "yes" or "no." The teacher will view such a reply as a "smart-aleck remark" and may retort with a verbal version of the semantic content: "I wasn't asking, I was telling you, 'Close the door'." The semantic content of question-commands and other utterances is largely a matter of going beyond the formal linguistic markers to information that is not linguistically formalized. Syntax, as Cicourel points out, offers some cues that can be used to construct the meaning of an utterance, but it is a very small part of what people use.

> The syntactic structure of the stimulus sentence obviously provides valuable information to the child, but this information may not be central to his performance because of the influence of interactional particulars experienced reflexively in the selling, or imagined as relevant (1973:126).

In his papers "Generative Semantics" and "Ethnomethodology," Cicourel (1973:74–140) proposes that a generative model of semantics is needed. Such a model would not be based on syntactic rules, but on the assembly of contexts that are recalled or imagined to give meaning to utterances. Syntactic rules are consulted by people and used to justify the semantic boundaries placed upon the utterance. Notions like sentences, grammatical rules, and syntactic rules are viewed as constructions invoked to bring closure. Hence, Cicourel alters the status of linguistic rules from causal agents to interpretive devices used by people to present their meanings as objective and as falling within conventional usage. Although Cicourel seemingly criticizes linguistics, in reality he is criticizing normative sociology.

Through his critique of linguistics, Cicourel is questioning the theoretical status of norms in sociological theory. Norms, like linguistic rules, have been reified and given an existence of their own. They have become divorced from situated usage. As a result, the judgmental work of using and recognizing norms in ongoing social scenes has been left out of sociological study. Sociologists, like linguists, see norms (rules) as giving meaning to behavior and all but ignore the work of assembling contextual particulars to give meaning to both rules and behavior. Both the sociologist and Chomsky work with a rule-governed theory of meaning wherein the formal rules of language and behavior determine the meanings of utterances and social action. Such a theory cannot adequately deal with ambiguous utterances and behavior because it creates a static world where everything has its formal, denotative meaning. The model is that of a dictionary—which, as it turns out, is faulty. The fault lies in the fact that to use a dictionary, one must supply a context. Jennings (1970) found that when one treats each word in a conversation as a dictionary entry, one uses tacit knowledge and contextual features to interpret and decide among the dictionary meanings. The use of a dictionary and other formal rules involves tacit knowledge and interpretive procedure to give the words meaning and to decide their applicability.

Cicourel's criticism of Chomsky's generative transformational grammar reveals some basic differences between it and ethnomethodology. First, for Chomsky, the semantic content of utterances is based on the rules of syntax. Ethnomethodologists view meanings as based in a context that includes but goes beyond the formal elements of language. Second, Chomsky stresses the rule-governing, formal aspects of language. From an ethnomethodological perspective, the rules of grammar are glosses that people use for finding and describing behavior and linguistic regularities. Rules have the status of interpretive aids as opposed to being causal agents. Cicourel expands this point to include the linguistic practice of taking the sentence as the basic unit of analysis:

> The generative semantics I want to develop in this paper will not view sentence boundaries as "natural," but as a particular normative practice that turns out to be rather convenient for developing and teaching rules of language (1973:83).

The account, rather than the sentence, is treated as the basic unit of analysis. An account takes in more than just single strings of sentences. When we are looking at accounts, sentences become minor conveyors of meaning. Pauses, ellipses, features of the setting, sounds, and physical posturing become important elements of analysis because they are used in the situated construction of meaning. By studying accounts rather than sentences ethnomethodologists restore the features of everyday language to the analyst's attention. When accounts are studied, everyday language takes on a certain ambiguity and looseness. It should be remembered, however, that the clean, formal language analyzed by Chomsky is produced by imposing a rule-structure on everyday language (Cicourel, 1973: 102). Third, ethnomethodology and Chomskian linguistics have different approaches to the study of nativeness. Native intuition consists of rules and deep structure elements that are more heuristic than empirically real. For the ethnomethodologist the study of nativeness is the study of interpretive procedures. Unlike deep strucure, says Cicourel, interpretive procedures are not heuristic devices.

> Instead they are part of all inquiry yet exhibit empirically defensible properties that "advise" the member about infinite collections of behavioral displays and provide him with a sense of social structure (or in the case of scientific activity, provide an intuitive orientation to an area of inquiry) (1973:51).

In addition, while the sense of social structure is a given for Chomskian linguistics, it is rendered problematic in ethnomethodology. It becomes a practical, ongoing accomplishment that is constitutive of everyday and scientific knowledge (see Chapter IV). The sense of social structure and the practices whereby "it" is produced can be visible only when they are no longer taken for granted (Cicourel, 1973:123). Finally, it should be noted that these points of difference between Chomskian linguistics and ethnomethodology are points of similarity between ethnomethodology and the branch of linguistics known as the ethnography of communication (Gumperz and Hymes, 1966).

Like ethnomethodology, the ethnography of communication is concerned with the study of everyday language as opposed to its formal aspects. The work of Gumperz and Blom on code switching (1971) and strategies of classroom interaction (1976) suggests the importance of context in deciding the meaning of talk and action. This work, like Cicourel's, points to the use of verbal and nonverbal cues by members of society.

The ethnography of communication, like ethnomethodology, is the study of everyday language use as opposed to its formal aspects. The work of Gumperz and Blom (1971) deals with code switching as a communication strategy. Heretofore, it had been thought that when bilinguals changed to another language, it was because they could not find the appropriate word in the intral language. Gumperz and Blom, studying Norwegians and, later, Spanish-English bilinguals, found that changing linguistic codes is a device used to communicate intimacy, seriousness, a change in status from formal to informal. In short, code switching serves as a cue telling the hearer to employ different background information to interpret what follows. Interpretive procedures are part of this phenomenon and may be the process behind the use of code switching in this manner. At the same time, code switching furnishes ethnomethodologists with some empirical support for the idea that interpretive procedures are invariant practices of language use.

The work in ethnography of communication and ethnomethodology support each other substantively. Bernstein's (1972:135-154) criticism of compensatory education supports the ethnomethodological notion of meaning by context. Bernstein points out that working-class students can and do use the elaborated code but only in certain contexts. It is up to the teacher to create contexts that will result in elaborated code usage. Labov's (1972) work on verbal insults and Mishler's (1972:267-298) work on teacher strategies complement studies by Mehan (1974) on teacher-student interaction and Leiter's (1974) study of elicitation practices used in screening interviews. The teacher strategies described by Mishler are not only similar to those described by Mehan, but are fashioned through the use of interpretive procedures. The strategies described by Mishler and Mehan are carried out through the use of the Et Cetera Principle (assuming the students can fill in the unstated meanings) and

Descriptive Vocabularies as Indexical Expressions (teacher assumes that students will embed her talk in a larger context made up of gestures, intonations, previous statements, etc.). In short, studies in the ethnography of communication and ethnomethodology are complementary in terms of substantive interests and findings. The ethnography of communication is another linguistic link to ethnomethodology.

In conclusion, ethnomethodology is not without its intellectual tradition. I have not attempted an exhaustive review of the fields that make up that tradition. These include person perception, psychology, cognitive anthropology, and Gestalt psychology. I have restricted myself to the phenomenology of Husserl and Schutz and linguistics because of their extensive contributions to the field. Phenomenology and linguistics have provided ethnomethodology with its basic phenomena, the rationale for studying it, and the direction that study has taken.

IV

The Members' Sense
of Social Structure

Ethnomethodology is the study of the three interrelated phenomena generally labeled commonsense knowledge: the stock of knowledge, the practices of commonsense reasoning, and the commonsense reality or the natural attitude. The topic of this chapter is the commonsense reality: the members' sense of social structure. It merits a chapter by itself because ethnomethodology is committed to the study of social phenomena "from the ground up." The radical character of ethnomethodology consists of its study of the very thing that is taken for granted by laymen and sociologists alike: the structure of commonsense reality and how it is produced.

The Sense of Social Structure

The members' sense of social structure is one of the mystical elements of ethnomethodology. Readers of the literature have difficulty understanding the perspective because of the elusive character of this concept. Part of the difficulty arises from the fact that the commonsense reality is referred to by a number of different terms. Some of them are: *commonsense knowledge of social structures, the everyday world, the mundane reality, the natural attitude of everyday life, the prejude du monde, formal structures of practical actions,* and *the sense of social structure.* All of these terms refer to the structure of commonsense reality as it is perceived, assumed, and taken for granted by members of society. Each term refers to the fact that all projects that take place in the "wide-awake working world" (Schutz, 1962:14) are founded upon the essential presupposition that the working world is an environment that is independent of perception. Later in this chapter, we shall see that this presupposition is the bedrock of all practical activities.

The term *sense of social structure* is used, by and large, by Cicourel and his students. It emphasizes the notion that both the layman and the social scientist treat the social world as a factual environment independent of perception. The "sense" in "sense of social structure" underscores the idea that the social world is a product of the very way we look at it and talk about it. The term is used to emphasize that even our experience of the social world as a concrete entity is a social product. Cicourel indicates this repeatedly by writing about the application of recipes, rules, and typifications in "concrete situations." He also uses the phrase "to prepare the environment for further inference and action." In both cases, he is referring to assembling a set of appearances into an environment that is perceived as independent of perception. Cicourel's use of the word "prepare" suggests that he views the facticity of the environment as a product of cognitive work performed by the individual. The use of "sense" in "sense of social structure," then, is intended to emphasize the idea that our experience of the social world as a factual environment is a cognitive product constructed by members of society.

Cicourel's definition of the sense of social structure is not very detailed or direct. The closest he comes to providing an explicit definition is the following selection from *The Social Organization of Juvenile Justice:*

> Both the "natural" and "laboratory" events studied by the sociologist are not established by asking first what a "natural order" is like, and then what would it take to generate activities members of society would label as "unnatural" or "natural." Instead the problems taken as points of departure are assumed to be "obvious" instances of *the* "real world" (1968:3).

The sense of social structure is the perception and the assumption that the social world is a "natural order." A natural order is objective; it is "out there" for people to see and interact with. A natural order is not perceived as the product of perception, but as something that is independent of the manner in which it is observed. When Cicourel refers to "what it would take to generate activities members of society would label as 'unnatural' or 'natural,'" he is suggesting that our sense of the social world as a "natural order" is something we produce—it is a social product. He is also suggesting that the commonsense reality is a cognitive bias that serves as an unquestioned condition of reality that is used by the layman and the scientist. The last line of the extract—"Instead the problems taken as points of departure are assumed to be 'obvious' instances of *the* 'real world'"—is Cicourel's way of saying that laymen and scientists take the facticity of the social world as a given rather than viewing that facticity as a social product.

To make the sense of social structure less nebulous, we require a specification of the properties of a "natural order." The formal properties of the sense of social structure are not described by Cicourel; however, Schutz (1962:218–229) and Garfinkel and Sacks (1970:346) provide two versions. Schutz's specification is his description of the natural attitude of everyday life. Instead of repeating the detailed discussion of Chapter I, I will present a set of idealizations that emerge from that discussion of the natural attitude.

1. Objects and events of the commonsense reality are "already there." The commonsense reality exists without our being present. It existed before we were born, continues to exist when we go to sleep, and will continue to exist after we die.

2. The entire world does not occupy our attention. Only those objects and events that are connected to our immediate projects are attended to and manipulated.

3. The objects and events of the commonsense reality are known in common with other men. They are "out there" for everyone to see; all one has to do is look.

4. The objects and events of the commonsense reality are as they appear to us. Their factual character is taken for granted until further notice.

These idealizations form a kind of prejudice toward the social world as a particular kind of world or reality. The natural attitude or the sense of social structure can be viewed as a cognitive prejudice that establishes the nature of the social world as a factual object. I use the term *prejudice* because the sense of social structure is both reality and the standard for judging what is real. There is no independent way of deciding what is real without invoking the natural attitude or its properties, which are also real. Every reality has its own standards for judging something as real; these standards, in turn, are a part of that same reality. In this way, realities can be said to "reflexively preserve themselves" (Pollner, 1970) by legislating in advance what is to be counted as real and how one is to do the counting. To use the scientific metaphor, every reality has its own standards of verification which apply only to that reality.

The commonsense reality is precisely this sort of prejudice, for it arranges for people to see the world as a factual environment at the very outset. The social world is not perceived by people as a set of random, unpredictable, unique events and appearances. Quite the contrary; it is perceived as being orderly, meaningful, and factual. Even events that are puzzling promise some explanation that awaits discovery.

The properties of such a world were further specified by Garfinkel (1957) in his early paper "Some Experiments on Trust" and later in his experiment on the documentary method of interpretation (1967:93–94). In these papers, Garfinkel uses the notion of the "perceivedly normal environment" to talk about the sense of social structure. He is referring to the properties of the social world (as a reality) as perceived by people within it. The six dimensions of the perceivedly normal environment are properties, situations, and events. They must be counted as "factual" from the perspective of members of society.

1. *Typicality.* Members of society can treat encountered events and objects as types or instances of classes of events. Objects and events are not unique, but are recognizable as the "same" thing again and again.

2. *Likelihood.* Members of society can assign subjective probability to the occurrence of events. People can assess the probability of something occurring—for example, "If I use my roommate's stereo without asking, he might get mad at me."

3. *Comparability*. Members of society can relate encountered events to other events in both the past and the future. They can compare present events to past events to arrive at an estimation of what future events might be like.

4. *Causal texture*. Members of society are able to detect antecedent conditions as the causes of present events and actions. Events and actions have causal relationships that are observable.

5. *Technical efficiency*. Members of society are able to detect means-ends relationships among events. They are able to locate and describe the way events are part of some means-ends relationship.

6. *Moral requiredness*. The above features are perceived by the member as natural features of a naturalistic order. They are perceived as having the force of moral necessity: events possess the above properties independent of one's wishes.

These are the properties of a factual environment. If these properties are not perceived in objects, events, and actions, those objects, events, and actions are not perceived as factual. Furthermore, these properties are not just applied to events; they are "managed" (Garfinkel, 1967:94). That is to say, they are properties of objects and events as a result of the active interpretive work of members of society. McHugh (1968) has shown that when that interpretive work (the practice of the documentary method of interpretation) is impaired, subjects can no longer assume the existence of the perceivedly normal environment. Subjects then actively invoke the six properties to restore a sense of normalcy to the situation. A more detailed discussion of this experiment is found in Chapter VI. Garfinkel's (1967:76–103) experiment on the use of the documentary method of interpretation and the replications by McHugh (1968) and Zimmerman and Pollner (1969) suggest that the properties of the social world are situated accomplishments of members of society through their use of a set of interpretive procedures that constitute the documentary method.

Before we turn to the methods used to elicit the sense of social structure, the sense of social structure itself needs further elaboration. This elaboration will consist of a set of examples of how the sense of social structure serves as an essential background for the accomplishment of everyday activities. I will present some examples of how laymen and sociologists "use" the sense of social structure—rely on it, if you will—as a precondition for their everyday activities. The "use" of the sense of social structure consists of taking it for granted—accepting (as given) the facticity of the social world. The practical activities of laymen and sociologists are based on this assumption.

The Layman's Use of the Sense of Social Structure

Laymen use the sense of social structure by attending to the world as a particular kind of reality and by taking that reality for granted. The use of the sense of social structure consists of assuming that the world is a naturalistic reality possessing the properties described by Schutz as the natural attitude of everyday life and by Garfinkel as the dimensions of the perceivedly normal environment. For the layman these properties are not situated accomplishments; they are simply there. The world has a factual character that is independent of the person's action or perception. To show this orientation or prejudice at work, I have selected some settings studied by ethnomethodologists: public schools, doctors' offices, and social welfare agencies. These examples have one common element: They show that the properties of the social world described by ethnomethodologists are used by laymen as a context for conducting their everyday activities.

TEACHERS AND THE SENSE OF SOCIAL STRUCTURE

In a study of teachers' placement practices in two kindergartens (Leiter, 1971), the author collected a set of verbal accounts from the teachers about their students. These accounts show that teachers experience their classrooms within the natural attitude of everyday life. In the first place, the teachers perceive their classroom situation as part of an organized world. Students are seen as having particular histories and individual abilities with which the teacher must deal.

I: What are they like when you first get them on the first day or week?

T: Right. They're all so different, starting with the children who, say, have been to two years of nursery school and whose parents have worked a lot with them and have been very interested, and they've had to share, and times when they've had to work on their own. And they walk into school as if they've been here already. They've done the same kinds of things. Then there are children who have had no nursery school but who have also had very interested parents who have . . . where they've learned to share and be patient and to listen and learned some basic skills. And then we have children who have—where many times in a large family where the parents haven't had time to work with them at all, and they haven't had any kind of school experiences and they're pretty much left to do what they please all day long, and there have been no expectations as to their behavior, they have no responsibilities and haven't learned even to take care of their room or to take care of their things or put anything away. And they come into the room, you know, just being every place at once; would take things out and not put them away, and this kind of thing.

So you start teaching them that, and you have to start with others on something else. It's just that they're all different and you can't really say—most of them you really couldn't say they weren't ready for kindergarten. We just have to be ready for them. And now there are a couple, like this one little boy I mentioned, that would have been better off at home a year. And there are some that I feel really should stay home a year before they start, but if you get them, then you've got 'm. Then you've got to get ready for them (Leiter, 1971:78–79).

The teacher does not perceive the children as blank slates. She depicts them as possessing abilities and histories. Furthermore, she conceives of these historical facts and abilities as "out there," something with which she must grapple ("We just have to be ready for them"). In addition, the features the teacher cites as the social and

personal histories of the students do not comprise the students'
entire biographies. They are selected features relevant to teaching
kindergarten: sharing, learning to listen to others, basic academic
skills, learning to put things away when one is through using them,
and having been in a school situation prior to kindergarten. These
features are chosen with regard to the practical problems confronting the teacher. The biographies are shaped by the pragmatic limits
of teaching kindergarten and thus illustrate that the teacher attends
to the world through a pragmatic orientation.

The teacher also deals with the classroom and its social objects
from a pragmatic viewpoint. The kinds of activities she plans for
the students are designed to be done without teacher supervision so
that she can teach reading or math to a small group of students
while the rest are playing. The following account illustrates the
teacher's pragmatic orientation and how it helps to shape the academic standards used in the classroom.

I: What constitutes being ready to read in terms of the readiness
program? What are the standards involved in that?

T: Being ready to read.

I: Yes.

T: All right, to begin with, things I've said: reasonable attention
span so they can sit in a reading group and, umm, be able to
work independently enough on follow-up activity while the
teacher is working with another group. These things are important.

These standards both reveal and are a product of the teacher's pragmatic orientation. We can say that such an orientation acts as a
resource in formulating the standards and becomes embedded in
them. In fact, they become "reasonable" standards only when
viewed within the context of the teacher's pragmatic motives. It
could be argued that the teacher merely couches the standards in
these pragmatic terms to give them the appearance of being "reasonable." That is to say, the teacher invokes pragmatic considerations as a tool for convincing others that the standards are "reasonable." This too is a use of the sense of social structure: By invoking

pragmatic considerations, the teacher is making the standards objectively reasonable. She is making them part of an objective reality.

The teacher assumes that objects and events in the classroom are intersubjective—that is, that they are out there for anyone who looks. She believes that objects and events exist independently of any individual's perception and takes their factual character for granted. For example:

I: Can you describe to me what the immature children are like and what the mature children are like?

T: Yes. The immature child has a very short attention span, has difficulty in paying attention. At first is usually not interested in much but himself or herself. Some just sit an' are very quiet, some may be shy. Some are the kind that are just all over, you know, they're poking at their friends, an' talking all the time constantly an' can't really follow through on anything. They just don't hear you. And then don't show much interest in what's going on. Once in a while they may raise their hand, and then again they may not. And very often you have to call them and try to encourage them, try to compliment them when they do well and all this. And there again, of course, they can't take too much at one time. And sometimes these children have emotional problems too, they're very babyish. They'll—they don't get along with the other children and they always have to be first. And, they tend to go from one thing to another. We have, for instance, free activity—they get to choose something, and they'll start something and they won't finish it and they'll want to do something else. Won't follow through too well. And, whereas the mature child can, as I said before, can pay attention and get along and adjust very well to a classroom situation. Will get along with other children and, follow directions and, always is— There's quite a marked difference, you can tell. I mean, if you didn't know anything about teaching and you walked in the room and noticed, you could tell which child is immature and which is mature. The characteristics are quite different. Am I telling you what you want to know?

The last three lines of the teacher's account show her use of the sense of social structure as a resource. For her, immature and mature students are intersubjective objects. They are out there for anyone to see. It could be argued that the teacher is invoking the sense of social structure to convince the interviewer that mature and immature students are not figments of her imagination. That is, the independence of objects from perception is invoked to convince others that the categories are factual. The sense of social structure, then, is being used to endow the concepts with their facticity. This constitutes an explicit use of the sense of social structure to produce the objective character of things in the social world.

In another recent study of classroom situations and the sense of social structure, Mehan (1974) examines the interpretive work done by teachers and students to produce a lesson on English grammar. Mehan begins his analysis by presenting the teacher's expectation for the lesson. Upon placing an object on a felt board, the teacher expected students to report the location of the object vis-à-vis other objects using a complete sentence ("The sun is above the tree"), but not phrases ("by it," "the tree") or gestures as answers. Mehan calls this expectation the Complete Correct Response. Mehan's analysis shows that throughout the lesson, the teacher's expectation underwent continual revision in terms of what she counted as a correct answer. The teacher, on the other hand, experienced herself as being consistent in her judgments of correctness and as maintaining the continuity of the expectation throughout the lesson. The teacher's perception of consistent treatment and of maintaining the expectation is her sense of social structure. The expectation has a sense of continuity over a variety of situated appearances. The sense of continuity refers to the sense of social structure, for if members of society could not maintain a sense of the object as the same object in different points in time, the social world would be meaningless. It would be made up of random, unique events and objects. The sense of social structure refers to the fact that members of society construct and maintain a sense of continuity of objects, events, and actions in the social world despite their situated appearances. Additional examples of this point are found in Chapter VI, where the work of constructing such continuity is discussed.

DOCTORS, PATIENTS, AND
THE SENSE OF SOCIAL STRUCTURE

A similar example of the member's sense of social structure is found in Skinner's (1975) study of doctor-patient interaction. Skinner tape-recorded doctors' examinations of their patients. After the examinations, she interviewed the doctors and patients separately about what each understood the other to have meant. She found that their accounts of the same conversation did not agree. Doctors and patients had different versions of what they understood the other to mean. At the same time, doctors and patients unanimously reported that they felt they were being understood by the other as well as understanding what the other said. This *sense* of being understood and understanding despite the lack of substantive agreement is the sense of social structure. Doctors and patients "use" it by assuming it is there all along and thereby treat "what is said" as observable to all parties, i.e., as intersubjective. By "using" the sense of social structure, the doctor and patient can treat the meanings of their conversations as intersubjectively known in common, and can produce the activity called a medical examination using the meanings as "objective" tools.

SOCIAL WORKERS AND
THE SENSE OF SOCIAL STRUCTURE

Zimmerman's (1974) study of case workers in a public welfare agency provides us with another example of the use of the sense of social structure. The case worker's job is to collect information used to assess the eligibility of a client applying for welfare. Zimmerman terms the variety of practices used to assess eligibility the "investigative stance." Included in the investigative stance is a complete skepticism about the client's eligibility (Zimmerman, 1974: 129). This skeptical outlook is not taken, however, toward official documents. They are treated as objective and factual: "Personnel simply treat a variety of documents as reports of plain fact for all practical organizational purposes" (p. 132). That is, information found in records is accepted without question. Zimmerman reports that when he suggested the possibility that the records could be faked, the case workers were incredulous. For them, the factual character of the records was taken for granted and was global in nature. Errors were possible, but they were regarded as *errors in reporting the facts* rather than as evidence of fabrication.

The case worker's treatment of documents as "plain fact" is the same orientation Schutz describes as the natural attitude. The case worker deals with documents from within the natural attitude. The information in the documents is treated as a set of intersubjective facts that are independent of any one person's action or perception. They are treated as facts of a naturalistic order that cannot be done away with (or faked) at will. Hence, Zimmerman's description of treating documents as "plain fact" is another example of the sense of social structure.

The case worker assumes the factual character of the documents she uses. Their facticity is taken for granted, and the contents are used as facts for checking out a client's claim. Documents are used to evaluate and establish the factual character of the client's claims of eligibility. For example, does a client have a bank record showing that he has the appropriate amount of money? The money does not exist without a record: a bankbook or letter of credit from a bank. The bankbook and letter of credit have the status of plain fact: They are assumed to be factual. There is no doubt expressed about their objectivity and the events they represent. Case workers "use" the sense of social structure by treating the facticity of documents as a given.

The reader may feel that the studies by Mehan and Skinner describe a different order of phenomena than that illustrated by the studies of Zimmerman and Leiter. A closer look at what we mean by facticity provides the necessary context for seeing that both sets of studies are addressing the same phenomena. One of the factual properties of objects is their recognizability over situated appearances. An object is factual when it is recognizable as the same object in a variety of situations or in spite of changes in its appearance. Without this property, objects and events would be idiosyncratic appearances in a swirl of other unconnected appearances.

Mehan and Skinner's studies document this aspect of the member's sense of social structure. The teacher's sense of being consistent over situational appearances and occurrences is the sense that her decisions are factual. For the teacher, those decisions have the same "plain fact" character that the documents have for Zimmerman's case workers. Skinner's doctors and patients treat the meaning of their exchanges as possessing a factuality that extends across situations. The meaning is experienced as being an intersubjective object, observable and understandable to all parties to the interaction. In short, the meanings are viewed as factual. The meanings of the teacher's expectations, the meaning of official documents, and the meanings exchanged in the medical examinations are perceived as objective tools by those who use them. Meaning is presumed to be out there for any competent member of the society to grasp. This presupposition constitutes the "use" of the sense of social structure in each of the examples presented. In all three settings, the presupposition of facticity forms the background of everyday activities. It is against such a background that mundane events occur and are recognized as social events.

Sociologists' Use of the Sense of Social Structure

The man in the street is not the only member of society who uses the sense of social structure as a resource. Social scientists use it as an unexplicated resource for doing sociology (Garfinkel, 1967; Zimmerman and Pollner, 1970; Cicourel, 1973). The commonsense world provides the sociologist with his substantive topics: crime and delinquency, mental illness, social stratification, power and politics, ethnic relations, ethnic identities, formal organizations, mass communications, and urban sociology. These areas of sociological interest are also areas of inquiry for members of society. Albert Cohen provides an excellent example of this convergence of topics and theories:

> The expression "delinquent subculture" may be new to some readers of this volume. The idea for which it stands, however, is a commonplace of folk—as well as scientific—thinking. When Mrs. Jones says, "My Johnny is really a good boy, but got to running around with the wrong bunch and got into trouble," she is making a set of assumptions which, when spelled out more explicitly, constitute the foundations of an important school of thought in the scientific study of delinquency. . . . In the language of contemporary sociology, she is saying that juvenile delinquency is a subculture (1955:11–12).

Cohen acknowledges the common conceptual foundation of sociologists' and members' theories of delinquency. He uses that commonality as a resource for launching into his study by inviting the reader to use his commonsense knowledge to understand what is to follow. Cohen's use of the sense of social structure lies in his assumption that he and the reader are addressing a common factual domain. Juvenile delinquency is a fact of life, and so are the processes and theories of how people become juvenile delinquents. Cohen, then, uses both his stock of knowledge at hand and the sense of social structure as a resource. His "use" of both is similar to the way members use commonsense knowledge: He assumes its use by others.

Cicourel (1968; 1973) and Douglas (1970) propose that social science concepts are inextricably grounded in knowledge of everyday life. The analytical concepts a theorist uses are not detached from commonsense knowledge through a process of abstraction. Instead, the sociologist relies on the reader to relocate the concept within the context of everyday life as a way of understanding its meaning. Cohen's remarks explicitly invite the reader to undertake and perform this filling of context.

The sociologist and the man in the street may entertain quite different theories of causation, but nevertheless, they agree on the facticity of both their respective theories and the phenomena they explain (Zimmerman and Pollner, 1970:81–82). For example, the sociologist and the layman may have different (or similar) theories about the causes of juvenile delinquency and crime in the streets, but they invariably agree on the factual nature of the problem and the processes that produce it. Similarly, the sociologist and the layman have theories about why minority groups and lower-class whites do poorly on I.Q. tests. Whether one subscribes to the cultural deprivation theory or the belief that students aren't learning because the teacher can't hit children who won't learn, an underlying facticity is assumed by members of society. The assumption of underlying facticity is revealed by the fact that even when members of society disagree on the nature of the problem (i.e., whether the problem is continuing inequality, rising violence, or low reading scores for the district), they treat whatever version they attend to as factual, as out there for anyone to see, and as something that needs to be corrected. Members of society are also able to point to disparate criteria and evidence in support of their particular theories. They always agree, however, on the *factual character* of the phenomena they are addressing. They all assume that the phenomenon (whether crime, education, ethnic relations, or divorce) exists—that it is independent of any one person's perception or method of inquiry. In short, "lay and professional members are mutually oriented to a common factual domain" (Zimmerman and Pollner, 1970:81).

This agreement means that the sociologist, like other members of society, uses the sense of social structure as a resource. In addition to choosing his topics of research (social stratification, crime and delinquency, race relations, complex organizations, or urban issues), the sociologist uses his sense of social structure in both of his major methods of study, the survey and the ethnography (Garfinkel, 1967; Cicourel, 1968; Zimmerman and Pollner, 1970).

SURVEYS

The sociologist's use of the sense of social structure and his stock of knowledge at hand as resources is most clearly seen in surveys.

Although surveys are designed to be objective and to produce macro-order phenomena, they are based on the sociologist's use of commonsense knowledge (Douglas, 1970). The sociologist uses his stock of knowledge at hand to select the wording of questions and to supply commonsense meanings to responses (Cicourel, 1964). The assumptions which underlie the standardized questionnaire betray the sociologist's use of the sense of social structure as a resource. The sociologist using a standardized questionnaire makes the following assumptions: (1) the meanings of the questions and the responses are the same for the researcher and the respondent; (2) the answers recover actual behavioral events and processes; (3) the questionnaire is administered in a standardized manner; and (4) the meaning of the questions is shared by the respondents.

These assumptions amount to treating the questionnaire as an interpersonal object. The researcher uses the intersubjective character of the questionnaire to get at a further set of facts: attitudes, past experiences, and behavior in specific situations. Accordingly, responses are given the status of factual observations. The responses are treated as an observation of attitudes, their properties, and their use. The concern with validity and reliability is a further illustration of how the sociologist uses the sense of social structure as a resource (Zimmerman and Pollner, 1970). Efforts to achieve greater reliability and validity presume a factual domain awaiting discovery through trustworthy methods.

Aaron Cicourel (1974) replicated a study of Jamaican fertility in Argentina to show that the "hard data" of survey research are a product of the researcher's use of commonsense knowledge and practical reasoning. To do this, Cicourel used open-ended questionnaires and instructed his interviewers to make ethnographic records of the interviews. The ethnographic details of the interviews were used to provide alternative interpretations of the hard data. Cicourel presented verbatim transcripts of the interviews, along with ethnographic details (as recorded by the interviewers). He then interpreted the data using the researcher's "formal" perspective. Following this interpretation, Cicourel provided an alternative interpretation using the ethnographic details from the interview. The disjunction between interpretations underscores the researcher's use of commonsense knowledge to analyze the data. The researcher does this, Cicourel argued, because survey research suppresses ethnographic details as epiphenomenal by treating the meaning of the responses as free from multiple meanings. Thus, the researcher relies upon his commonsense knowledge to supply a single meaning to each response and to supply enough details to build his analysis.

Furthermore, the ethnographic particulars used by the researcher are not revealed to the reader. When the reader is confronted with the tables and analysis, he must supply ethnographic details to build a correspondence between them (Cicourel, 1964; 1974; Garfinkel, 1967). Hence, the researcher relies not only on his own member's knowledge, he relies upon that of the reader as well. The researcher's use of social structure is not a product of special training (Garfinkel, 1967). It is the product of his membership in society, for he uses his sense of social structure to produce both everyday and scientific activities. To quote Cicourel:

> The researcher's use of the particulars he selectively labels "data" is part of a broader activity whereby he sustains an everyday existence within which the researcher proceeds and on which he trades implicitly. Every description of scientific activity relies on this existence even though the researcher does not acknowledge that he must sustain this common sense world in connection with his claims to knowledge about an environment of objects that relies on implicit, culturally organized verbal and non-verbal conditions (1974:113–114).

Cicourel ethnographically demonstrates the researcher's use of commonsense knowledge and reasoning to produce and analyze tables from surveys. He does this by first presenting tables from his survey data via standardized coding. Then he presents ethnographic data from the interviews. The tables are then interpreted using first the researcher's commonsense knowledge and then the ethnographic details of the interviews. Cicourel demonstrates how the researcher can produce alternative interpretations of "hard" data using the ethnographic data of the interview situation. For example, from one table, one can infer that men and women of little education, like men and women with high education, prefer small families.

The finding of a correlation between education and family size or church attendance and family size or income and family size does not prove that the researcher has examined the everyday conditions and experiences of family life or that he has ascertained how decisions are made or avoided (1974:118).

Cicourel points out that even standard macro-variables like rural-urban differences are interpreted in a context created by the researcher's background knowledge. A standard finding, for example, is that people who live in urban areas prefer smaller families. The use of commonsense knowledge is essential because variables like urbanization do not identify the specific characteristics of urban living that lead to everyday decision making.

. . . variables like urbanization are too comprehensive and do not identify the characteristics of urban living that lead to small families. *We can refer to the crowded conditions of urban areas—and Buenos Aires certainly fits this image, for housing is hard to come by and marriage is often delayed for years until a couple in the lower- or middle-class can find an apartment.* But how these people reason about such decisions is not clear, nor is it clear what logic working-class families use in considering their housing situations before deciding (by fiat?) on the number of children they will have (Cicourel, 1974:122).

I have underscored areas where the researcher relies upon his and the reader's use of commonsense knowledge. Neither the table nor the researcher's analysis captures the practical reasoning used by the people being studied. This points to another way the sociologist uses commonsense (or practical) reasoning as a resource. The theories constructed by the sociologist imply but do not recommend the study of the use of practical reasoning. When sociological theories propose that action is the result of decision making by members of society (i.e., whether to have large or small families, or to use illegitimate means to attain cultural goals), they imply practical decision making but then study "social factors" rather than the decision making itself. Practical decision making remains a tacit resource of sociological theory; it exists by implication, but not as a topic of sociologic investigation. As a result:

We are forced to imagine and we must persuade the reader to imagine or invent possible social settings; and we tacitly elaborate
ethnographic settings to animate the tables we employ for claims to
knowledge (Cicourel, 1974:140).

Cicourel's work is important because it reveals how the researcher
uses his commonsense knowledge to produce data. The reader
should observe that the researcher "uses" the sense of social structure
in the same manner as other members of society. He relies upon it
as the tacit background for accomplishing his everyday work and
for recommending its factual character to others. The survey researcher uses his commonsense knowledge as an aid to perception
to construct questions and fixed-choice alternatives that are "meaningful" by using himself and others as informants. Commonsense
knowledge is also used to interpret the data and to "animate" tables
through the construction of ethnographic settings. Finally, the survey researcher relies upon the reader's use of his sense of social
structure, commonsense knowledge, and practical reasoning to accomplish a behavioral connection between the tables and the researcher's interpretation. One way of discovering this for oneself is
to read an article using survey research and to observe the imagery
in the form of interactional events one supplies. Through the construction of such interactional events from memory or imagination,
the reader becomes a participant in the research enterprise. Through
his use of commonsense knowledge and practical reasoning, he
makes the connection between numbers and theory.

ETHNOGRAPHY

Ethnography forms another research setting for studying the use of
commonsense knowledge as a tacit resource. The ethnographer assumes that the social world is observable and that it can be described
objectively. The purpose of the ethnographer is to describe objective
social reality from the standpoint of the member of society. The
ethnographer begins with the social world as it appears to the
member of society and, after describing the perspective of the peo-

ple, the attempts to produce an objective account of the society's structure. The ethnographer, then, does not simply describe the perspective of members of society. He also attempts to use that perspective to arrive at an objective account of how the society operates. To do this, the ethnographer tests the reports of his informants against his own observations and against reports of other informants. He may even use a small survey as a check for accuracy. The ethnographer treats the reports of his informants as "reports about an objective reality." Testing these reports is further based on the idea of getting the facts straight, again assuming that the society exists as a factual object (Zimmerman and Pollner, 1970:90–92). Furthermore, informants' accounts often take on the status of descriptions by colleagues. This is seen in the practice of stating an argument and then reinforcing it with a quotation from an informant. The following extract from Glaser and Strauss' *Awareness of Dying* (1966:222) is an example of this common practice in ethnographies:

Loose sedation orders give the nurse enough latitude to administer potentially lethal doses in the hope of achieving painless comfort. In this way she can help the patient die. One nurse said, "It may kill her but why not let her go free of pain?" Another said, "None of the nurses believe in euthanasia but it's just that as you give these heavy doses of narcotics you think that this may be the last one she can take" (1966:222).

The accounts by the researcher and his informant are descriptions that make features of the setting observable to the reader and the researcher. Using informants' accounts to reveal selected features of the setting constitutes the researcher's use of the sense of social structure as a resource. The informant's sense of social structure is not approached as a topic of study. Instead, the researcher relies on the informant's sense of social structure to produce interpretations of the setting. These interpretations, in turn, become data for the researcher. At no time does the process of constructing descriptive accounts and the sense of social structure become a topic of study if we ask, How does the informant construct accounts of the society? and How does the informant create and sustain the sense that the society and the events he describes have a factual character?

The ethnographer uses the sense of social structure, commonsense knowledge, and practical reasoning to gather his data. When the researcher initially attempts to enter a setting, he uses his commonsense knowledge to formulate recipes for gaining access. When two colleagues of mine were trying to gain entrance to a county sheriff's department, they began with a combination of letters and personal introductions. The letters were sent on the assumption that the sheriff's department keeps records so that when they called for a personal appointment, the person in charge would have something to look at before they arrived. Once they were granted an appointment, they had to convince the sheriff that they were not doing an exposé of the department. To do this, they used commonsense reasoning and social skills any member of society uses to convince someone else of his sincerity.

Once in the setting, the researcher must continue to use his social skills as a member to stay in. Methods books like those by Goode and Hatt (1952), Selltiz et al. (1965), and Denzin (1974) picture the researcher who uses his scientific reasoning to decide what kind of role to play in the setting. Goode and Hatt (1952), for example, suggest that the researcher should decide at the outset whether to be an observer, a participant-observer, or a combination of both. They further recommend that once the researcher makes his decision, he should stick to it throughout the research. Such a formulation is not "wrong" as much as it is incomplete. They do not tell the reader that such decisions rest on commonsense rather than scientific grounds. The decision is often based on "what anyone knows" about the setting under study, on fragmentary ethnographic data, or on the recommendation of an informant. They also do not tell the reader that very often the role the researcher plays changes over the course of the study and sometimes within a single day. Finally, the decision of what role the researcher will play is often made by other members of the setting. For example, when I was studying the placement practices of kindergarten teachers (Leiter: 1971; 1974), I thought I would just observe. However, one of the teachers placed me in the role of teacher's assistant, making me a participant-observer. Furthermore, I found that my role changed over the course of a single day. I would enter the classroom as an observer and watch the beginning of class from behind the students as they sat on the rug in front of the teacher. Then the teacher might, for example, ask me to correct the boys' math work, thereby redefining my role as that of a participant-observer. When I finished that task, I would switch back to observing the teacher and students interact. To do this, I had to follow her around the room. As I walked among the students, some would detain me to ask a question about the work they were doing. Once again, I became a participant-observer as I answered their questions. To remain in the setting, I had to switch roles rather than remain in a consistent one throughout the research. I could not say to the teacher, "That's not my job. I'm just an observer, and I must maintain the continuity of my observations." Nor could I say to the student who detained me, "Go away, kid, I'm observing. I'll catch you later." The point of this is to suggest that the manipulation of the research role does not end once the researcher is in the setting. It continues throughout the research, and is based on commonsense knowledge and practical reasoning (Cicourel, 1964; Boese, 1971; Mehan, 1972; Leiter, 1974).

Ethnographers' use of commonsense knowledge and commonsense reasoning is not news. Ethnographers in sociology and anthropology have been candid, up to a point, about their use of commonsense knowledge and practical reasoning. In some cases (Dalton, 1959; Whyte, 1955), their frankness is reserved for brief forwards or for methodological appendices to their ethnographies. In other cases (Casteneda, 1970; 1971; Briggs, 1970), researchers have written their ethnographies in a manner that lets the reader observe their fieldwork methods. While anthropologists recognize that they are creating social reality through the process of doing an ethnography, the process (the use of commonsense knowledge and practical reasoning) is seldom the topic of study. Sociologists and anthropologists who use ethnographic field methods have not turned the ethnographic situation itself into a setting for the study of how social reality is created.

Cicourel's *Social Organization of Juvenile Justice* (1968) is one example of research that shows how the investigator's use of commonsense knowledge produces findings. In the account that follows, Cicourel reveals his use of commonsense knowledge within the context of the analysis. The italicized sections highlight the impressionistic particulars and ethnographic details used by Cicourel to accomplish his analysis.

The establishment of the category "first offense" and the juvenile's appearance and general demeanor before the police officer are integral features of the conversation, even though I can only document the "first offense" part of the picture. I can only tell the reader that my impression of the youth was that of a neatly dressed person. The conversation itself, even when stripped of its paralinguistic properties, suggests a casual or "light" exchange. My impression of the conversation was that the police officer did not regard this offense as a "serious" matter; the parents would report to the Juvenile Bureau, and a "lecture" given to the juvenile would be repeated in the parents' presence in order to impress the juvenile and his parents with the future consequences of such conduct. *The issue was not to establish guilt, but to deliver a "lecture" on the evils of criminal acts.* Having observed this police officer at work on many occasions for over two years, *I can describe her as "confident." The tone of her voice suggested to me that she did not regard the case as "serious." Her remark that "I understand you had something to do with stealing . . ." was said in a "casual" way. The statement "Well, what about this" can be viewed as an invitation to the juvenile to engage in self-recrimination about his act, reveal his remorsefulness, and afford him the opportunity to indicate that he is "sorry" and will not "do it again."* The officer continually tries to have the juvenile voluntarily express his remorse, his plans for reform, and the comment "Now he's out a tool kit, right" seeks to prod the juvenile into a remorseful statement. The response of "Yah" is not enough for the officer. She pushes the issue once more by asking: "Would you like to be out something like that?" She then seemed impatient with the juvenile and proceeded to spell out her concern without waiting for answers each time. During this part of the exchange, the juvenile sat with his head down, looking rather ashamed, while the officer indicated the terms of the disposition—repayment of the loss to the victim and (not quoted) a "talking to" by his parents. *The remark, "Now right is right," triggered off a very long "lecture" by the officer that I could not record. It was like a sermon on the importance of being honest and the sacredness of the property of others.* This "sermon" was suggested in the earlier statements quoted: "Would you like to be out something like that?" and "If you do something wrong you ought to pay for it" (1968:124).

Cicourel embeds his analysis in the commonsense knowledge and ethnographic details he used to produce it. The reader has access to the sociologist's use of commonsense knowledge within the context of the analysis: the impressionistic particulars and ethnographic details. The ethnographic and impressionistic details are described to reveal, rather than hide, their context-dependent character to the reader.

D. Lawrence Wieder's (1974) study of a halfway house also shows the researcher's use of commonsense knowledge as a resource. The first part of his book, consisting of a conventional study of deviant behavior in a halfway house for paroled narcotics addicts, describes the patterns of deviant behavior and the rules which produce them (the convict code). The second part of his book contains a study of how he discovered and produced the patterns of deviant behavior and the convict code. This part of Wieder's book analyzes the use of commonsense knowledge by the residents and the researcher. Wieder's use of commonsense knowledge is described in Chapter VI.

Wieder turns the research act into an occasion to study the researcher's use of commonsense knowledge. He, like Cicourel, provides the ethnographic details used to produce his analysis. He also describes the practical reasoning (the use of the documentary method of interpretation) used in making sense of those details. Through Wieder's and Cicourel's analysis, the reader is privy to the commonsense knowledge and practical reasoning used to accomplish social science research. Furthermore, these two studies suggest that the visibility of commonsense knowledge and practical reasoning is not a methodological problem. Neither Cicourel nor Wieder use any "new" methods of research; they both simply shift their theoretical orientations. They can make commonsense knowledge observable because they make it the topic of their respective investigations (Cicourel, 1964; Garfinkel, 1967).

LAY AND PROFESSIONAL USE
OF COMMONSENSE KNOWLEDGE

The purpose of the preceding discussion and its accompanying illustrations has not been to debunk the use of commonsense knowledge and practical reasoning. None of the researchers cited are criticizing common sense or its use. Mehan and Skinner are not proposing that teachers are liars or that doctors and patients *do not really* understand each other. Zimmerman and Leiter are *not* trying to undermine the case worker's and the teacher's faith in the facticity of documents and students by suggesting that this facticity is misplaced. All of these studies describe that faith in facticity and how it is used by members of society. None of the studies cited in this text seek to replace the sense of social structure with some other reality. As we saw in Chapter I, such a replacement hinders rather than facilitates social interaction. The studies in this chapter show that Schutz's description of the natural attitude is not simply a philosophical polemic. The natural attitude of everyday life is a description of how the *social world* is experienced by all members of society in the everyday working world they inhabit. The natural attitude, along with the properties of the perceivedly normal environment, is a specification of people's sense of social structure. This does not mean that the sense of social structure is the only reality people are capable of experiencing, as Casteneda (1970; 1971) has so eloquently argued; but it is *social reality*.

The discussion of how sociologists use the sense of social structure is also intended to explicate the phenomenon rather than to debunk those who produce it. Although the sense of debunking may be present "between the lines," it is more a product of the position toward common sense taken by sociologists than an effort to debunk sociology by ethnomethodologists. In Chapter I, we saw that as a result of limiting commonsense knowledge to the stock of knowledge at hand, sociologists generally debunk it. When commonsense knowledge is expanded to include the sense of social structure and the practices of commonsense reasoning, we see that sociologists use commonsense knowledge in the same manner as laymen. The debunking character of this finding is a result of initially viewing sociology as competitive with commonsense knowledge. Ethnomethodology sees sociology as the *study* of commonsense knowledge as it is used by both laymen and sociologists. As a result, ethnomethodologists do not debunk the sociological use of common sense as a resource. They find the sociological practice of debunking and using commonsense knowledge strange.

> It's not wrong; it's a very curious enterprise. There is no irony. The sin is not that you are wrong. The sin is that you circle back to use the same devices of practical reasoning to recommend the scientific character of a finding, which makes it a very puzzling—not wrong—but a very puzzling enterprise with respect to how these scientific arguments now come to be seen (Hill et al, 1968:29).

I am not suggesting that sociologists should avoid using commonsense knowledge. Such an undertaking would be impossible since all three methodologies of the social sciences involve interaction between the researcher and the subject. That interaction is produced through the use of commonsense reasoning, the sense of social structure, and the stock of knowledge at hand. The researcher relies on the subject to endow his questions, situations, and instructions with facticity, just as the researcher does when he interprets the responses. There is virtually no mode of inquiry in which the facticity of the subject matter is *not* assumed. Lay and professional inquiry are predicated on the assumption that the objects and events studied are independent of perception. That is, they are presumed to exist independent of the methods used to make them observable. Ethnomethodologists are not exempt from using commonsense knowledge in their studies of how it is used by others. The major difference between ethnomethodology and sociology is that for the ethnomethodologist, commonsense knowledge is a topic of study as well as a resource.

The Sense of Social Structure:
A Topic

Ethnomethodology studies how members of society sustain a sense of social structure. The question that confronts us now is, How do we turn commonsense knowledge and the sense of social structure into a topic of study? To answer this question, I will first present a method for turning the everyday world into a topic. Then, I will present some examples of how ethnomethodologists study commonsense knowledge, practical reasoning, and the member's sense of social structure.

THE OCCASIONED CORPUS

Basically, one turns the member's sense of social structure into a topic by looking at the social world in a way that almost turns the commonsense world on its head. Zimmerman and Pollner's (1970) formulation of the "occasioned corpus" approximates an ethnomethodological method for the social scientist. Viewing a setting or the social world as an occasioned corpus makes the social world "anthropologically strange" (Garfinkel, 1967) in order to turn the everyday world into a topic. The occasioned corpus is the theoretical stance through which the social world can be approached so as to both turn it into a topic and reveal the ethnomethodological phenomena of interest. This method does not tell a person using the occasioned corpus *what* he will see in the social world but merely *how* to look at it so that he can see.

Zimmerman and Pollner instruct users of the ethnomethodological perspective to view the social world (or social settings) as an occasioned corpus. That is, they should treat the social world as consisting of elements that are brought together to form a corpus through the use of a set of practices. Social settings are reduced to two parts: elements of the occasioned corpus and the practices that members of society use to make the elements observable and recognizable. The elements of the occasioned corpus are defined by Zimmerman and Pollner as:

> . . . those features of a setting that members rely upon, attend to, and use as the basis for action, inference and analysis on any given occasion (1970:96).

The ethnomethodologist is instructed to view the elements as unique to the particular occasion in which they are assembled. The elements of the occasioned corpus may not be generalized to other settings by the analyst. When the elements are thus viewed as unique, the setting's features, along with their factual properties, are turned into accomplishments produced *by members*. By restricting the analysts' generalizing, the method focuses on how members produce the generalizability of objects and events. When the elements of the occasioned corpus are viewed as unique to the occasion in which they are assembled, the factual and rational properties of the elements (typicality, likelihood, causal texture, technical efficiency, comparability, moral necessity, efficacy, intelligibility, etc.) are turned into products.

In addition to their uniqueness, the elements of the occasioned corpus do not form a closed, fixed set.

> The occasioned corpus is a corpus with no regular elements, that is it does not consist of a *stable* collection of elements (Zimmerman and Pollner, 1970:95).

This means that the features of a setting cannot be bounded. There is an open structure (Cicourel, 1973) that results in the possible indefinite elaboration of the features of a setting. The closure that members bring is a product—and a temporary one at that. It can be opened, and new elements added or taken away at any time. Such openness implies that as the elements change, the setting does too.

The second part of the occasioned corpus is a set of practices that members use in assembling its elements. These practices are situation-specific, possessing properties which are invariant to the situation. Zimmerman and Pollner do not tell us what the practices are, for that is not the purpose of the occasioned corpus. On the contrary, the purpose is to provide the ethnomethodologist with a method for turning the sense of social structure into a topic. It is up to the researcher to use this method to locate the practices members use to create and sustain their sense of social structure. The practices used to create and sustain the factual character of the social world form the central topic of Chapter VI.

Before presenting a review of how ethnomethodologists use the occasioned corpus, I will describe some additional steps involved in its use. First, the ethnomethodologist must suspend the notion that behavior is rule-governed or produced by complying with rules (Garfinkel, 1967; Zimmerman and Wieder, 1970). The second step is to observe that members of society describe and explain the factual character of the social world by invoking notions like "action produced through conformity to a rule" (Zimmerman and Wieder, 1970:288). For example, during his study of the halfway house, Wieder found that the residents used the idea of "following the code" to explain the behavior of other residents. Zimmerman (1970:232–233) found that social workers used the notion of people following a rule of "first come, first served" to depict and render observable the orderly features of their everyday activities. The third step is to "treat the appearances of described and explained patterns of orderly social activities as appearances produced, for example, by and through such procedures as analyzing an event as an instance of compliance (or non-compliance) with a rule" (Zimmerman and Wieder, 1970:288). The ethnomethodologist is asked to treat the notion of a factual environment as a set of *appearances* produced by people's sense-making methods. These additional steps, along with those previously mentioned, allow the ethnomethodologist to step back and "re-view" (Douglas, 1970:15) phenomena heretofore taken for granted: the methods whereby the stock of knowledge is brought to bear and the factual properties of the social world are produced.

An example of viewing the world as an occasioned corpus is Wieder's study of "telling the convict code." The elements of the halfway house studied are the patterns of deviant behavior and the convict code. Both are features of the setting which are known to its members and used as a basis for action, inference, and analysis.

Wieder's topic is how the residents and staff make these elements observable to each other and to him as a researcher-member. The factual character of the behaviors and the code is treated as a set of appearances produced by the residents, the staff, and himself. The situated practice whereby this is accomplished is called "telling the code." Residents and staff invoke the notion of people following the convict code to explain their behavior and the behavior of others. When the behavior is connected to the code, the behavior acquires its deviant meaning; it is perceived as orderly, repetitive, and independent of the particular people in the halfway house. The work of connecting the behavior to the code is called the "documentary method of interpretation." In Chapter VI, the residents' and staff's use of the documentary method of interpretation will be described.

For the moment, it is important to note how Wieder's approach is an example of using the occasioned corpus. First, he treats the features of the setting as elements of a corpus that are brought together and assembled. Second, the code and the behaviors have the same properties as the elements of the occasioned corpus. Wieder describes how the meaning of the behaviors can be elaborated indefinitely and how the code as a scheme of interpretation "elaborates itself" through the researcher's use of one piece to interpret other pieces. The meaning of the behaviors is unique to the situation and generalizable through the use of the documentary method of interpretation. Third, Wieder treats the orderly and factual character of the code and the deviant behavior patterns as appearances which are produced by the staff and residents through a set of practices. He provides the reader with descriptions of his use of the documentary method of interpretation as well as its use by the staff and residents.

TREATING COMMONSENSE KNOWLEDGE
AS A TOPIC

A fairly typical remark made about ethnomethodologists is that they are always "twisting things around." Ethnomethodologists seem to take conventional topics and make them strange by phrasing them in what seems to be an odd manner. Critics view this practice as doctrinaire, an attempt to impose in-group terminology on conventional sociological problems. Actually it is an attempt to study commonsense knowledge and commonsense rationalities as topics. The inversion or twisting of conventional problems represents an effort to treat what has heretofore been the sociologist's hidden resource as a sociological phenomenon. The results of these efforts will be discussed in Chapter VI. For the moment, however, a discussion of the topics may provide more substance to the phrase "treating commonsense knowledge and commonsense rationalities as topics."

A basic element of sociological theory is the notion of ascribed status. The sociological literature describes statuses like sex as ascribed or inherited; that is, they are statuses into which one is born and remains throughout one's life. Discussions on sexual deviance, for example, are based on this fundamental idea. Thus homosexuals, lesbians, and transvestites are people who are deviating from the fundamental statuses of male and female. Male and female remain the basic statuses to which even deviants belong and from which their deviation is judged. A sexual deviant is still essentially male or female but is not behaving in accord with cultural definitions of the sex. Although a substantial body of anthropological and sociological literature suggests that definitions of sexuality are culture-specific, even here the concept of male and female remains the anchoring point. After all, the different cultural definitions are about male and female as intersubjective objects.

It is here that the ethnomethodologist asks a different question, one which turns the sense of social structure into a topic. How do members of society create the intersubjective character of their sexual statuses, male and female? In short, the intersubjective or objective character of sexual status is viewed as a set of appearances produced by the individual. To be perceived as a male or a female is an ongoing, managed accomplishment from the ethnomethodological perspective.

To be a given kind of person, then, is not merely to possess the required attributes, but also to sustain the standards of conduct *and appearance* [my emphasis] that one's social grouping attaches thereto. The unthinking ease with which performers consistently carry off such standard-maintaining routines does not deny that a performance has occurred, merely that the participants have been unaware of it (Goffman, 1959:75).

The ethnomethodological task which follows from this conception of status consists of describing the practices members of society use to present themselves as particular status-objects in an interpersonal environment.

Garfinkel (1967:116–185) presents a case study of the "managed achievement of sex status." An "intersexed person" called Agnes presented herself at UCLA for an operation to remove a fully grown set of male genitals and to have a female vagina constructed in its place. Before the operation, Agnes was studied by a group of physiologists, psychologists, and Garfinkel from November 1958 to August 1959. The physiologists were interested in knowing how a female could develop a set of male genitals. The psychologists interviewed Agnes and administered a number of tests to establish what her "real" psychological identity was. They were also interested in why a person raised as a male would change sexual identities. I mention these interests because Garfinkel's was strikingly different. He wasn't interested in why but in *how* Agnes successfully presented herself as a recognizable female. He describes the "passing practices" Agnes used to actively and deliberately manipulate her appearances before others. Her sexual status is treated as a total accomplishment achieved by manipulating the way people viewed her as a social object. In fact, Garfinkel argues that Agnes herself took this view and used it to discover for herself how people create their perceived sexuality. The "passing practices" Garfinkel describes ("anticipatory following," being a "secret apprentice," and relying upon what people knew and didn't know) are *not* a set of rules or strategies for creating one's sexual identity. Instead, they are accounting practices. As Garfinkel explains:

To enumerate Agnes' management devices and to treat her "rationalizations" as though they were directed to the management of impressions and to let it go at that, which one does in using Goff-

man's clinical ideal, euphemizes the phenomenon that her case
brings to attention. In the conduct of her everyday affairs she had
to choose among alternative courses of action even though the goal
that she was trying to achieve was most frequently not clear to her
prior to her having to take the actions whereby some goal might in
the end have been recognized. Nor had she any assurances of what
the consequences of the choice might be prior to or apart from her
having to deal with them. Nor were there clear rules that she could
consult to decide the wisdom of the choice before the choice had to
be exercised. *For Agnes stable routines of everyday life were "disen-
gageable" attainments assured by unremitting, momentary, situated
courses of improvisation. Throughout there was the inhibiting presence of talk, so that however the action turned out, poorly or well,
she would have been required to "explain" herself, to have furnished "good" reasons for acting as she did. . . . I have used the
case to indicate why it is that persons would require this of each
other, and to find anew as a sociological phenomenon how "being
able to give good reasons" is not only dependent upon but con-
tributes to the maintenance of stable routines of everyday life.
. . .* (Garfinkel, 1967:184–185). [Emphasis mine]

The italicized portions of this quotation indicate the phenomenon of ethnomethodological interest. It consists of people's accounting practices for rendering the factual character of their activities and their sexual identities observable. Note that Garfinkel
is not denying that people experience sexuality as a "natural fact
of life." Rather, he views the "natural fact of life" character of one's
sex as a product of accounting practices, something people produce.
Thus, the member's sense of social structure, along with his commonsense knowledge, has been turned into a topic consisting of the
practices used in its production. Garfinkel's study reveals additional
social phenomena behind what we typically study.

Mel Pollner's *On the Foundations of Mundane Reason* (1970)
deals with the sense of social structure. Pollner calls the member's
sense of social structure "mundane reason." Mundane reason is
founded on the presupposition of a factual and determinate world.
It is this "prejudgement which permits the sense and possibility of
a world in the first place" (Pollner, 1970:33). To study how the

presupposition of mundane reason is accomplished, Pollner examines a setting wherein mundane reason routinely becomes problematic: traffic courts. The routine occurrence of "conflicting accounts" constitutes a "crisis" in mundane reason. When two or more accounts arise, each claiming to be *the* version of "what really happened," the presupposition of mundane reason is brought into question. Since the presupposition of a factual and determinate world independent of perception predicts unanimity of accounts, conflicting accounts challenge that presupposition.

The crisis implicit in the challenge, however, does not develop. The presence of conflicting accounts does not throw members into a solipsistic doubting of reality.

> Specifically, on the occasion of conflicting accounts, mundane reason preserves its foundating presupposition by rendering problematic not the facticity of the object, but the methods through which the intended object's features are made observable (Pollner, 1970:viii).

Mundane reason preserves itself reflexively by rendering the *accounts* problematic in light of the world's facticity. In short, at the very moment when the world's facticity is rendered problematic, that same facticity is invoked to render the accounts problematic, thereby preserving the facticity. Pollner uses the occasion of conflicting accounts to reveal the essential presupposition of the facticity of the social world and to describe the methods used to preserve it. In this way, Pollner has taken the member's sense of social structure and turned it into a topic of study. The sense of social structure, with its essential presupposition of facticity, is no longer used as a tacit background for producing everyday activities. Instead, the nature of that background and its production by members is the topic of sociological investigation.

A final example of treating the factual properties of the social world as a topic are two studies I did of teachers' accounts and placement practices (Leiter, 1971; 1974). For the last several years, there has been a debate over the educational practice of ability grouping. One faction argues that children learn better when they are in groups that are homogeneous, i.e., where students are of the same academic and social level. The other faction argues that heterogeneous groups better develop students' abilities and are more equitable because minority group students are not isolated. It is further argued that ability group titles create teacher expectations which become self-fulfilling prophecies (Rosenthal and Jacobson, 1968).

Underlying both sides of the debate is a common presupposition: that students possess factual properties of being bright, slow, average, mature, or immature. The debate centers on the "proper" environment for students possessing these and other factual properties. For an ethnomethodologist, the underlying presupposition becomes the topic of study. An ethnomethodologist would study the methods of observation and reporting used by teachers, parents, counselors, and school officials to produce these properties.

The study of placement practices (Leiter, 1974) in the kindergartens of two elementary schools examines the presupposition underlying the debate on ability grouping. Both sides of the debate rest on the presupposition of the facticity of students. That is, the arguments for and against homogeneous classrooms rest on the notion of students as possessing factual properties and abilities. The only question being debated is, What is the best environment for students who are bright, average, and slow? For the purposes of my study, I was interested in how the facticity of students as possessing abilities is produced in the classroom and the kinds of practices used by the teacher to place students into the next grade. I elicited a set of accounts and analyzed them, both for their properties and for the interpretive procedures used by the teacher to produce the factual character of the students and their abilities. In the classroom, I observed and recorded the teachers' methods of observation and reporting student activities. I located a set of elicitation practices teachers used when they interviewed students in the classroom and during developmental screening tests for incoming students. Through the use of elicitation practices, the teachers produced a set of facts about the student. Another method of locating students' abilities involved using routine classroom activities as schemes of interpretation. This practice consisted of converting mundane classroom activities (putting blocks away, choosing free activities, painting, playing with blocks or games) into mini-tests by supplying tacit meaning to these activities. For example, painting a picture could be turned into a "color test" by asking the student to name the colors in his picture. When a teacher wanted to observe whether a student was a "behavior problem," she would put him in an activity that tested his ability to get along with others, such as playing with blocks with other students. There were not enough blocks for each student to build his object at the same time, so students either had to work in teams or share the blocks.

Social typification also formed a scheme of interpretation used by the teachers. Social types like "mature child," "immature child," "behavior problem," "bright child," and "slow student" were used to place students in ability groups and into first grade. This practice formed the basis for both kinds of classroom organization, ability group tracking and personality tracking. Social types, along with the tacit knowledge embedded in their use, were employed to justify placement of particular students in certain classes and groups.

This investigation of teacher placement practices (Leiter, 1971; 1974) is also a study of the members' sense of social structure. The placement of students is a result of "what kind of student" he or she is. The factual properties of any student are viewed as products of the teachers' methods of observation and reporting. These methods, as well as their use by the teacher, were the main topic of study. Thus, the members' sense of social structure was turned into a topic of study.

REVIEW

For many readers, the phrase *sense of social structure* is symbolic of the cultlike, mystical quality ascribed to ethnomethodology. In writing this chapter, I have tried to remove this mystique by showing how it forms a part of the topic of ethnomethodological study. I began with a description of its properties through Schutz's formulation of the natural attitude of everyday life. The members' sense of social structure was shown to be the perception (and experience) of the world as an intersubjective, historical reality independent of the manner in which it is addressed. Studies by Mehan (1974), Skinner (1974), and Zimmerman (1974) showed that members of society use the sense of social structure as described by Schutz to produce everyday activties. This consists of assuming that the sense of social structure is a natural fact of life. The members' sense of social structure provides the taken-for-granted facticity necessary for constructing everyday activities.

Members of society use the sense of social structure as a tacit resource for accomplishing their everyday activities. The sociologist, because he is a member of society, is not exempt from this unavoidable practice. Cicourel's (1974) study of Argentine fertility, Cohen's (1954) study of delinquency, Wieder's (1975) study of a halfway house, and others show how the sociologist's use of the sense of social structure is identical to that of the man in the street. The intention is not to debunk sociology—for what sense is there in debunking an unavoidable practice? All the examples are intended to show is that: (1) what Schutz calls the natural attitude of everyday life is the members' sense of social structure; (2) once viewed this way, the sense of social structure is no mystery; and (3) the study of how members produce a sense of social structure is the study of how the foundations of social reality are produced.

Turning the members' sense of social structure from a resource into a topic requires a shift in perspective. The occasioned corpus was introduced as a method for accomplishing this. The method consists of viewing the social world as a set of appearances, the facticity of which is produced through a set of practices. Every setting is treated as a set of unique, open-ended elements assembled through the use of a set of practices. The studies by Garfinkel, Pollner, and myself implicitly used this method. Garfinkel viewed Agnes' sex as a set of appearances which had to be assembled or produced on every occasion, using a set of practices. Pollner's study of traffic courts treats the construction of "what really happened" as an occasioned corpus; the facticity of the social world is preserved via members' use of accounting practices. In my study of teachers' placement practices, the factual properties of students are treated as being assembled by the teacher through her methods of observation and reporting.

In Chapter VI we will discuss the practices whereby the sense of social structure is sustained. Now that the sense of social structure is not so mysterious, we can move on to the next step in explaining ethnomethodology: the explication of indexicality and reflexivity. These two properties of the social world are central to creating a sense of social structure. For ethnomethodologists, the sense of social structure is an ongoing accomplishment because these two properties are unavoidable in the social world. In Chapter V indexicality and reflexivity are defined and the implications of their presence are discussed.

V

Indexicality
and Reflexivity

As has been said before, ethnomethodology examines the ways in which societal members create a sense of social structure through interpretation. Social reality, along with its sense of being a naturalistic entity independent of perception, is the ongoing accomplishment of the methods people use to observe and describe the society in which they live. Thus, the sense of social structure is not something that is accomplished once and for all, needing only occasional repair. Instead, the facticity of the social world is maintained by interpretive work that is without interruption or remedy. There is no "time out" from the use of interpretive procedures and the production of social reality (Garfinkel and Sacks, 1970:356). As properties of talk, behavior, and objects, indexicality and reflexivity make the meaningful character of the social world the product of continual interpretation.

Because objects and events are indexical, their meaningful character, including their substantive sense, is a continual accomplishment. Producing a sense of facticity or giving objects and events a meaningful character does not consist of negotiating the fit between sign and rule—as in conventional referential theories of meaning, wherein meaning is a product of following rules (Wieder, 1970: 107–135). Objects and events are made meaningful when they are embedded in an ethnographic context that is without specified boundaries and made up of ethnographic particulars which are also indexical. Common understanding, from within the ethnomethodological perspective, is not a product of shared agreement. Rather, a sense of common understanding is derived when an object or action is embedded in an assembled context (Bar-Hillel, 1954; Schutz, 1962; Garfinkel, 1967; Wieder, 1970; Cicourel, 1973).

Indexicality and Reflexivity:
Definitions and Properties

INDEXICALITY: TSORIS

When Garfinkel was asked to define ethnomethodology at the Purdue Symposium (1968), he said that it begins with a set of obstinate, unavoidable troubles that do not go away—what in Yiddish is called *tsoris*. Indeed, ethnomethodology does begin with a set of paradoxes and troubles which sociologists, philosophers, and laymen have known about for years and which have resisted all attempts at remedy. The first and most fundamental paradox centers on the concept of indexicality.

Indexicality refers to the contextual nature of objects and events. That is to say, without a supplied context, objects and events have equivocal or multiple meanings. The indexical property of talk is the fact that people routinely do not state the intended meaning of the expressions they use. The expressions are vague and equivocal, lending themselves to several meanings. The sense or meaning of these expressions cannot be decided unless a context is supplied. That context consists of such particulars as who the speaker is (his biography), the relevant aspects of his biography, his current purpose and intent, the setting in which the remarks are made, or the actual or potential relationship between speaker and hearer (Bar-Hillel, 1954; Garfinkel, 1967; Husserl, 1969; Cicourel, 1973).

Husserl (1969) called such phrases "occasional expressions" because understanding their specific sense involves supplying the details of the occasion during which the expression is used. Bar-Hillel called them "indexical expressions" and proposed that their meaning is understood only through reference to the "pragmatic context" in which they are used (1954:363). He used the word *indexical* to note that expressions or words act as indices for the context required to make specific sense of those expressions. By their equivocality, such expressions "index" a context—which, in turn, provides them with a more precise sense.

Linguists "discovered" indexical expressions when they attempted to construct mechanical transcriptions and found that phrases isolated from specific contexts can take on different meanings (De Mauro, 1967:40). Phrases are not experienced as plurisemantic by the speaker-hearer. De Mauro explains why:

> A phrase is not normally plurisemantic for the hearer but for him it is not isolated: he hears it in a precise setting made up of all he knows about the person who pronounces it, about his past experiences, his plans, about what the author of the phrase intended and so forth. . . . This enormous bundle of information, not linguistically formalized, helps the rapid selection of meaning best adapted to the situation in which the phrase was pronounced. Isolated from this framework, every phrase may be plurisemantic (1967:40).

De Mauro's statement presents the basic concept of indexicality. The talk we use to describe the social world is made up of expressions which are basically equivocal. The member of society, however, does not experience them as plurisemantic because he is continually embedding such talk within a context he has assembled to decide its meaning. This context is indefinite in scope, as indicated by the fact that De Mauro uses the term "and so forth" at the end of his list of contextual particulars. A classic example of an indexical expression is the following:

The book is in the pen.

When heard as a statement spoken by one secret agent to another, the meaning becomes "The code book has been reduced to microfilm and is in the barrel of a fountain pen." When spoken by the farmer's wife as the farmer is looking for something, the same phrase becomes "That dirty book you're looking for is in the pig pen."

The construction of meaning does not end with these contexts. Each context can be indefinitely elaborated. For example, one can go on and ask, "Which code book, ours or theirs?", "Which pen?", "Whose pen?" and so on. The farmer context can also be elaborated, for it could refer to a breeding book as much as to a dirty or a clean book. The contexts I have supplied to "The book is in the pen" are open-ended because they consist of indexical expressions. Contexts such as these can lead to more than one gloss. Thus, they cannot be regarded as equivalent to dictionary meanings. As a result of such indefiniteness, the contexts cannot be viewed as another set of rules; unlike rules, their meaning is not bounded. Furthermore, the context supplies more than just the meaning content of an indexical expression. It also supplies the sense of the meaning. That is, "The book is in the pen" does not have to be heard in the concrete sense of a book being physically inside a pen. Depending on the context supplied (and/or the hearer's interpretation), it can be heard in a metaphorical sense, such as "The writer's conception is at the stage where the writing flows smoothly and rapidly."

Everyday talk consists of such phrases—phrases whose specific sense cannot be decided without supplying a context. The contextual particulars that make up the context are assembled by the member to decide the specific sense of the talk. Once assembled, the talk is perceived as possessing stable meaning. Anything can be used as a contextual particular; hence, the context is said to be open-ended. Furthermore, the context itself is made up of indexical expressions, which means that sense has to be made of the context as well. The context, then, is not fixed, nor does it function as a set of context-free rules for determining meaning. The following examples from the ethnomethodological literature and sociology will serve both to clarify the preceding ideas and to define indexicality as it is used by ethnomethodologists.

T: But anyway he wasn't low enough to be considered, well he would have been low enough (lowers her voice) but he's Mexican-American and this district has to be very careful who they put into the retarded program. I guess it's the state now who won't put a Mexican-American into the program unless it's even lower because they've been accused of discriminating against (raises her voice). But I'm not so sure that it would have been the best thing for him anyway because he's a child with limited ability and the less frustrated he can be the better off he'll be.

I have purposely removed the above remarks from their context in order to illustrate several points about indexicality made in the preceding paragraphs. In the first place, to say that the teacher's remarks are indexical is *not* to say that they are senseless or that the reader could not make sense out of them. The reader can make sense of the first line by consulting and using the rest of the passage as a context or by imagining a set of circumstances involving the speaker (a teacher) and the person discussed (a student). The notion of indexicality, as it is used by ethnomethodologists, does not disagree that the reader could make sense of the teacher's remarks. Nor is the specific sense of the remarks at issue, because a number of meanings are derivable from them.

What ethnomethodologists focus on is *how* the reader makes sense of the teacher's remarks: the methods people use to construct meaning. Indexicality is not used to point to the utter meaninglessness of the social world, as some (Coleman, 1968; Gordon, 1974) have asserted. Indexicality points to the accomplished nature of meaning. Doubtless the reader has already constructed a meaning out of the teacher's remarks by assembling a context consisting of elements of the passage and whatever ethnographic knowledge of the society he recalls or imagines. By supplying the following ethnographic details, I may confirm or revise the reader's sense of the passage. The remarks were delivered by a kindergarten teacher during an interview that was part of my study of teachers' placement practices in two elementary public schools (Leiter, 1974). The teacher's previous remarks were, "I did have him tested for IQ because I was concerned that he was retarded and he's borderline and we can't—." I am not arguing that the reader cannot make sense of the passage without these ethnographic details. Indexicality does not refer to the meaninglessness of talk. Quite the contrary, it refers to the multiple meanings of talk and to the fact that meaning is assigned by assembling an ethnographic context for the talk (which includes using details of the talk as part of the context).

The second point this passage illustrates is that speakers also perform contexting activity to remedy the indexicality of their talk. In other words, the teacher builds an ethnographic context to give her remarks a specific sense. The phrases "he's borderline" and "but anyway he wasn't low enough to be considered" are indexical, for in addition to having more than one meaning, they are vague. They require additional information to be supplied by the reader. The teacher supplies a specific meaning by assembling a context consisting of the following ethnographic details which are features of the setting: (1) the ethnic origin of the student (T: "He's Mexican-American") and (2) the practical circumstances of the school district (T: "and this district has to be very careful who they put into the retarded program").

The third point illustrated by the teacher's account is that the ethnographic context itself is indexical because it consists of indexical expressions. The teacher's description of the practical circumstances of the school district does not provide the reader with a precise sense of what the school district has to be "careful" about or what "being careful" involves. In short, there are several meanings one can supply to this expression: they want only genuinely retarded students; the classes are so crowded that careful screening is necessary; they don't believe in the program and therefore send only the most severely retarded children to it, and so on. The point is that indexicality is an essential, unavoidable property of talk. It resists all attempts at remedy because any remedy possesses the same property. The contexts supplied by the teacher to remedy the indexical character of her talk are themselves indexical, requiring further contexting by the speaker or the hearer.

The context, then, has an open-ended character. The notion of context used by ethnomethodologists and linguists like Wittgenstein (1953) and De Mauro (1967) does not consist of a fixed, well-bounded set of elements. In the tradition of Gestalt psychology and phenomenology, the elements of the context or background are continually shifting or capable of shifting and thereby changing the meaning of that which is being contexted. Cicourel puts it this way:

The notion of particulars [context] used here differs from the notion of distinctive features in at least two important ways: almost anything the member attends to can be a particular; and no grouping of particulars crosses specific settings to form measurable sets of features unique to different objects and events to which meaning is assigned. The resulting openness, ambiguity and uncertainty will strike most readers as absurd because it robs him (sic) of the kind of measurement procedures considered the hallmark of rigorous research in the behavioral and social sciences. Yet the open character of such a theory of meaning suggests the basis for misunderstanding in everyday communication as well as its unique flexibility (1973:92).

Such flexibility is illustrated by the fact that when the teacher seeks to clarify the context with still another one, it too is indexical.

> T: I guess it's the state now who won't put a Mexican-American into the retarded program unless it's even lower because they've been accused of discriminating against—(Leiter 1971:187).

To see how this context relates to the school, we must supply additional ethnographic particulars of the school: to wit, the student population is over 50 percent Chicano. Thus, the teacher's account illustrates the notion that indexicality is without remedy. The ethnographic context used to supply meaning can be indefinitely elaborated because each further elaboration also contains indexical particulars. That the reader could have arrived at an interpretation of the teacher's account using a different set of ethnographic particulars merely supports Cicourel's notion that anything can serve as a contextual particular. The indefinite elaboration of the context produces the experience of talk as being always meaningful. That is the paradox: It is precisely the indefinite elaboration of the context that produces our experience of meaning as factual. "The range of the open possibilities of meaning of each element is narrowed by mutual specification" (Wieder, 1974:200). The research focus for ethnomethodologists thus becomes the variety of practices whereby members of society produce a context and thus the factual sense of meaning.

When a sociologist does a field study, he finds himself dealing with indexical expressions. The talk of members in the setting is indexical, and so is their behavior. The researcher is constantly confronted by the fact that the everyday talk of members of a setting takes on meaning that is peculiar to that setting. The meaning of the talk and the observed behavior would change if that "same" talk and behavior took place in another setting. To remedy this, the sociologist-anthropologist assembles ethnographic details of the setting into a context for providing a specific sense to the talk and behavior. The researcher may not always present the entire context to the reader during his analysis, but he nonetheless uses it as a resource (Cicourel, 1964; 1973; Garfinkel, 1967; Wieder, 1974). How an ethnographic context has been assembled is usually not apparent in a completed study. Only when researchers have discussed how they conduct their research is the process laid open for inspection by others.

The following account by Howard Becker, for example, relates how he found the meaning of the term "crock":

> When we first heard medical students apply the term "crock" to patients we made an effort to learn precisely what they meant by it. We found through interviewing students about cases both they and the observer had seen, that the term referred in a derogatory way to patients with many subjective symptoms but no discernible physical pathology. . . . The derogatory character of the term suggested in particular that we investigate the reasons students disliked these patients. We found that this dislike was related to what we discovered to be the students' perspective on medical school: the view that they were in school to get experience in recognizing and treating those common diseases most likely to be encountered in general practice. "Crocks" presumably having no disease could furnish no such experience (1970:35).

Becker's solution to finding the meaning of "crock" was to assemble an ethnographic context. The context consisted of determining who said it (medical students), about whom (patients), in what setting (clinical rotation in medical school), and with what purpose (to gain experience in treating and diagnosing diseases). Thus, Becker used the same procedure as the layman to remedy indexical expressions. His context had the same effect as one constructed by the man in the street: It provided a specific sense to the expression and revealed another feature of the social world to the observer.

Wieder (1974:189) reports a similar situation. A resident in a halfway house for paroled addicts was asked by a staff member to organize a baseball team. The resident replied, "You know I can't organize the baseball team." To hear that remark as meaning, "You know I can't cooperate with the staff—that would be a violation of the code," one must supply a specific context consisting of who said it (a resident), to whom (a staff member), on what occasion (group meeting), and the social relationship between the speaker and the hearer (parolee and parole agent). Change these contextual particulars, and the meaning of the expression also changes. As Wieder writes:

> If the remark "you know I can't organize the baseball team," had been uttered by one staff member vis-à-vis another staff member, I would have heard the remark as something else entirely. Depending on *which* staff member was talking and *which* staff member was listening, the remark could have been heard as "You know that it is your job, since you are on the recreation committee and I am not". . . . Each utterance upon which my analysis of the code was based was meaningful in the ways it was said socially-in-a-context. Each utterance gave sense to the context and obtained sense from its place in that context . . . (1974:187–188).

It may seem to some readers that the preceding discussion diverges from Bar-Hillel's discussion of indexicality (1954). The differences center on the implications of the notion for the treatment of context. Bar-Hillel is using the notion of indexicality to address logicians and general semanticists who complain that everyday language is not precise because of indexical expressions. They further propose that this state of affairs can be eliminated by using expressions that are context-free as opposed to context-dependent. Bar-Hillel points out that indexical expressions are essential for communication.

> The use of indexical expressions seems therefore to be not only most convenient in very many situations—nobody would doubt this fact—

but also indispensable for effective communication. Indexical language will continue to be used by scientists, philosophers and everybody else alike (1954:369).

Garfinkel and Bar-Hillel agree not only on this point but also that the attempts to eliminate indexical expressions are doomed to failure because they too contain indexical expressions. Bar-Hillel puts it this way:

> Reichenback, if I have understood him rightly, claims to have developed a method for complete elimination of indexical expressions. . . . Since this method is very intricate and interwoven with his peculiar theory of token-quotes, a criticism of which is beyond the limits of this paper, I shall state only somewhat dogmatically that a thorough investigation of this method has shown me that an elimination according to it requires additional knowledge on the part of both producer and recipient, in conformity with our former results (1954:374).

In short, because Reichenback's method requires a context consisting of knowledge of Reichenback's theory of token-quotes, it is indexical. These are the similarities between Bar-Hillel's use of indexicality and that of ethnomethodologists.

The major difference or extension is the notion of the open-ended context. The context that is assembled to decide the meaning of an indexical expression can be indefinitely elaborated because of the indexical property of the ethnographic particulars that make it up. The context is not fixed and stable; rather, the foci and fringes are constantly changing. To quote Pollner:

> The proverbial "appeal to context" as a means for determination and resolution of "ambiguities" is inadequate because the context is as "ambiguous" as the sense of the very aspects it is employed to decide. Indeed, given that the context is functionally related to the sense of the aspect in question, the aspect is a feature of its own context (1970:82).

The ethnographic particulars that form the context are context-dependent. The meaning of the context itself, then, is not something that is automatically settled once and for all; instead, it is a practical accomplishment. Bar-Hillel, however, does not treat the context as problematic in this way. By proposing that the context is also indexical, ethnomethodologists are proposing that the meaning of the context is a constant construction. The context should not be treated as a set of meta-rules governing meaning. Indexicality, as used by ethnomethodologists, is really closer to Husserl's notion of "occasional expressions" (1969). It should be remembered throughout this discussion that I am not proposing that people experience meaning as an infinite elaboration of contexts. People experience meaning as factual because of the indefinite elaboration of context as object. The indefinite elaboration provides a sense of concreteness. This is best documented by examining some representative studies. The studies that follow are intended to illustrate the indexical properties of behavior, talk, and events, as well as to illustrate the ethnomethodological approach to the study of indexicality.

GOOD REASONS FOR "BAD" CLINICAL RECORDS

A classic study centering on indexicality is Garfinkel's "Good Organizational Reasons for 'Bad' Clinic Records" (1967:186–207). It began as a study of decision making in a hospital and how patient careers are constructed. Garfinkel and his graduate students were coding a large number of clinic folders in an effort to retrieve the basis of decision making that produced patient careers. As they were coding the folders, they noticed a dwindling information return. Information on age, sex, and marital status was obtained for nearly all of the cases. The information dwindled, however, as they moved into those coding categories dealing with patient careers. The files were incomplete and vague, thus preventing the retrieval of the information they sought. Garfinkel used the term *normal troubles* to refer to the incompleteness and vagueness of the files.

"Normal, natural troubles" are troubles that occur because clinic persons as self-reporters actively seek to act in compliance with rules of the clinic's operating procedures that for them and from their point of view are more or less taken for granted as right ways of doing things. . . . The troubles we speak of are those that any investigator—outsider or insider—will encounter if he consults the files in order to answer questions that depart in theoretical or practical import from organizationally relevant purposes and routines under the auspices of which the contents of the files are routinely assembled in the first place (1967:191).

Normal troubles are thus: persistent, regular, uniform, and with "the flavor of inevitability" (191-192). These properties led Garfinkel to conclude that normal troubles could not be eliminated by revising the coding scheme or by inventing some other methodological practice. Rather than try to eliminate them, Garfinkel embarked upon the study of normal troubles and the interpretive work of reading records as phenomena of sociological investigation.

One source of normal troubles is the pragmatics of record keeping in the clinic. First, it takes time for nurses to keep records. Time spent keeping records is time spent away from other kinds of work. Second, because the records can be used to supervise the nurses, they are given deliberate vagueness. By making the contents vague, the person responsible for the entries can defend them and establish their meaningful character on his own terms. Third, the file slots act as a set of instructions for gathering information. The categories on the file can be read as a script outline that instructs the record keeper "what" information to gather and "how" to gather it. The quotation marks around "how" and "what" indicate that both are products of interpretation.

Garfinkel found that the major source of normal troubles was the indexical or occasional character of the entries. The entries are a set of hints, and "reading" them requires having to supply an ethnographic context to decide their specific sense.

We start with the fact that when one examines any case folder for what it actually contains, a prominent and consistent feature is the occasional and elliptical character of its remarks and information. In their occasionality, folder documents are very much like utterances in a conversation with an unknown audience which, because it already knows what might be talked about, is capable of reading hints (1967:200–201).

Garfinkel found that his coders continually invoked operations of the clinic to decide the sense of the folder contents. Thus, rather than revealing the patterns of interaction and operation of the clinic, reading the folders required that just such a context be supplied by the reader. It was the reader, then, who was the active agent. Accordingly, the sense of the file folders changed with the kinds of readings or ethnographic contexts being supplied.

Garfinkel used indexicality to focus on the phenomena of reading and understanding the file folders. His interest is not in indexicality *per se,* but specifically in what a person has to do to understand the files. Although Garfinkel does not provide us with examples of how coders or members of the clinic read file folders, he does provide a description of the work involved. The reader must view the contents "as tokens—like pieces that will permit the assembly of an infinitely large number of mosaics" (Garfinkel, 1967:202). This points to the open-ended property of indexical expressions that makes the construction of their meaning continual and open to revision. The reading of the clinic folders is accomplished through the use of the documentary method of interpretation (see Chapter VI). The folder contents are arranged to represent an underlying pattern of meaning—which, in turn, gives meaning to the entries. Rearranging the contents produces a change in the underlying pattern and a change in the meaning of the entries:

> A subsequent entry may be played off against a former one in such a way that what was known then changes complexion (1967:204).

In summary, the following aspects of Garfinkel's paper should be noted. First, by referring to the troubles as "normal," Garfinkel is establishing the essential character of occasionality. He is saying, in effect, that indexicality is without remedy, that there is no corrective that will eliminate it as a property of talk and behavior. Second, "reading" the clinic folders is a practical accomplishment of the reader. Whoever reads the folders must supply an ethnographic context consisting of what he knows or assumes about the clinic activities. The number of contexts, and hence readings, that can be supplied is infinite. Third, Garfinkel's interest in occasionality does not lie in specifying its properties. Indexicality is important as a pragmatic source of ongoing interpretation whereby the factuality of folder contents and clinic activities is secured.

READING TEST SCORES

Garfinkel's programmatic statements concerning the unavoidable character of indexicality and the open-ended character of contexts have been implemented in my study (which was reported in *Sociology of Education Journal*, Summer 1976) of the placement practices kindergarten teachers use to assign students to ability groups and to the next grade (Leiter, 1974). I had the opportunity to observe how teachers read the results of standardized tests. One of the stated reasons for the use of standardized tests is to eliminate the teacher's use of subjective knowledge. As Goslin writes:

The most widely used technique for achieving objectivity in a written test is the multiple choice question in which the respondent is forced to choose one of several answers, thus eliminating subjective judgements on the part of the grader as to the correctness of the answer (1966:15).

Such attempts to remedy the teacher's subjective knowledge have not only failed but are doomed to fail because standardized test scores are not unequivocal for the teacher. While they eliminate one level of equivocality, as Goslin notes, they create another one that is important for the teacher. Unlike the researcher who is interested in the distribution of scores for different populations, the teacher's task is to determine ability and promote students into the next grade. The teacher wants to find out *what* each student knows. The test scores do not tell the teacher what she needs to know because they do not recover the kinds of social and academic knowledge used to take the test or the reasoning used to apply the knowledge.

> Given that the score and the score sheet are the only records of the testing session, there is little way to take the child's background knowledge into account. There is no way to record the recognitions, linkings, explanations, and stories about the items that routinely go on in a testing session. Most certainly there is no way that such behavior can be taken into account in raising or lowering the score (Roth, 1972:277).

The scores, like the folder contents in Garfinkel's study, are occasional expressions (Husserl, 1969). To use the scores, the teacher must render them meaningful by embedding them in just the kind of knowledge the test scores are supposed to replace. This unending circle suggests what Garfinkel (1967) and others (Garfinkel and Sacks, 1970; Pollner, 1970; and Wieder, 1974) have proposed: The traditional remedy for indexical expressions (the substitution of objective expressions) is itself indexical.

This is not a theoretical statement. It is grounded in observations of how a teacher actually interprets the test scores of her students. Neither is the statement ironical in intent. Instead, its purpose is to direct the researcher's attention to how the teacher makes the test scores meaningful and how she secures their objectivity. The implication for ethnomethodological research that emerges from this finding is not to dismiss it as "bad logic" or as an example of the faulty character of commonsense knowledge, but rather to study the interpretive process created by the presence of indexical expressions.

The test scores are made meaningful and objective by the use of ethnographic particulars to form a scheme of interpretation. Ethnographic particulars are the concrete, context-bound versions of contextual particulars mentioned by Garfinkel (1967), Husserl (1969), and Cicourel (1973):

> The general significance of indexical expressions, therefore, is to be found in their use by members for locating speech and non-oral

communication within a larger context of meaning by instructing the speaker-hearer to link the expression to: clock-time; the type of occasion in which it occurred; the speaker and relevant biographical information about him; the place; the intentions of the speaker; and the kinds of presumed common or special knowledge required for endowing the expression with obvious and subtle meanings (Cicourel, 1973:88).

Together these things constitute the teacher's background knowledge. Before presenting some examples of how the teacher used ethnographic particulars, it is appropriate to cite her description of the test. The teacher's conception of the test and what it measures is part of the background knowledge used to interpret the scores.

I: What I wanted to ask first of all, like which of the tests are these?

T: This is the Murphy-Durell

I: Uhh Huhh could you—

T: Reading Readiness Test.

I: Uhh Huhh (okay) what does that consist of?

T: Well, I'll just read the—briefly? Well, there's a Phoneme part which is a series of, well, four pictures in a row and they have to choose the two that begin with a certain sound you're saying. And you say "sss" and then if it's sink, and soap, they circle them and there are forty-eight of those. Forty-eight possible. Then the next part of the test is Letter Names, just purely letter recognition. Capital letters—all twenty-six—and then the other part is small letters and they have to choose from five. Then there's the Learning Rate Test where you actually teach them ten words and wait an hour and see what they can retain on that; well, I guess that's it. (Leiter, 1976:60).

How the test came to be given in the school is then described by the teacher:

I: Okay, is this particular test now given routinely? I mean is this just—

T: This is the first time and we will be giving it for the next four years and this is—I mentioned the ———— materials?

I: Yeah I was wondering is this part of that?

T: This is a condition of her letting us, allowing us to use her materials was that we test the children with this particular test and she chose it. I guess—I understand she went through thirty or forty tests to find the one that she felt would be best.

I: Umm humm (go on)

T: So umm, we just did it at the end of the year. We didn't do it at the first of the year.

This section suggests the pragmatic as opposed to the theoretical grounds for testing in the schools. Although it is common to cite educational rhetoric (and the teacher tacitly invokes this when she talks about "thirty or forty tests"), in this instance the teacher is revealing more pragmatic grounds. She acknowledges that the test is not routinely given in the kindergarten but that it will be given for the next four years. The teacher's remarks suggest the purely fortuitous and pragmatic grounds for later routinization of the test. With routinization, the test takes on a "moral quality" which is quite independent of the pragmatic grounds cited by the teacher. The pragmatic reasons for using the test raise a problem with regard to the standardization of the test—specifically, its interpretation. As Garfinkel pointed out in the previous section, different pragmatic purposes lead to different interpretations of the same materials. Hence, what may be unequivocal for the researcher using the test for his purposes can become equivocal for the teacher with her pragmatic interests.

A person reading the contents of the test folders has to use his background knowledge to link the scores to the anecdotal information contained in the files (Garfinkel, 1967:186–207). In the cases that follow, we will examine a teacher's use of background knowledge to interpret the test scores of her students. The cases illustrate the following points: (1) the impossibility of eliminating indexicality, (2) the open-ended character of contexts, (3) the properties of background knowledge, and (4) the objective character of the test scores, produced through the use of background knowledge.

CASE I

The student under discussion here is a Chicano (a person whose native language is Spanish and who is a member of a family where Spanish is the primary, although not the exclusive, language spoken in the home). Her scores on the test are presented, followed by the teacher's interpretation of them.

Student A

Phonemes	11th percentile
Letter Names #1	28th percentile
Letter Names #2	38th percentile
Letter Names T	32nd percentile
Learning Rate	42nd percentile
Total Score	18th percentile

T: 1 Now A was one of the little Spanish-
2 speaking gals and ahh she will be going
3 to junior first. She did really well in
4 the learning rate test which shows her—
5 well for her we felt she did well. She's
6 right in the average group on learning
7 rates so she can learn if the word is
8 presented to her as a whole and she can
9 remember it. And we watched her as she
10 took the test and she did really remember:
11 she went right to the word, she didn't
12 have to guess or anything. Now on the
13 Phonemes, the auditory part, she was low
14 but a lot of this could have to do with
15 language you know. And so considering
16 her attention—she has an excellent
17 attention span—she really wants to learn,
18 and she wants to do well. So I would tell
19 the junior first teacher we're placing A
20 there for more language development but
21 maybe in the middle of the year she can go
22 to the first grade. She might not
23 have to stay in your room a whole year.

24   That's what I would tell you if you
25   were going to be her junior first teacher:
26   to watch and see if she can learn to
27   read just by sight and umm maybe this
28   won't be so important for her (Leiter 1976:61).

The following ethnographic details are assembled by the teacher to form and thereby accomplish her interpretation of the student's scores. First, the teacher used a social type as a scheme of interpretation for making sense of the scores. The teacher placed the student as a particular social type ("Now A was one of the little Spanish-speaking gals") and later used this social type to interpret the scores in lines 12–15.

Second, the student's placement as a certain type of student, in turn, rests on a feature of the student's biography which is also used to interpret the test scores. Part of the teacher's interpretation of the learning rate score is accomplished by using the student's biography as a scheme of interpretation (lines 3–5). Lines 3–5 suggest that the scores are being interpreted in the context of the student's biography—the fact that her native language is Spanish.

Third, the test procedure itself is also part of the teacher's background knowledge which is used for making sense of the scores, as seen in lines 3–9. Recall the teacher's earlier description of this part of the test ("Then there's the Learning Rate Test where you actually teach them ten words and wait and see what they can retain on that"). The similarity between the teacher's description of what the Learning Rate Test is designed to measure and her remark describing A's performance on the test ("so she can learn if the word is presented to her as a whole and she can remember it") suggests that she is using her sense of the testing procedure and what the test measures as a tacit resource for interpreting the score and for providing future prospects for the student.

Fourth, the student's behavior while taking the test forms part of the background knowledge used to interpret the scores. At the beginning of the interview, the teacher explained how the test was given, and, in doing so, provides us with a context for analyzing her later remarks.

T: Now I wanted to explain that we gave the test in small groups of six. Or seven was the most we had. We had a parent helper so that we could really watch to make sure—to observe whether it really appeared that they understood and went right to the answer. That's why we—you know if you give it to a huge group of children you're never really sure whether they lucked out or whether they really went right to the answer. So I feel that most of these—when I look at them, I can remember whether he was one that just guessed the whole time or whether he really knew and if so how well he did knowing that, you know, so I'm glad we did it that way (Leiter 1976:61–62).

The teacher's statement indicates that she is sensitive to the truncated nature of the test scores. This sensitivity is suggested by her comment "That's why—you know if you give it to a huge group of children you're never really sure whether they lucked out or whether they really went right to the answer." At the same time, this transcript suggests that this sensitivity is used as an interpretive resource for assigning meaning to the student's score.

With this background, let us return to the teacher's interpretation of Student A's test scores, where this sensitivity becomes useful background knowledge. When the teacher says, "And we watched her as she took the test and she did really remember: she went right to the word, she didn't have to guess or anything," she is using her background knowledge to provide the test score with a specific sense. That sense or meaning she is providing by placing the score within this context is that of the score as the product of the student's "knowledge," and hence valid. Note that it is the teacher who is providing the score with this sense. This sense does not reside in the score itself, for the score does not inform the reader whether it was the product of knowledge or of random guessing.

Fifth, the teacher's personal experience with the student in the classroom also forms part of the background knowledge used to interpret the scores. When the teacher remarks, "And so considering her attention—she has an excellent attention span—she really wants to learn, and she wants to do well," she is invoking her experiences with the student in the classroom and using them in the form of "in-order-to motives" (Schutz, 1964) to interpret the test scores. In

summary, this case illustrates the point that the background knowledge used by the teacher comes from a variety of sources and that
its use provides the test scores with their specific sense.

CASE 2

Student B is a girl in the morning kindergarten class whose placement was determined by the results of her performance on and during the test. The decision confronting the teachers was whether she
should be assigned to junior first grade. Her scores on the test were:

Student B

Phonemes	66th percentile
Letter Names #1	99th percentile
Letter Names #2	94th percentile
Letter Names T	96th percentile
Learning Rate	24th percentile
Total Score	76th percentile

Below is the teacher's interpretation of these scores, along with some
context as to how the scores were to be used:

I: 1 Did you use these scores, you've al-
      2 ready had your placement in terms of
      3 your high low group.

T: 4 We didn't have these. The only—
      5 the way that they would affect any
      6 of our placements is like the ones
      7 I told you that I would alert
      8 the teachers: they might either
      9 go ahead or perhaps come back.

I: 10 uh huhh

T: 11 And in one case in the morning on the
     12 basis of test scores and watching the
     13 child take the test we put her in
     14 first grade—on that basis. We had
     15 been watching her all along. She

16 really has you know—we just in fact
17 at the first of the year (She's Ro's)
18 and we just shook our heads. This
19 little gal was really mousey and quiet
20 and did everything slowly and so we
21 referred her for IQ testing. We thought
22 she might be retarded. And from then
23 on she just started amazing us on
24 what she was able to do. Of course,
25 when they tested her individually like
26 that they found out she had a high IQ
27 and she started really perking up and we
28 got her to talk more and found out that
29 she had absorbed everything that'd been
30 going on in the classroom. She's just
31 a quiet child.

I: 32 Uhh huhh
    33 —very fearful child. She's scared to
    34 death to go down the ramp and this
    35 kind of thing. And so she really
    36 was doing well and then when she took
    37 the test we watched her. She went
    38 right to the answers. The only part
    39 of the test that she didn't do well on
    40 was the Learning Rate Test and she had
    41 a little—oh one of the little boys had
    42 pulled her hair or something right be-
    43 fore the test and she was crying practi-
    44 cally through the whole test. And she
    45 ended up average on it but she would
    46 have done better. So in her case the
    47 test score was just—it was the final
    48 thing. Then we put her in first.

I: 49 What were her scores?

T: 50 Ohh (turning page and showing scores)
    51 let's see. To begin with . . . this
    52 was the learning rate where she didn't. . . .
    53 And she was sure of everything that she
    54 did, you know. It wasn't a haphazard
    55 kind of thing; she went right to the
    56 answers. So umm Ro notified the parents
    57 right away.

Before the teacher even begins to interpret the test scores, she provides the interviewer with a context as to how the results came to be used in determining this student's placement in first grade (lines 11–31). Note that she does not simply display the numbers to the interviewer, expecting them to speak for themselves. Rather, she begins by embedding both the student's testing and the decision to use the scores as the basis for first grade placement within a set of context-bound ethnographic details (lines 18–35). The ethnographic details assembled by the teacher are (1) the teacher's first impressions of the student ("At the first of the year, she's Ro's, and ahh we just shook our heads"); (2) the student's classroom performance ("This gal was really mousey and quiet and did everything slowly"); (3) additional impressions and conclusions drawn from her classroom performance ("and so we referred her for IQ testing. We thought she might be retarded"); (4) the student's performance on the IQ test, which is also set within a context ("Of course, when they tested her individually like that they found out she had a high IQ"); (5) the student's performance in class after the IQ test ("and she started really perking up and we got her to talk more and found out that she had absorbed everything that'd been going on in the classroom"); (6) a new impression of the child held by the teachers, which is different from the previous one and had anecdotal context ("She's just a quiet child, very fearful child. She's scared to death to go down the ramp and this kind of thing").

The teacher then turns to the student's scores. Her interpretation of them rest on her use of background knowledge. Student B's scores are thoroughly embedded within the test setting. Student B's behavior during the testing period is used to interpret the scores and to provide them with a sense of "validity," as the product of the student's knowledge. There are two instances of this use of background knowledge:

(1) T: . . . and then when she took the test we watched her. She went right to the answers.

(2) T: And she was sure of everything that she did, you know. It wasn't a haphazard kind of thing; she went right to the answers.

The second instance strongly suggests that the teacher is using the student's behavior during the testing to provide the scores with the sense that they are the product of Student B's knowledge. In that instance, the teacher's comment, "and she was sure of everything that she did," can be read as saying, "The scores were the result of what she knew, not guessing"; thus, the teacher is providing the scores with their validity.

The most dramatic use of background knowledge occurs with the interpretation of Student B's performance on the Learning Rate Test. The interpretation was as follows (39–46):

> T: The only part of the test that she didn't do well on was the Learning Rate Test and she had a little—oh one of the little boys had pulled her hair or something right before the test and she was crying practically through the whole test. And she ended up average on it but she would have done better.

Here the background knowledge consists of a context-bound incident occurring before the test and the student's subsequent behavior during the test. The phrase "context-bound" indicates that the incident is tied to a setting by the teacher. In fact, the statement, "She ended up average on it but she would have done better," suggests that the teacher intends the anecdote to serve as a context for the student's score. The teacher's use of this background knowledge is no small matter, for it normalizes a rather large discrepancy in the student's performance—a discrepancy that could cast doubt on the validity of the other scores. In this way, background knowledge serves to sustain the facticity of the teacher's perception of the student and her performance.

During the interview the teacher contrasted the two cases that follow, thereby revealing the background knowledge she used to interpret the scores. The test scores for the two male students contrasted are listed below, followed by the teacher's interpretation. For the reader's convenience, the teacher's interpretation will be interrupted to examine each of the cases.

Student C

Phonemes	44th percentile
Letter Names #1	26th percentile
Letter Names #2	34th percentile
Letter Names T	30th percentile
Learning Rate	42nd percentile
Total Score	30th percentile

Student D

Phonemes	58th percentile
Letter Names #1	50th percentile
Letter Names #2	64th percentile
Letter Names T	58th percentile
Learning Rate	66th percentile
Total Score	64th percentile

T: 1   C did about what we figured he would
2   do by the time we'd get to the test.
3   He was the one that we thought would
4   just go to town, you know, an' really
5   we thought he would be one of the
6   brightest in the class. An' he
7   didn't perform to our expectations.
8   The test showed us about what we ex-
9   pected it would show us by the end of
10   the year. Now I thought I would com-
11   pare him to D. C's going to first
12   grade mainly because he has good work
13   habits and he does seem to still show
14   that kind of—I don't know I just
15   feel he can do better than this. I
16   really do—and I don't—I think there's
17   a lot of pressure at home to do well
18   and the mother wants badly for her
19   children to achieve. It's a Black
20   family, she wants to maybe she told
21   me she wanted, you know, prove her
22   family could earn their way an' ahh
23   contribute something to society.

24 So there may have been a lot of pres-
25 sure and he may just have gotten con-
26 fused. Anyway, he's still going to
27 first grade because I think he has
28 what it takes an' his work habits are
29 good. Now D who actually did better
30 than C on the test—these scores indi-
31 cated C who sat there and took the
32 test instructions in and did the test (Leiter 1976:62).

Let us examine the background knowledge of Cases 3 and 4 used by the teacher to interpret C's scores. First, part of the background knowledge consists of information about the student gathered through daily contact in the classroom. This background knowledge is contained in the teacher's opening statement (lines 1–10), which serves to place the scores in a context by identifying the person taking the test and how he has performed during the year. The last remark in this example, "the test showed us about what we expected by the end of the year," as well as her next statement citing the student's "work habits," suggests that the test scores are intentionally being placed in the context of the teacher's knowledge of the student's classroom performance. Through such background knowledge, the test scores are provided with their specific sense of being "no surprise" to the teacher.

Second, in lines 14–26, the teacher uses what she knows about the student's family life as background knowledge; specifically, she sees the scores as the product of "confusion" rather than ignorance. The teacher is using her own folk theory of social behavior to interpret the score. This theory contains notions about the effect of aspiring parents upon their offspring, as suggested by her remark, "So there may have been a lot of pressure and he may have gotten confused." This theory, and the ethnographic details which form part of its data, are used by the teacher as a scheme of interpretation for providing the scores with their specific sense, much as the sociologist uses similar theories.

Third, lines 30–32 show the teacher using Student C's behavior during the testing period as a scheme of interpretation. Here, as in the previous case, the scores are provided with the sense that they are valid.

This point is perhaps more dramatically demonstrated by turning to the teacher's interpretation of D's scores. In the first ten lines of the interpretation that follows, the teacher uses D's behavior in the test setting as an interpretive resource. The teacher reconstructs his behavior and then uses it to assign meaning to the student's scores.

T: 1 D it was a struggle every minute of
    2 the testing period to get this out
    3 of him. This was . . . yeah . . . he did,
    4 he answered the questions by himself.
    5 I didn't answer them for him, but I
    6 had to sit there and point my finger
    7 just to keep his attention on the
    8 right line and to make sure he was in
    9 the right place. An' he'd be under the
    10 table and up on top. So even though D
    11 is capable of doing this well academically,
    12 his emotional problems, his immaturity
    13 keep him from I mean it just—he's just
    14 not ready for reading. He can't
    15 sit that long. He's not ready emotionally.
    16 He's ready academically, I mean he
    17 knows the stuff an' he could be bright
    18 but he has a lot of problems. And he
    19 is one that we did not refer for counsel-
    20 ling but I would definitely alert the
    21 junior first teacher to refer for counsel-
    22 ling. He's a lot like this all the time.
    23 So that's why I thought you might notice
    24 these, you know.

I: 25 Umm humm

T: 26 You know since he did do better than C
    27 why C is going one place and he's the
    28 other. And that's where teacher's
    29 judgment comes in a lot (Leiter 1976:63).

In this interpretation, D's scores are first embedded within the testing situation. The student's behavior is used to point to an underlying pattern which goes beyond the test and which undercuts what might be regarded as good results from within another context (lines 10–18). The student's behavior is treated as documenting his underlying "immaturity" and "emotional problems." This underlying pattern, in turn, is used to document the student's inability to enter the first grade program. The underlying pattern also has the effect of nullifying what are, to the teacher, good scores. This is demonstrated by examining the teacher's interpretation in light of the following statement about the reading readiness program, taken from another interview.

I: What constitutes being ready to read in terms of the readiness program? What are the standards involved in that?

T: Being ready to read?

I: Uh huhh, yes.

T: All right, well to begin with things I've said: reasonable attention span so they can sit still in a reading group and able to work independently enough on followup activities while the teacher's working with another group—these things are important (Leiter 1976:63).

The grounds invoked by the teacher are very similar to her interpretation of D's scores. This similarity suggests that her use of background knowledge is connected to tacit assumptions about the reading program, which are used as a tacit resource for interpreting the scores. Another piece of background knowledge used to interpret D's scores is his daily behavior, as suggested by the statement, "He's a lot like this all the time" (line 22).

To summarize, what is termed the "teacher's judgment" (lines 28–29) consists of using background knowledge to form a context for interpreting the scores. The background knowledge used in these two cases consisted of ethnographic details of the student's home life, his behavior in the classroom, his behavior in the testing session, assumptions about the school reading program and its social organization, and theories of social behavior.

BACKGROUND KNOWLEDGE
AND THE INTERPRETIVE PROCESS

The teacher's use of background knowledge consisting of various ethnographic details was found in every instance of deciding the placement of the students. Thirty cases (the entire class) were examined, and background knowledge was used to interpret the scores of each student.

The preceding cases and their discussion reveal several properties of background knowledge and its role in the interpretive process of creating facticity. One of the features of background knowledge is its occasionality. That is, background knowledge too requires a context for its understanding. This is because bits and pieces of background knowledge are themselves context-dependent. The understanding of background knowledge itself depends on what the reader or auditor assumes or knows about the setting.

The second feature of the teacher's use of background knowledge is that it relies on tacit knowledge. This feature, which is related to the first, is that the teacher's use of background knowledge carries with it unstated but intended additional information which is also used as an interpretive resource by the teacher. Recall that in Case 1, when the teacher said, "Now on the Phonemes, the auditory part, she was low but a lot of this could have to do with language you know," she was using a tacit theory of how taking a test in one's second language can affect the results as an interpretive resource for deciding the sense of the scores. This use of tacit knowledge is linked to the assumption that the auditor will fill in unstated but intended information.

The third feature of background knowledge is the diversity of the ethnographic details which constitute it. While background knowledge was used in every case, the specific ethnographic details comprising it varied. The conclusion to be drawn from this finding is that background knowledge (specifically, the ethnographic details making it up) is both heterogeneous and situation-specific. That is, (1) some specific ethnographic details are used in only one case, (2) others are used in more than one case but not all, and (3) when their use is repeated, their sense and the sense they make of the score is not identical across cases. The uniformity of these properties suggests that background knowledge is heterogeneous and situation-specific.

The four cases presented also suggest the role of background knowledge in the interpretive process. Numbers are equivocal when they are simply presented. It is only when they are provided with a context that they begin to take on meaning. Douglas (1970) and Cicourel and Kitsuse (1963) propose that sociologists have long used official statistics without asking what is the interpretive process (the use of commonsense concepts and the practices of common-sense reasoning) whereby the statistics are assembled. They also argue that sociologists have used their background knowledge and commonsense reasoning as an unexplicated resource for members (lay and professional). Doing "practical sociological reasoning" (Garfinkel, 1967) is a topic of study for ethnomethodologists.

The role of background knowledge revealed by the four cases is to provide the numbers with a specific sense by embedding them within a context. This role of background knowledge in the interpretive process was demonstrated in all four cases. The most dramatic was the teacher's interpretation of Student C and D's scores:

> T: These scores indicated C who sat there and took instructions in and did the text. D it was a struggle every minute of the testing period to get this out of him. That was . . . yeah he did, he answered the questions by himself but I had to sit there and point my finger just to keep his attention on the right line and to make sure he was in the right place. An' he'd be under the table and up on top.

Here the teacher's use of background knowledge is used to provide one set of scores (C's) with the sense of validity. Student D's behavior while taking the test, on the other hand, undercuts and alters the meaning his scores have for the teacher. A person reading those scores without such background knowledge would assign a different sense to them. Thus the specific sense of the scores—their meaning—depends on the background knowledge used to interpret them. This becomes a practical problem when one considers that the student's next teacher does not have access to the background knowledge used to interpret the scores and send the student into her class. She has to supply her own background knowledge, either through construction of normal forms or her own observation.

The factual character of a social object rests, in part, on its being seen as the same object in spite of situated variations. The work of creating and sustaining the facticity of an object involves normalizing situated discrepancies so that the object is still seen as the same object. There are two examples that illustrate the teacher's use of background knowledge to normalize situated discrepancies in the students' performances that could potentially change the teacher's perception of the student. The most dramatic example of this role of the use of background knowledge was in Case 2 (lines 38–46):

> T: The only part of the test that she didn't do well on was the Learning Rate Test and she had a little—oh one of the little boys had pulled her hair or something right before the test and she was crying practically through the whole test. And she ended up average on it but she would have done better.

Background knowledge, then, provides scores and objects with factual status. The facticity or objectivity of the scores thus is determined through the use of background knowledge.

The use of background knowledge results in embedding the test scores within a context so that the scores take on an objective appearance. That objective appearance is the accomplishment of subjective activity. The use of background knowledge, then, not only provides test scores with their specific sense (meaning), it also sustains the teacher's sense of social structure through the normalization of discrepancies which would destroy the congruence of the student as one particular kind of social object. While sociologists and educators imply that the use of background knowledge undermines the objectivity of the test, we have shown that it is through the use of background knowledge that the objectivity of the test is *secured*. An otherwise truncated account of the student's capacities is rendered into a rich immediate context.

SUMMARY

In the previous chapter, the sense of social structure was discussed. From the ethnomethodological perspective, the sense of social structure is a continuous, ongoing accomplishment. One reason for its ongoing nature is the indexicality (occasionality) of behavior and talk. The behavior and talk that we see, hear, and perform amounts to an unending set of indexical expressions. That is to say, their meaning is relative to the context in which they occur. Without a context, behavior and talk become plurisemantic; more than one meaning can be assigned to them. To decide which meaning among many we choose, talk and behavior occur in an ethnographic context of who the speaker is; his biography; his purpose and/or intent; the setting in which the remarks were made; and the present setting. As Cicourel writes:

> Indexical expressions force all members to retrieve by recall or invention particular ethnographic features from context-sensitive settings that will provide acceptable normative meanings to present activities and accounts of past activities (1973:85).

Although troublesome, indexicality cannot be eliminated. Every remedy for indexical expressions contains the same property. Cicourel's remarks and the previous examples provide a reason for this. The ethnographic details assembled to form a context are "features from context-sensitive settings." That is, they are context-dependent for their specific sense. The contents of the files were indeed meaningful for those who used them while also being indexical. By supplying contexts consisting of what they knew or assumed about how the clinic operated, they rendered the folders meaningful for Garfinkel and his coders. The ethnographic particulars used by the teacher to turn the test scores into objective accounts of the students' abilities are just as equivocal as the scores they interpret. For example, the teacher used the phrase "going straight to the answers" as an ethnographic particular to sustain the factual character of the test as a product of knowledge rather than guessing. The phrase is an indexical expression which, in addition to the teacher's meaning, can also indicate guessing. In spite of the continued presence of indexicality, the scores remained meaningful through the teacher's interpretation. In these cases, and others to be discussed, indexicality and meaningfulness exist side by side. Indexicality, then, is a normal trouble (Garfinkel, 1967) that orients the ethnomethodologist to his central topic: the interpretive procedures whereby societal members create and sustain a meaningful, factual environment of objects.

Reflexivity

Next to the sense of social structure, reflexivity is the second most misunderstood concept in ethnomethodology. Reflexivity is obliquely described in the literature, as the following examples suggest.

> Accounts of "plain fact" character of documents are done by members of the organization for members of the organization; they are integral features of the situations they make observable and hence organize (Zimmerman, 1974:134).

> Members' accounts are reflexively and essentially tied for their rational features to the socially organized occasion of their use, for they are *features* of the socially organized occasions of their use (Garfinkel, 1967:4).

For the nonethnomethodologist, such definitions merely state that accounts are influenced by the setting in which they are delivered. This view was recently articulated in Scott and Lyman's (1968) paper "Accounts." Reflexivity is more than that, however. It is a property of social phenomena which, like indexicality, makes social facts the product of interpretation.

Actually, the examples showing how reflexivity is described are better than one realizes at first. When defining reflexivity, it is best to remember what makes indexicality an essential property: The contextual particulars are themselves indexical. This sets up the property of reflexivity. Accounts, whether verbal or behavioral, accomplish one thing. They reveal features of the setting to the observer. However, accounts are also made up of indexical expressions, the sense of which depends on supplying ethnographic knowledge of the setting. Accounts and settings, then, mutually elaborate each other. The account makes observable features of the setting—which, in turn, depend on the setting for their specific sense. The features of a setting that are revealed by descriptive accounts and behavior do not just explicate the setting; they, in turn, are explicated by the setting.

Seen against this background, Zimmerman and Garfinkel are saying the same thing. Behavior and talk are simultaneously *in and about* the settings they describe. Accounts that sustain the "plain fact" character of documents are not delivered from an objective point outside the setting. Rather, they are obtained from *within* the setting, using indexical expressions and activities whose sense depends on the very setting in which they are performed. These same activities and expressions organize the setting; through their use as schemes of interpretation, the features of the setting are made observable. Garfinkel is proposing that because accounts consist of indexical expressions, they depend on the setting for their meaning. At the same time, a feature of any setting is the production of accounts. The setting gives meaning to talk and behavior within it, while at the same time, it exists in and through that very talk and behavior.

REFLEXIVITY OF TALK AND BEHAVIOR

Having defined reflexivity, let us provide examples of the property and spell out its implications. The first example is from a study of teachers' accounts, "Telling It Like It Is" (Leiter, 1971). During the study of teachers' placement practices (Leiter, 1974), I gathered a set of teachers' descriptive accounts of their students. One such account is presented below as an example of the mutual elaboration between account and setting. A teacher provided the following ac-

count as a part of her answer to the question "What are some of the
behaviors that you would call poor behavior?"

T: 1   . . . any behavior that's caused by real
        2   serious emotional problems or conflict;
        3   we just take them out of the room rather
        4   than constantly be, you know, disciplin-
        5   ing them.
I: 6   What would constitute a severe problem
        7   that would have to be treated that way?
T: 8   All right. We had one little boy at the
        9   first of the year who—Well he started
     10   out right at the first making noises and
     11   couldn't sit still and up and down. And
     12   half the time you wouldn't know where
     13   he was and we'd have to chase him down.
     14   And then in the meantime the rest would
     15   be getting restless. And then he, if
     16   you—our usual form of discipline in the
     17   class is if you're really bad you have
     18   to sit in the "thinking chair," which means
     19   that you have to leave the rug and sit in
     20   one of the chairs where you won't be near
     21   anyone. —Well we couldn't even get him
     22   to sit down in the chair. He would run
     23   from us and we'd try to bring him to the
     24   chair.
     25   And the kind of child that you can't
     26   discipline. I mean the children will do
     27   things wrong and they know it. But if
     28   you tell them "Go sit in the 'thinking
     29   chair,' " they'll go and do it. Or if you
     30   tell them "Go sit outside at the table
     31   until you quiet down," they'll go and do
     32   it. But this is the type of child who
     33   will say "no I won't," and then you have to
     34   chase him down and he's just as liable to
     35   run out of the room and run home. And
     36   then eventually it got worse: he would
     37   threaten the children and picked up a
     38   pair of scissors and was going after them.
     39   So this is when we have to get him out

40 of the room. And he was disturbed psycho-
41 logically.
42 Then we have had another little boy who
43 is very, very immature: and he was a
44 November birthday; just a little, little
45 boy. And he was either practically sitting
46 in my lap half the time or running around
47 the room. And just making it—if they're
48 so bad that you can't keep the rest of the
49 class involved; if they're disturbing
50 the rest of the class, that's when I feel
51 it's necessary to get them out of the room,
52 refer them for counselling because usually
53 when the behavior of the children is bad
54 they'll stop when you talk to them or
55 when you put them over in the corner they'll
56 sit there for a while. But you can run in-
57 to a couple like this that cannot even
58 be disciplined (Leiter 1971:208–209).

The reflexive property of this account lies in the fact that while it makes features of the setting observable, those features and the account are made meaningful by the setting. To make this mutual elaboration observable, one should note that the teacher is using two cases to context what she means by "any behavior that's caused by serious emotional problems or conflict." Case 1 is discussed in lines 1–41 and Case 2 in lines 42–56. Each case consists of a description of the student's behavior (lines 9–13 and 21–24 in Case 1 and 45–47 in Case 2). The teacher supplies contexts for the behaviors as well. The first context is:

. . . And then in the meantime the rest would be getting restless . . . our usual form of discipline in the class is if you're really bad you have to sit in the "thinking chair," which means that you have to leave the rug and sit in one of the chairs where you won't be near anyone . . . the kind of child that you can't discipline. I mean the children will do things wrong and they know it. But if you tell them "Go sit in the 'thinking chair,'" they'll go and do it. Or if you tell them "Go sit outside at the table until you quiet down," they'll go and do it. . . . So this is when we have to get him out of the room. . . .

The context in the second case consists of:

> . . . he was a November birthday; just a little, little boy. . . . And
> just making it—if they're so bad that you can't keep the rest of the
> class involved; if they're disturbing the rest of the class, that's when
> I feel it's necessary to get them out of the room, refer them for
> counselling because usually when the behavior of the children is bad
> they'll stop when you talk to them or when you put them over in
> the corner, they'll sit there for a while. . . .

These contexts make features of the classrooms observable. The first
context renders the routine forms of discipline and students' reactions to discipline observable. That is, from this account we can say
that one form of discipline is to isolate a student from his peers by
having him sit in a chair. The account also reveals how students re-
act to this type of punishment: Some sit in the chair when told,
while a few wander around the room. Lines 14–15 and 47–50 reveal
the practical task of the teacher: keeping the attention of twenty-
nine students while one is undermining her efforts by his behavior.
The second case reveals the criteria for identifying immature students.

These features of the setting are made observable by the teachers'
accounts—which, in turn, depend upon the setting for their specific
sense. The features elaborated by the accounts are indexical particulars that require some knowledge of the setting for their specific
sense. Without the setting as a context, their meanings are potentially equivocal. "Sitting in a chair away from the group" is a feature of the setting and at the same time depends upon the setting
for its specific sense. There is nothing inherently punishing about
sitting in a chair on the back edge of a rug. But when one surrounds it with features of the setting (can't hear the teacher as well,
can't get help from fellow students, cut off from teacher's eye contact, teacher treats it as punishment, peers treat it as punishment),
then it does become "punishment." The practical tasks of the teacher
achieve their status as such from the nature of the setting—a school.
If it were a day-care center where there was no instruction, the
teacher might not need the students' attention. Even within the
classroom setting, there are situations in which the teacher leaves

students to their own devices and does not want their attention. During "activity time" the teacher expects students to work on art projects and games *by themselves,* with little or no supervision from her. The "practical circumstances of keeping students' attention" achieve that status when further setting particulars are supplied; for example, during a lesson, all of the students are seated on the rug while the teacher is giving a lesson. In short, while the account explicates the setting by making some of its features observable, the setting, in turn, explicates the account.

This reflexive property is visible *within* the account itself. The reader should note that the teacher is illustrating a point with two cases, which are further contexted with features of the setting. These elements mutually elaborate each other in that they receive their specific sense by being played off against each other. The selected features of the classroom are made observable by the behavior of the students. These features, in turn, give that behavior its deviant sense. For example, note the inference the teacher draws from placing a student in the "thinking chair": "you have to leave the rug and sit in one of the chairs where you won't be near anyone. . . ." For the teacher, the chair's significance is that it takes the student away from the group. The chair's meaning thus elaborates the sense in which the student sitting in it is a deviant—he can't behave and is distracting the group. While the student's behavior makes this feature observable, the feature, in turn (along with its tacit meanings as drawn from the setting), provides us with the deviant character of the behavior.

The second context is also mutually elaborative of (and is elaborated by) the particulars of the case. The criteria for judging a student as "immature" and the practical circumstances of keeping the class's attention provide a context for the behavior of the student. The behavior ("he was either practically sitting in my lap half of the time or running around the room") is rendered deviant in its sense through the teacher's use of these ethnographic features. Using them as perceptual aids, a student sitting on the teacher's lap during a lesson is specifically seen as "deviant" rather than "affectionate." The behavior explicated the practical circumstances by providing a context to see them as such, while the practical circumstances (along with setting), in turn, are used to see the deviant sense of the behavior.

We can say that reflexivity is a property of accounts. It consists of the mutual elaboration between the account and the setting. Accounts reveal features of settings, and settings, in turn, provide the specific sense of accounts. Furthermore, within accounts there is a mutual elaboration between context and that which is being contexted. In both instances, reflexivity is the result of the indexical property of objects, events, and particularly talk. Reflexivity is produced through the unending chain (or circle) of indexicality. The following example from Wieder's (1974) study of the convict code illustrates the reflexive relationship between account and setting in more detail, particularly with reference to the implications of the property for the conduct of sociological research.

Wieder studied how a particular social environment is constructed. The social environment is a halfway house for paroled narcotics addicts. Wieder begins with a description of the product and then shows the reader how it is produced by residents, staff, and researchers. The social reality, as experienced by members of the setting, was one that matched sociological descriptions. There was a set of deviant behavior patterns which were typical, repetitive, and uniform. They were "caused" by residents following a set of rules, the convict code—or, as it was referred to in the halfway house, "the code." In the second half of his study, Wieder describes the phenomenon called "telling the code."

"Telling the code" is the use of maxims of the convict code, along with the idea of people following the code, to interpret the behavior of residents in the halfway house. The residents, staff, and Wieder invoked the code to find the meaning and reasonable character of acts performed by the residents. The code was invoked to supply specific sense to residents' behavior and to provide that behavior with the sense of being trans-situational. Wieder describes the staff and residents' telling the code in the following manner:

Telling the code rendered residents' behavior rational for staff by placing the acts in question in the context of a loose collection of maxims which compelled their occurrence and by portraying the consequences for those residents who did not comply with these maxims. By describing resident conduct in terms of the normative order that generated it, staff depicted residents as reasonable, acting like any man would act under the circumstances. . . . That is, one could say that residents employed this narrative to point out that an event, or "our relationship," or the behavior of that other resident, or the resident's own behavior were instances of patterns which were long standing, which had been seen before and which would be seen again. One would also then say that residents were "telling the code" in showing, or perhaps to show, that the particular event under consideration would have been enacted by any resident . . . (1974:156, 164–165).

Telling the code amounted to doing folk sociology. The "sociological explanation" was used by members of the halfway house to produce social reality. How this was accomplished is discussed in Chapter VI. For now, our interest lies in Wieder's analysis of how he told the code. Wieder describes how he came upon both the code and the deviant behavior patterns. His description shows that without one he could not know the other.

Wieder discovered the code and the deviant behavior patterns in bits and pieces. The code was never recited to him maxim by maxim. Instead, elements of the code were presented apart from each other and separated from the objects and events they were purportedly about. This last condition means that even if a resident had recited the complete code, Wieder (or any other researcher) would have been left to fit the code to observed behaviors. He proceeded to use what bits and pieces he had acquired as perceptual aids in recognizing additional elements of the code:

An example of the use of this method is provided by the interpretation of a remark I overheard during my first week at halfway house. I passed a resident who was wandering through the halls after the committee meetings on Wednesday night. He said to staff and all others within hearing, "Where can I find that meeting where I can get an overnight pass?" On the basis of what I had already learned, I understood him to be saying, "I'm not going to that meeting because I'm interested in participating in the program of halfway house. I'm going to that meeting just because I would like to collect the reward of an overnight pass and for no other reason. I'm not a kiss-ass. Everyone who is in hearing distance should understand that I'm not kissing up to staff. My behavior really is in conformity with the code, though without hearing this (reference to an overnight pass), you might think otherwise." I thereby collected another "piece" of talk which, when put together with utterances I had heard up to that point (which permitted me to see the "sense" of this remark) and used with utterances I had yet to collect, was employed by me to formulate the general maxim, "Show your loyalty to the residents" (1974:185).

Wieder's method is one that any ethnographic-member uses to discover the culture of the group he is studying. The key feature of the method is its reflexive character: the discovery of something new (or old) on the basis of what is already known. Recognizing elements of the code depends on knowing something about them and using that something to recognize instances of what is already known or instances of new elements. In this way, the code is said to reflexively elaborate itself (Wieder, 1974). Telling the code, then, is a process of mutual elaboration wherein old elements are used to gather new ones—which, in turn, provide each other with their specific sense.

This mutual elaboration extends to the behavior in the halfway house. The code rendered features of the setting (deviant behavior patterns) observable while simultaneously obtaining its meaning from the setting. Wieder writes that he could not have grouped the behaviors of residents into the deviant behavior patterns if he did not have the code as a scheme of interpretation. In other words, the behavior of residents was indexical. Grouping the behaviors into the particular deviant pattern was accomplished by seeing them as a product of following the code. If one imputes a different set of motives (a different code, if you will) to the residents, the meaning—and hence, the classification of their behavior—is altered. Not only would the names of the patterns change, but so would their deviant sense.

For example the behavioral particulars accounted for by the rule, "Show your loyalty to the residents," were analyzed in my description as doing "distance, disinterest and disrespect," "passive compliance," and "demands and requests." Without the organizing motivational scheme of the rule, "Show your loyalty to the residents," the particular observed behaviors organized under the names' titles (e.g., "doing disinterest and disrespect") would not have been collected under those titles and would, in turn, have been seen by me and anyone else (e.g., the staff) as meaning something different than they were seen to mean (Wieder, 1974:193–194).

Thus, the code and the setting mutually elaborate each other. The behavior patterns (their grouping and their sense of being deviant) are discovered through the code, while the meaning and existence of the code are known through the behavior. Both reveal and are revealed by each other because both are part of the setting.

The reflexive character of the code is seen in the fact that it is both in and of the setting. The code is not told from outside the setting; it is told from within. Telling the code is an act performed within the setting it describes. It is another set of indexical expressions which are used to context other behaviors and which, in turn, are contexted by the setting. By the "setting" I mean the behaviors, what the setting is, who is in the setting, the typical motives of the members, and so on.

Wieder's study not only illustrates reflexivity as a property of behavior and talk, it also spells out some of the implications. First, reflexivity and indexicality are two essential properties of objects and events. Reflexivity is essential not only because it is without remedy but also because of the meaningful character of objects and events. Reflexivity ties objects and events to settings in such a way that they are not experienced as plurisemantic by an observer.

But when the elements of a setting occur in their natural position and are juxtaposed with one another, the behaviors and talk mutually fulfill and determine one another. The range of the open possibilities of meaning of each element is narrowed by mutual specification (Wieder, 1974:200).

Thus reflexivity, with its circularity, is essential for the meaningful character of social reality.

Second, the causality of rules must be reconsidered in light of reflexivity. The place of norms as part of a deductive cause-and-effect relationship is called into question by Wieder's data. The rules of proof in deductive logic require the literal description of variables. That is, the dependent and independent variables must be capable of being described independently of each other and of the setting (Wilson, 1970). Wieder's data suggests that the code does not meet this deductive criterion. Instead of being describable and observable independently of the setting and the behaviors it "causes," the code's sense is derived from them and, in turn, provides them with their specific sense. This finding challenges sociology's attempt at deductive theory by reminding us, as Weber (1947) did, that social phenomena are *fundamentally* different from natural phenomena. The fundamental difference is the property of indexicality. Social behavior is context-dependent. This difference alters the theoretical and empirical status of rules from causal agents to interpretive devices used by the observer to render behavior understandable. The use of rules as interpretive devices is discussed in Chapter VII. Third, as we shall see in the section that follows, reflexivity and indexicality form the basis for an alternative theory of meaning in the social sciences.

Meaning by Context

The properties of indexicality and reflexivity form the basis of a theory of meaning and common understanding that is quite different from the one used by contemporary sociologists. Social interaction, according to normative sociology, is possible because the members of society share a common language. In *The Social System,* Parsons is explicit:

> Thus for the interaction process to become structured, the meaning of a sign must be further abstracted from the particularity of the situation. Its meaning, that is, must be stable through a much wider

range of "ifs" which covers the contingent alternatives not only of ego's action but of alter's and the possible permutations and combinations of the relations between them (1951:11).

For Parsons social interaction is stable because the meanings of language and behavior are detached from particular situations by a process of abstraction. Ethnomethodologists, on the other hand, use the properties of indexicality and reflexivity to construct a theory of meaning wherein the stability of interaction and meaning is accomplished by embedding (rather than removing) language and behavior in particular settings (contexts). Before we proceed to the ethnomethodological theory of meaning by context, however, more must be said about the current sociological theory of meaning—meaning by rule (Wieder, 1970).

Throughout much of the sociological literature, there runs an assumption of common cognitive consensus. Homans' definition of sentiment clearly contains such an assumption:

> Sentiment need not be verbal symbols—a kiss is not verbal—but all sentiments do resemble language in that their connection with what they refer to is shared by a particular community and not all mankind (1961:33–34).

What is shared, according to Homans, are the substantive meanings of the symbols. This sharing of substantive meanings is brought about by the internalization of rules—rules governing the appropriate use of language categories. Common cognitive consensus is essential; without it, members would not be able to jointly recognize the meanings of norms and situations as being the same (Wilson, 1970).

Furthermore, this sharing of meanings is an essential assumption in sociological research. The use of field methods, surveys, and experiments rely on it. Experimenters assume that the instructions and stimuli mean the same thing to all subjects (Cicourel, 1964; Friedman, 1967). It is further assumed that the experimental situation, as well as the talk done within it, are mutually understandable by the participants. Survey research relies on the same assumption:

that the questions and the alternatives have the same meaning for the subjects and the researcher. In the course of their work, researchers encounter different interpretations of their instructions and questions by subjects, and often curse themselves for not having anticipated a particular difference in interpretation. In spite of these pragmatics, researchers using experiments and surveys recommend their findings on the basis of standardization. Field work relies on common cognitive consensus only to the extent that it is assumed to exist between the researcher and the people he is observing. Field work relies on this assumption less than the other forms of investigation because its very method brings the field worker into contact with evidence that common cognitive consensus as normatively described does not exist.

Language and meaning in contemporary sociology form, in effect, a social version of Jerome Bruner's (1956) theory of categorization (Wieder, 1970; Handel, 1972). Categorization, or the classification of objects into groups, is essential for the stable character of social reality. Without categories, the world would be without shape and without order. Everything would be unique. We impose stability upon the world by categorizing—by linking and grouping objects into classes. The process of categorization consists of matching features of an object with criterial attributes. *Criterial attributes* are differences that serve to distinguish objects from one another. According to Bruner, anything that makes a difference to an individual can serve as a criterial attribute. Such attributes are formed by the individual and used to group objects into classes. Contemporary sociological theory and ethnosemantics add a social component to Bruner's individualistic theory by proposing that the criterial attributes are part of a society's culture and are therefore shared, learned, and transmitted (Wieder, 1969; 1970). The program of ethnosemantics consists of learning the cultural map of a people by eliciting their cognitive categories (Eglin, 1974).

By concerning themselves solely with denotative meanings, ethnosemanticists are subscribing to a theory of meaning by rule. They are, in effect, equating everyday categories with the categories of formal logic, the meanings of which are determined by rules. Parsons (1951:11) does the same thing by equating the stability of meaning with its detachment from "the particularity of the situation." For Parsons and the ethnosemantics, stable meaning is equated with the context-free meaning of terms used in formal logic.

It is at this point that ethnomethodologists part company with conventional theory.* They do not agree with the theory of meaning by rule because everyday language and its categories are not identical to those of formal logic. Schutz states the difference this way:

> On the level of everyday experience, however, logic in its traditional form cannot render the services we need and expect. Traditional logic is a logic of concepts based on certain idealizations. In enforcing the postulate of clearness and distinctness of the concepts for instance, traditional logic disregards all fringes† surrounding the nucleus within the stream of thought. On the other hand, thought in daily life has its chief interest precisely in the relation to the fringes which attach the nucleus to the actual situation of the thinker. This is a very important point. It explains why Husserl classifies the greater part of our propositions in daily thought as "occasional propositions" (1964:76).

Schutz is proposing here that the meaning of commonsense categories is not found in the formal meanings governing their use but rather in the "fringes" or context. This distinguishes everyday language from that of formal logic. Instead of using terms that are context-free, the man in the street uses terms that are context-dependent. Everyday categories and terms are indexical expressions that depend on context rather than rules for their specific sense.

The distinction made by Schutz is also found in Mannheim's *Ideology and Utopia* (1936). Mannheim proposes a distinction be-

---

* Ethnomethodologists are not the only ones who do not subscribe to the theory of meaning by rule as a description of everyday language use. Wittgenstein (1953), Austin (1961), DeMauro (1967), and Blumer (1969) also object to common cognitive consensus and propose a theory of meaning by context.

† *Fringes* refers to the context or connotative meanings, while *nucleus* refers to the denotative meanings.

tween scientific and prescientific terms. The former have context-free meanings, whereas the latter are context-dependent.

> This so-called prescientific, inexact mode of thought however (which paradoxically the logicians and philosophers also use when they have to make practical decisions) is not to be understood solely by the use of logical analysis. It constitutes a complex which cannot be readily detached either from the psychological roots of the emotional and vital impulses which underlie it or from the situation in which it arises and which it seeks to solve (2).

Mannheim not only makes the same distinction as Schutz, he proposes that when the scientist leaves his theorizing and returns to the world of everyday life, he uses the prescientific vernacular to accomplish his everyday plans and projects. Occasional (indexical) expressions are thus used by both laymen and professionals in everyday life.

Schutz and Mannheim are proposing that the categories of everyday language are different from those of formal logic. The basis of this proposal is that everyday typifications are expressions that are context-dependent. By proposing a theory in which meaning is determined by rules, social scientists have substituted a scientific thought mode for the commonsense mode used in everyday life. This substitution does not permit the study of the construction of social reality as done by the man in the street or the sociologist. The existential nature of social reality requires that the meanings and properties of everyday typifications be studied on their own terms. It is through the use of these typifications (as opposed to logico-deductive categories) that members of society create the facticity of social reality.

The macro-sociologist may say, "That's all well and good if that is your topic, but when I deal with large-scale social phenomena like suicide, crime, and birth rates, I don't need to be concerned with the everyday meanings that people use." Schutz (1962) and Douglas (1970), however, argue otherwise.

In the first place, sociological constructs are "second-order constructs." That is, they are constructs about members' sense making and are produced through members' methods for making sense of situations and events.

> The thought objects constructed by the social scientists refer to and are founded upon the thought objects constructed by the common sense thought of man living his everyday life among his fellow men. Thus, the constructs used by the social scientist are, so to speak, constructs of constructs made by the actors on the social scene . . . (Schutz, 1962:6).

Take, for example, the concept of personality. Inkles (1968) uses a definition of personality that "lies on the insistence that all forms of social organization have personal meaning or psychological implications for the participants . . ." (Inkles, 1968:10). Here personality refers to the meanings social organization has for the individuals in a society. Personality, thus, is a second-order construct because it depends upon the sense-making activity of people. If people do not make sense of social organization, then the very basis of personality is eliminated.

In the second place, social facts, such as rates of crime, suicide, mental illness, voting behavior and the regularities of attitudes, have their point of origin in the commonsense categories and commonsense judgments of people (Cicourel and Kitsuse, 1963; Garfinkel, 1967; Cicourel, 1968; Douglas, 1970). Suicide and crime rates are products of decisions made by police, coroners, doctors, and lawyers in defining an event as a "suicide" or a "crime." This decision making becomes one of the topics discussed in the following chapter. These decisions are produced through the use of commonsense typifications and ethnographic particulars which are assembled into contexts through the use of interpretive procedures.

The theory of meaning that emerges from the indexical property of language and behavior is meaning by context. According to such a theory, meaning is not a product of a set of internalized rules but is constructed by assembling an ethnographic context of interpretation for occasional expressions. The ethnographic context is not another form of context-free rules because it too consists of indexical expressions. As the context changes, so does the meaning of the object and the event. The context, from this perspective, does not consist of a fixed set of particulars. Instead, it is revisable at any time. In addition, one does not need to construct the same context to understand the other person or to sustain the sense of understanding him. Common understanding is not the result of sharing substantive meaning. It is a product of assembling contexts of interpretation.

Skinner's (1975) study of how doctors and patients understand each other suggests that common understanding is not the result of substantive meanings that are shared by the participants. Instead of tracing the source of problems of understanding between doctors and their patients, Skinner's interest was in how understanding was produced. She tape-recorded and observed medical examinations at community medical clinics in a large Southwestern city. At the conclusion of each examination, Skinner interviewed the doctor and the patient. During this interview, she asked both of them to state what each meant by his own statements and questions and what he took the other to mean. These interviews were also tape-recorded. All the doctors and patients reported that they understood the other and were understood in turn. Upon examination of the interview transcripts, however, Skinner found that doctors and patients differed on what they understood the other to mean. Take, for example, the following exchange between a doctor and his patient and their interpretation (Skinner, 1975: 100–102):

EXAMINATION

Dr: How much of the Benedryl are you having to take.

Pt: Mmmm less, I take something Friday, Saturday. I didn't take any yesterday. I haven't taken any today cause I didn't felt you know nauseated, today or yesterday.

INTERPRETATION

I: How about when he asked you how much Benedryl you'd taken. What do you think he was asking you that for?

Pt: Well I guess to see had I taken any of the medication 'cause a lot of people when they give it, give 'em medication, and sometimes I do that when they give me medication I won't take it, take it home and throw it in the drawer and that'd be the last time you'd see it until I get ready to clean up and then I throw it away.

Dr: Some people say are saying they're well say that they're doing all right. But actually they're having to take the medicine every—just as often as they can in order to suppress their symptoms. And you're, you're what they're trying to say is yeah your treatment's working (laugh). And you might assume when they say that that they're well and they, they're not well. They're just uhh that your treatment's working. She said that she hadn't taken the Benedryl in a couple of days so I figured that she's all right.

Doctor and patient reported that they understood each other. Yet the basis of that common understanding was not a substantive sharing of meaning. The doctor and the patient have substantively different interpretations of the intent behind the doctor's question and the meaning of the patient's response. Thus, we are led to speak of a sense of common understanding rather than of understanding. The basis for this sense of understanding is the ability to supply a context for what is said. The doctor and his patient embed the intent of the question within an ethnographic context: how patients typically do not take the medicine prescribed and think they're well because they are taking so much that they are suppressing symptoms. It is important to note that the ethnographic contexts are not the same and that the meaning each derives comes from the particular context constructed. This suggests that common understanding is a product of assembling a context of interpretation. It does not depend on sharing the substantive nature of the contexts. As long as the doctor and patient can continue to supply contexts, even different contexts, they are able to sustain a sense of understanding. The context acts as a perceptual aid in seeing the meaning of the other's talk and in providing that talk with the sense of being out there for both to see. The use of rules and social types in this process is one of the topics discussed in the following chapter.

Skinner's study has an important limitation: It does not deal with the joint construction of meaning over time. Because she did not follow one group of patients through a series of examinations, Skinner was unable to observe how meaning is managed across and between examinations. An examination does not come to a complete end when the patient leaves. The end is temporary; the examination is reopened the next time patient and doctor meet. Thus, each subsequent examination becomes an occasion in which doctor and patient mutually repair and discover new meanings. Without this temporal flow, Skinner's study can be easily misinterpreted as saying that the construction of meaning does not involve the problem of preserving the continuity of meaning.

Indexicality and Ethnomethodology

Indexicality and reflexivity are not, by themselves, topics of ethnomethodological inquiry. They are properties of behavior, settings, and talk which make the ongoing construction of social reality essential. Because behavior is potentially equivocal, people are continually creating its specific sense by embedding it in a context. The fact that the behavior and the context mutually elaborate each other not only creates a sense of specificity for the meaning, it also creates an unending circle of interpretation. As a result, the meaning of objects and events, as well as our perception of them, is conferred upon them. From the ethnomethodological perspective, the facticity of the social world is a continual accomplishment through the use of interpretive procedures.

All of the studies in this chapter document this relationship. Although Skinner demonstrates the indexical properties of talk, the purpose and topic of her study is to describe the interpretive procedures people use to sustain a sense of common understanding. Her study suggests that assembling a context to create a sense of social structure does not depend on a common context. Leiter's (1974) study demonstrates that indexicality is without remedy because the remedy (substituting standardized test scores for the teacher's use of subjective knowledge) is indexical. The main topic of his study, however, is how the teacher secures the objectivity of the scores through the use of background knowledge. Garfinkel's study of clinic records begins with a description of their indexical properties, but his emphasis is on *how* his coders and clinic members read the folders. Wieder's (1974) study uses the properties of indexicality and reflexivity to show that the meaning and organization of the behaviors in a halfway house are accomplished by using the convict code as a scheme of interpretation. The code has to be used in this fashion because it does not predict what responses will be made by residents, since the maxims of the code are indexical. The maxim "show your loyalty to the residents" does not inform the researcher how residents will enact it during group or other occasions. The researcher cannot predict whether the residents will be tense and hostile or slouching in their seats; both are equally plausible.

> Instead of predicting behavior, the rule is actually employed as an interpretive device. It is employed by the observer to render any behavior he encounters intelligible i.e., as coherent in terms of patterned motivation (1974:179).

So although indexicality and reflexivity are not topics by themselves, they are used to point to the continual construction of social reality. The central topic of ethnomethodology is the methods people use in that process.

VI

Topics in Ethnomethodology: Accounting Practices and the Documentary Method

A source of confusion for many readers is the fact that the study of members' sense-making methods does not take a single form. There is seemingly no unified approach taken by ethnomethodologists. Garfinkel (1967), Pollner (1970), Zimmerman (1970) and Leiter (1971) study accounting practices used to construct descriptive accounts. The *use* of rules by members of society is another way of studying members' sense-making methods and commonsense reasoning. Emerson (1969), Leiter (1969), Zimmerman (1970) and Wieder (1974) have studied how members of society use rules. A third form of studying members' methods is found in the works of Sacks (1965) and his associates (Schegaloff, 1968; Turner, 1972, Goldberg, 1975). Theirs is the study of the methods used to construct everyday conversations and the development of a generative model of turn-taking. Aaron Cicourel and his students (Cicourel et al., 1974) study a fourth area: how members understand everyday conversations.

While the form and even the topic of study may differ, two themes unite all ethnomethodological studies: the sense of social structure as the managed accomplishment of members of society and the study of the methods used in that accomplishment. These themes, in turn, have their basis in the ethnomethodological version of the problem of social order.

The Problem of Social Order: An Alternative View

Each topic of ethnomethodological study is a specialized way of addressing the problem of social order as formulated from within the ethnomethodological perspective. The problem of social order forms a schema for reading the ethnomethodological literature. The elements of the ethnomethodological problem of social order have been described in previous chapters. It does not consist of providing causal explanations for patterned social action. Instead, we will deal with the ways members of society assemble settings and behaviors so as to create and sustain a sense of social order as it is experienced commonsensically. Members of society are continually engaged in displaying and detecting the orderly features of the social world, which are experienced as the sense of social structure. Social order, for ethnomethodologists, refers to a *sense of social order. Order,* refers to the factual properties of objects and events. The problem of social order, from the ethnomethodological perspective, deals with how people create and sustain the factual character of the social world as a patterned object independent of perception.

Unlike the natural sciences, the social sciences cannot take for granted the social world as a *natural object.* Because objects and events in the social world depend on recognition by members of society for their existence, the social world must be regarded as an existential product (Walsh, 1972; Schutz, 1962; 1964). As a result of this difference, the social scientist has an additional field of study available to him: the factual character of the social world as a product of members' sense-making practices. The solution to the ethnomethodological problem of social order is that facticity is socially produced through methods of interpretation used to observe and report events. As Zimmerman succinctly puts it:

> We generally hold the view that the social world exists in-and-through the practices members employ to make it observable and reportable. In as plain and bold language as I can summon the social world as an *object of ethnomethodological* investigation consists, is identical with, is nothing more than, the practices members employ to make it observable and accountable (1971:4).

Admittedly, this version of social order turns commonsense reality on its head. This is done so that commonsense reality can become a topic of study. By adopting this version of social order, the sociolo-

gist is able to suspend his belief in the facticity of the social world
in order to study the methods of interpretation whereby societal
members accomplish that facticity in interactional settings. It would
be a mistake to view Zimmerman's statement as a rejection of commonsense reality. Zimmerman and the other ethnomethodologists
whose works are discussed are adopting this analytical stance in order to study a particular phenomenon: the interpretive procedures
societal members use to provide themselves and others with the
continual sense that the social world is an object independent of
perception.

Accounts and Accounting Practices

The preceding version of the problem of social order forms a rationale for treating members' descriptive accounts as a topic of
study rather than as mere rationalizations of their circumstances.
Descriptive accounts contribute to the sense of social order in everyday life. Wieder and Zimmerman (1976) make this clear by invoking a sociologist from another planet who visits earth and no-
tices that people are constantly describing and explaining to each
other what they have done. The interplanetary sociologist files the
following report:

Each human group is characterized by the fact that its members
appear to be almost continually engaged in describing and explaining themselves. Virtually all humans can tell such stories although
their stories are not accorded equal attention and respect by their
fellows. While this invidious comparison of stories should be a topic
of further research, I can report the following observations. . . . In
any case, human stories, whether told by ordinary people or by
those professionally charged with such story telling, play similar
roles. They are stories *about* the society and events *within* it. Simultaneously, they organize and accomplish the features of society and
the events they report. Thus the features of social scenes and the activities that comprise them—whatever their substantive character—

are made to happen *in and through the telling* because this is the way humans instruct each other on how to see the organization of their social world (1976:106–107).

The stories that people are continually telling are descriptive accounts. Through their telling, they organize and render observable the features of society and social settings; they are thus *mini-ethnographies*. I use this term because descriptive accounts and ethnographies serve the same purpose. They share similar topics (what people do and why they behave the way they do), and are constructed using the same methods of interpretation. When members of society tell ethnographies to each other in the form of verbal reports, they seek to communicate their understanding of events to each other. While they are communicating their understanding to others, they are simultaneously rendering the event observable and understandable to themselves. For example, as a graduate student, I took an undergraduate course in social stratification. Some of my undergraduate friends were also taking the course, and as we left each class they asked me for a recapitulation of the lecture. While I was telling them my version, I was making observable to myself and to my friends features of the lecture. The person who listens to these ethnographies, like the anthropologist, uses them to construct an understanding of the event. People, like ethnographers, use the details of the ethnography to create the meaning and their understanding of the event. Descriptive accounts, like ethnographies, form perceptual aid for assigning/finding meaning in objects and events.

The details that make up lay ethnographies are also similar to those used by an anthropologist to understand what he sees and are then reconstructed to fit into his ethnography. The details of lay and professional ethnographies include settings, people in the settings, typical behaviors, typifications used, typical motives for behaving, objects, events, remarks made by others, and so on—the list is potentially endless. Because they are context-dependent, these and other ethnographic details are used by lay and professional members to understand "what happened" from within.

Like the ethnographies of informants, members' ethnographies are selected, truncated versions of what happened. They do not contain all the details, but just enough to give some sense to the event. For example, when someone is asked about an event or is casually asked "What ya do today?" the report that follows is not a blow-by-blow account. Instead, what is rendered is a truncated version of what really happened. A mini-ethnography is offered, one which is made up of enough details to provide the other with a sense of the event.

These ethnographies are accounts. *Accounts,* in turn, are any intentional communication between two or more people that covertly or through practical analysis reveal features of a setting and serve the pragmatic interests of the participants (Tobias and Leiter, 1975). Since most ethnomethodologists work with verbal accounts, they too require definition. Verbal accounts are defined as talk that is both intended and heard as "talk about a factual environment of objects" (Pollner, 1970). Data, for ethnomethodologists, are generally verbal accounts.

Accounts of all types produced by members of society constitute the major phenomena studied by ethnomethodologists. Accounts are important because they are the means by which members of society create and sustain their sense of social structure. The very nature of accounts as social phenomena makes this so. To construct an account is to make an object or event (past or present) observable and understandable (*accountable* in Garfinkel's terms) to oneself or to someone else. To make an object or event observable and understandable is to endow it with the status of an intersubjective object. In short, one is creating everyday reality. Accounting is the looking and telling that constitutes the work of creating a sense of social structure. The members' sense of social structure, to put it briefly, is created and sustained through accounts. This may seem to leave out the study of social interaction, but it does not. The connection between accounts and social interactions will be made in the next chapter.

The ethnomethodological interest in accounts is not in their content. The interest lies in locating and describing the accounting practices members use to render objects and events observable as objects and events in and of an intersubjective world. In the course of analyzing accounts for the practices used in their production and in the production of a sense of social structure, ethnomethodologists make reference to the content of accounts. Specifically, they make reference to the features of and behaviors in settings made observable by the account. However, their attention is focused on the *accounting practices* used to make those features and behaviors observable as intersubjective, i.e., factual objects and events.

ACCOUNTING PRACTICES

Accounting practices are basically a method of observation and reporting which renders objects and events observable, objective, and rational. Obviously, such a definition takes in a lot of territory. The rationale for such a broad definition is found in the following statement by Garfinkel on the aim of ethnomethodological studies:

> Their study is directed to the tasks of learning how members' actual ordinary activities consist of methods to make practical actions practical circumstances, common sense knowledge of social structures and practical sociological reasoning analyzable . . . (1967:vii).

My study of teachers' placement practices (Leiter, 1974) illustrates this approach to the study of accounting practices. The student in the elementary school is not just a student. He or she is a bright, average, or slow student; a behavior problem; a mature or immature student. These "facts" are important for teachers, students, and their parents because student careers with different outcomes are fashioned from these facts. These facts are also social products. That is to say, the factual character of students as certain kinds of students who possess particular abilities is produced through the teacher's methods of observation and reporting. Through the use of accounting practices, the properties of students (bright, average, slow, behavior problem, mature, immature) attain their factual status. One accounting practice I found was the "use of routine activities of the classroom as schemas of interpretation" (1974:38–41).

> For example one of the teachers was observed helping a student put the blocks away after activity time. She asked the student to put the larger of two blocks on one shelf and the smaller on the other shelf. The student put the wrong block on the top shelf. The teacher then asked him to put a square block on the first shelf and a round one on the second. The student couldn't tell the difference between the two blocks. At the end of the day I overheard the teacher relate this interchange to her colleague. In her account she generalized the child's performance to difficulties in shape perception and eye-hand coordination (1974:38).

Routine activities like cleaning up after activity time, painting pictures, choices of activities, participation in activities like playing with blocks, and the kinds of roles they play in games with roles— all are used as interpretive devices for locating students' abilities. The use of routine activities in this manner is accomplished through the teachers' interpretation of the activities. By seeing something more in those routine activities than their surface appearance of painting, playing with blocks, cleaning up and playing in doll houses, the teacher converts the activities into mini-tests for locating and describing students' abilities. In this way, the indexical properties of the activities serve as a tacit resource that occasions interpretive work—which, in turn, creates the factual character of students as "students with abilities." In short, the use of routine activities as schemas of interpretation is an accounting practice—a method of observation and reporting that produces social objects.

Accounting practices like the one described above are produced through the use of a few fundamental processes. The ethnomethodological literature focuses on the documentary method of interpretation (Mannheim, 1952:53–63; Garfinkel, 1967) and the interpretive procedures (Schutz, 1962; Cicourel, 1973). These two processes are assumed to be the basis for more situated practices of understanding and interaction. It is also assumed that the two processes are in some way related to each other. Unfortunately, these assumptions are not documented in the literature. What one finds is a set of situated practices that are not linked to these fundamental processes. Furthermore, the relationship between the documentary method and the interpretive procedures is not explicated. Without an explication of these two assumptions, ethnomethodology has become confusing for readers of its literature. Clarification of the relationship permits an understanding of these processes and also serves to delineate the relationship between accounting practices and the sense of social structure.

An Ethnomethodological Background Assumption: The Documentary Method and the Interpretive Procedures

When ethnomethodologists read and speak about the documentary method of interpretation, they are referring to a set of practices. They assume that there is more to the *documentary method* than its formal definition: treating a set of appearances as standing on behalf of an underlying pattern. This background assumption has also been made by nonethnomethodologists. James Coleman (1968: 126) criticized Garfinkel by saying that the documentary method was not "news." What would have been "news," Coleman wrote, would be an empirical description of the practices which he, along with others, assume constitute the method.

A corollary of this background assumption is that the documentary method of interpretation and interpretive procedures stand in some kind of relationship to each other. Interpretive procedures, as defined by Cicourel, are a set of commonsense methods that members of society use to sustain a sense of social structure necessary for articulating rules with "concrete" situations. Like the documentary method of interpretation, interpretive procedures are used to create and sustain the factual character of the social world. Cicourel (1973) refers to the documentary method but provides no explicit connection, save to call it an interpretive procedure in a loose sense. Zimmerman and Pollner (1970) refer to accounting practices which members of society use to create the facticity of the social world, but they do not mention the status of either the documentary method or the interpretive procedures as accounting practices. Thomas Wilson (1970) proposes that the documentary method is the basic process of producing social interaction. He, too, makes no mention of the interpretive procedures, even though the two have the same theoretical status in other parts of the literature. The reader is left with the impression that there are two sets of practices. As a result, the reader assumes the two are related, but the nature of the relationship remains tacit.

The Theoretical Relationship

I propose that the interpretive procedures (Cicourel, 1975; Schutz, 1964) are the constitutive practices of the documentary method of interpretation. Furthermore, it is not an accident that the two are related in this manner. The relationship is theoretically essential from within the ethnomethodological perspective. This theoretical necessity stems from the manner in which the documentary method is defined and the logic of its use.

THE DOCUMENTARY METHOD OF INTERPRETATION

The documentary method of interpretation was first described by Karl Mannheim (1952:52–63) and Alfred Schutz (1967). Mannheim described it as a method of locating the world view (*Weltanschauung*) that produced some act or object. According to Mannheim, the documentary method is more efficient than the objective and expressive methods. It is more efficient than the expressive method because, by virtue of the documentary method, the meaning of an act or object could be grasped by using a few features rather than all of them, as required by the expressive method. The documentary method is better than the objective method because, while objective meaning is unique to the object or gesture, the documentary method supplies meanings that are not dependent upon a single gesture.

Schutz (1962; 1967) discussed the documentary method in connection with Weber's concept *Verstehen*. Weber (1968) proposed that sociology was fundamentally an interpretive science, committed to the study of the subjective meanings people impute to others' actions. *Verstehen* is a method whereby the sociologist treats action as a product of the subjective meaning imputed by the actor, and then uses that subjective meaning to understand the meaning of someone's behavior. Schutz proposed that *Verstehen* is not unique to social science. It is a method used by members of society to render the behavior of others meaningful. That is, members of society convert into meaningful action by viewing it as the product of subjective meanings imputed to the actor. Furthermore, like the sociologist, members construct typologies of subjective meanings and use them to interpret the behavior of others. Schutz proposed that the members' use of *Verstehen* should be a sociological topic.

Garfinkel (1967:76–103) expanded Mannheim's and Schutz's proposals. First, he defined the documentary method:

> The method consists of treating an actual appearance as "the document of," as "pointing to," as "standing on behalf of" a presupposed underlying pattern. Not only is the pattern derived from its individual documentary evidences but the individual evidences, in their turn, are interpreted on the basis of "what is known" about the underlying pattern. Each is used to elaborate the other (1967:78).

Garfinkel then proposes that through the use of the documentary method of interpretation, the facticity of the social world is created and sustained. The use of the documentary method produces a sense of social structure by providing objects and events with consistency, or the sense that they are the same over time. It is also the process whereby behavior is experienced as meaningful action *a la* Weber: behavior that is meaningful to the person performing it. The members' sense of social structure would not be possible if objects were simply of the here and now rather than connected to the transcendent social scene. Objects and events would lose their facticity if they were just part of the here and now, for they would become idiosyncratic appearances. John Baldwin reported (personal communication) that when he first went to the field to observe the social behavior of spider monkeys, he could not find a pattern. He perceived their behavior as random movement through the trees. Only after Baldwin gave the monkeys names could he perceive and describe their social behavior. He achieved a "connectedness" of the object over temporal and circumstantial changes in its appearance; he was able to identify monkeys seen at one time as the same monkeys seen at another time. Only then could he record the pattern of their social life. Without such connectedness between the here and now and the transcendent social scene, the monkeys' behavior seemed random.

The use of the documentary method is also the process whereby behavior is experienced as meaningful action *a la* Weber (1947). If behavior were not experienced in the Weberian sense (meaningful to the actor), it would be perceived as random movement without meaning or patterning. Experimental psychologist D. O. Hebb (1946) provides some supporting evidence. Hebb conducted an experiment on the effects of anthropomorphizing research animals. He had two groups of students study the same chimps. He told one group that they were to write up their observations without anthropomorphizing the animals' behavior. The other group was told they could use anthropomorphic terms. Hebb then examined the reports. The first group saw no patterning in the chimps' behavior. They reported that the chimps were unpredictable and bit the members of the group. The observations of the second group stressed the patterning in the chimps' behavior.

Third, Garfinkel also extended Schutz's proposal that the process of *Verstehen*—as a member's method of understanding—should become a topic of study. He designed and conducted an experiment to uncover the practices of the documentary method. Garfinkel's design consisted of telling a group of students that they were participating in an experiment to discover alternative methods to psychotherapy. Each subject was told to think of a problem, state it, and ask advice, to which he would receive a "yes" or "no" answer from a psychotherapist in an adjoining room. Upon receiving the advice, the subject had to disconnect the microphone connecting him with the psychotherapist and then assess the answer with a tape recorder running in his room. When he had completed his assessment, the subject was to reconnect the microphone to the psychotherapist and ask his next question. The "psychotherapist" in the adjoining room was actually an experimenter, and the "answers" he gave to the subjects' questions were preselected by random procedure and given independent of the subjects' questions. This experiment was designed to "exaggerate the features of this method in use and to catch the work of 'fact production in flight'" (Garfinkel, 1967:79).

The results of Garfinkel's experiment will be presented later; for now let me summarize the argument at this point. The documentary method must include a set of practices for producing facticity. Unless the situated appearances of objects and events are *somehow* connected with the transcendent social scene, they cease to be objects to which the dimensions of the "normal" environment apply. They lack: typicality, likelihood, comparability, causal texture, technical efficiency, and moral requiredness (see Chapter IV for definitions). The "somehow" of the previous statement *is* the documentary method of interpretation. The member connects the situational appearances of an object or event with the transcendent social scene by using the documentary method. When the member uses the present appearance of an object as the "document of" or "as pointing to" some underlying pattern, he accomplishes connectedness and, simultaneously, the facticity of the object as an object in and of the social world.

This relationship between the documentary method of interpretation and the members' sense of social structure means that the documentary method must *by definition* include a set of practices for accomplishing facticity. The members' sense of social structure involves, and depends upon, the stability of the object over and in spite of variations in situational appearances. The documentary method of interpretation establishes such stability; it connects situational appearances with the transcendent social scene.

The logic of its use provides another reason why the documentary method must include a set of practices to produce facticity. From the analyst's perspective, the facticity of objects and events may be viewed as a product of the members' use of the documentary method. *From the member's perspective,* he is not working with appearances, but with facts which have factual meaning. *To use* the documentary method, then, involves presuming and relying upon the facticity of the social world at the outset while simultaneously creating that facticity through the use of the documentary method. An example is found in Zimmerman and Pollner's (1969) replication of Garfinkel's experiment. Subjects were told that they were participating in a communication experiment. Each was led to believe that two subjects at a time were to communicate with each other by passing slips of paper with one of ten sentences selected from an English grammar book through a slot in a partition. Actually, the subject did not have a partner. An experimenter was on the other side; he selected the sentence to be sent to the subject at random. One of the subjects perceived the deception and announced it to the experimenters. Instead of leaving, she continued with the experiment *as before*. She treated the events as "real" events, not as "faked" events. The subject's transcript shows that she continued to treat the sentences as "sentences sent by someone communicating with her." The interpretive work used by the subject to make sense of the sentences remained unchanged. She continued to use the documentary method of interpretation, as she did prior to discovering the hoax. Her use of the documentary method is based on assuming the events to be real (i.e., perceiving the sentences as "sentences sent by someone trying to communicate with her"). Without making that assumption, she could not "find" the meaning in the sentences. Thus, to use the documentary method, one must presume the facticity of the social world while simultaneously creating it.

Additional support for this proposal is found in McHugh's (1968) replication of Garfinkel's experiment. McHugh tried to eliminate the use of the documentary method by using a prearranged sequencing of "yes-no" answers into sequences of five "yeses" followed by five "nos." While this procedure did not eliminate the use of the documentary method, it altered the subjects' use of its practices *vis-à-vis* their use of the six dimensions of the perceivedly normal environment (typicality, likelihood, causal texture, comparability, technical efficiency and moral requiredness). Upon coding the transcripts, McHugh found in the regular transcripts the subjects used the practices of the documentary method, rarely invoking the six dimensions of the perceivedly normal environments. However, in "anomic" transcripts, subjects generally did use these six dimensions. The conclusion McHugh draws from this finding is that when the practices of the documentary method are used undisturbed, the facticity of the social world is taken for granted. When the practices are interrupted, that facticity can no longer be assumed, and the subject actively seeks to restore it by invoking the six dimensions. This finding supports the notion of the documentary method as both presupposing *and* creating the facticity of the social world, for when its practices are disrupted so is the facticity of the social world. At the same time, the diminished use of the documentary method by McHugh's subjects, while invoking this facticity, suggests that the use of the method rests on the ability to assume the world's facticity.

Members sustain a sense of social structure by connecting their "here and now" with the larger social scene. Using the documentary method relies on treating both the observed behavior and the underlying pattern as facts-in-the-world. Garfinkel, in his definition of the method, suggests this when he refers to the underlying pattern as a "presupposed underlying pattern" (Garfinkel, 1967:78). It is in this sense that the documentary method both creates and presupposes a factual world. Because the documentary method of interpretation simultaneously presupposes and creates the facticity of the social world, it must contain a set of practices for accomplishing that facticity.

It is my contention that the practices produced in these experiments are the interpretive procedures. Specifically, the practices Garfinkel describes as his "findings" are in fact descriptions of the interpretive procedures. In order to render forthcoming analysis of Garfinkel's findings clearer, the interpretive procedures will be defined and discussed.

THE INTERPRETATIVE PROCEDURES

Cicourel's interpretive procedures emerge from and incorporate elements of the works of Bar-Hillel (1954), Schutz (1962; 1964), Chomsky (1965), and Garfinkel (1957; 1967). The details were described in Chapter II. Cicourel's accomplishment lies in extending and elaborating the interpretive procedures *vis-à-vis* language use to describe how people create a sense of social structure. With the idea of interpretive procedures, Cicourel has attempted to link people's everyday knowledge with their production of a factual environment of objects. The everyday stock of knowledge used by people is made up of bits and pieces of information that are as indexical as the language used to recall and store it (Mead, 1934; Schutz, 1962). Therefore, the situated relevance of the stock of knowledge must be accomplished through the use of interpretive procedures. As Cicourel explains:

> But normative rules are not self-contained instructions for assigning meaning to an environment of objects and events. The child must learn to articulate general rules or policies with particular objects and events so as to show that the context-restricted features experienced can be accounted for by the claim that they are governed by general rules or policies. Notice, however, that normative rules do not exist for providing the speaker-hearer with instructions on how this articulation occurs between particular features experienced and the general rules or policies said to govern the adequate explaining or meaning of the particular objects and events (1973:84–85).

The problem discussed above applies to constructing accounts and to sustaining a sense of social structure. In delivering an account, a member is faced with the problem of taking "concept-restricted" events and features that are part of his own experience and making them intersubjectively observable to others as events and features out in the world. Language by itself cannot accomplish this any more than general rules can; the meanings of words are context-bound. Hence, interpretive procedures are used to provide context-bound meaning across context. To quote Cicourel:

> The interpretive procedures prepare and sustain an environment of objects for inference and action vis-a-vis a culture bound worldview and the written and "known in common" surface rules [norms, values] (1973:52).

Cicourel's formulation of the interpretive procedures has been confusing to readers for several reasons. First, in describing them, Cicourel does not use a constant metaphor. They are referred to alternatively as "properties," "assumptions," and "instructions." Second, as Cicourel has (1978:88) noted, the interdependence of the interpretive procedures is obscured by describing them analytically. Third, the number of interpretive procedures varies from paper to paper. Cicourel's initial formulation (1973:147–151) lists six, but his latest paper lists four (Cicourel, 1973:85–88).

In order to remedy some of these difficulties, I have chosen to recast the interpretive procedures as a set of interrelated assumptions. Interpretive procedures are commonsense assumptions, and it is through the activity of making them that members are able to create and sustain a factual environment of objects. Because they are commonsense assumptions, they must be made continuously. Unlike the assumptions of formal logic, which need to be invoked only once, commonsense assumptions are promissory. They must be continually enacted because they must be geared and regeared to the unfolding events of the everyday world. Cicourel states that "interpretive procedures prepare the environment for substantive or practical considerations" (1973:49), thus submitting that they are not used in pure intellectual speculation. Rather, they are used to accomplish everyday projects of action in the real world.

The following, then, is offered as a recasting of Cicourel's (1973: 85–88) formulation of the interpretive procedures.

1. *The Reciprocity of Perspectives.* In their communications, members assume that if they were to change places, each would see what the other sees from his perspective. Members also assume that while they are biographically unique, the experiences of each are sufficiently congruent to permit them to ignore any differences that might be due to personal experiences and perceptions "until further notice." Furthermore, when discrepancies do arise, the presumed underlying congruence permits them to *use those differences as a scheme of interpretation for understanding* each other. Each may impute differences in biography and perception to the other as a way of understanding how he could come to a different interpretation of an object or event.

2. *Normal Forms.* This interpretive procedure instructs each member to assume (and expect) that the other will emit utterances that are recognizable, intelligible, and embedded within a body of tacit common knowledge—"what anyone knows" (Garfinkel, 1967). Also involved in this interpretive procedure is the tacit instruction that one understand what is being said.

3. *Et Cetera Principle.* To sustain the "normal forms" appearance of talk despite deliberate or presumed vagueness due to the routine practice of leaving the intended meanings of expressions unstated (Cicourel, 1973; Garfinkel, 1967), the speaker assumes that (1) the hearer can fill in the unstated but intended meanings of the speaker's expressions (the Et Cetera assumption), and (2) the hearer assumes that the speaker will say something at a later point in the conversation that will clarify the ambiguous expressions (retrospective-prospective sense of ocurrence).

4. *Descriptive Vocabularies as Indexical Expressions.* Members assume that in providing (and deciding) the specific sense of the expressions used in their conversations, they must go beyond the surface form and kernal meanings of words and link them to a context consisting of such particulars as who is the speaker, his biography or relevant aspects of his biography, his purpose and intent, the setting in which the remarks are made, or the actual or potential relationship between speaker and hearer (Cicourel, 1973; Garfinkel, 1967).

The Practices of the Documentary Method

GARFINKEL'S EXPERIMENT REEXAMINED

As I have stated previously, Garfinkel conducted an experiment to locate and describe the practices of the documentary method—and describe them he did. The findings section of his paper contains ethnographic descriptions of the practices. Garfinkel also provides two protocols from the experimental sessions, but the reader is not shown the practices described in the findings section.

A reexamination of Garfinkel's findings connected to the transcript reveals that (1) the ethnographic descriptions have an empirical basis and (2) Garfinkel's practices are the interpretive procedures.

First, there is the practice of formulating the questions through a retrospective-prospective review of the conversation. Garfinkel found that his subjects did not use questions made up in advance. Rather, each question was the product of reflecting back upon the previous course of the conversation and assuming future answers by treating the answer as answers-to-questions. All of the examples are from Garfinkel (1967:80–85).

> S: He may not be too strongly opposed now because we are only dating, but perhaps he sees future complications that he would really like to get off his chest at the moment. I am ready for my third question now. If after having my conversation with Dad and he says to continue dating her, but at the same time he gives me an impression that he is really not, he really does not want me to date her, but he is only doing it because he wants to be a good dad, should, under these circumstances, should I still date the girl?

The subject's fourth question is formed by reflecting back on the previous course of the conversation ("if after having my conversation with Dad and he says to continue dating her . . .") and then forming the question in light of the previous conversation and future possibilities. The retrospective-prospective work described by Garfinkel is a direct description of the retrospective-prospective sense of occurrence and the use of the Et Cetera Principle, where the speaker assumes that the hearer can fill in the unstated but intended meaning of his utterances and where the hearer assumes that the speaker will say something later that will clarify a previously vague utterance. That Garfinkel's subjects treated the answers in this manner describes the use of the interpretive procedure as *normal forms,* for in treating the answers as answers to questions, Garfinkel's subjects were assuming that the utterances were both understandable and understood by the experimenter.

The second and third practices described by Garfinkel illustrate how his subjects handled incomplete, inappropriate, and contradictory answers. "Where the answers were unsatisfactory or incomplete the questioners [subject] were willing to wait for later answers to decide the sense of the previous ones." Another way of handling incomplete answers was to treat them "as incomplete because of the deficiencies of this method of giving advice" (Garfinkel, 1967:90). In the following example the subject's third question (see previous example) is answered by the experimenter.

E: 1 My answer is yes.

S: 2 Well I am actually surprised at the
     3 answer. I expected a no answer
     4 on that. *Perhaps this is because*
     5 *you are not quite aware of my dad*
     6 *and his reactions* and he seems to be
     7 the type of person that is sensitive
     8 and therefore he is very careful in
     9 the way that he will handle things.
    10 Even though he might have said go
    11 ahead and date her I perhaps would
    12 feel guilty in knowing that he
    13 really did not want me to continue
    14 to date her. Though I don't know
    15 that it would actually help the situ-
    16 ation any. *So well, perhaps we will*
    17 *look into this further and that is*
    18 *another question.* I am ready for the

19   fourth question now. If after having
20   this discussion with Dad and getting
21   a positive answer from him but at
22   the same time felt that this was not
23   his honest opinion do you think that
24   it would be proper for me to have my
25   mother have a serious talk with him
26   and therefore try to get a truer
27   reaction to Dad's opinion on the situ-
28   ation?

The subject's assessment is in part produced by using the two practices described by Garfinkel. First, he uses the practice of invoking the differences in perspective caused by the experimental design (lines 4–6). Second, he then uses the practice of waiting for a later answer to decide the sense of the present one (lines 16–18). Both of these practices are interpretive procedures. The practice of invoking differences in perception as a scheme of interpretation is the use of the *reciprocity of perspective:* using congruency of relevance (or lack of it) as a scheme of interpretation for normalizing discrepancies. The practice of waiting for later answers to decide the sense of previous ones (lines 16–18) is the *Et Cetera Principle:* The hearer assumes that the speaker will say something later on that will clarify unclear meanings of the conversation. The other practices used by the subject in producing his assessment are (1) assigning the advice a scenic source (lines 2–3) by treating the answer as coming from the experimenter in answer to his question and (2) retrospective-prospective review to form his next question in lines 15–22. Here the subject uses elements of the previous answer (19–23) to form his next question.

The fourth practice reported by Garfinkel is the use of institutionalized features of the collectivity as a scheme of interpretation. This practice consists of making specific references to social structures and then using them to decide the sense of the advisor's answer. "Such references, however, were not made to any social structures whatever. . . . References that the subjects supplied were to social structures which he treats as actually or potentially known in common with the advisor" (Garfinkel, 1967:93). For example:

S: If I was to fall in love with this girl and want to make plans for marriage do you feel that it is fair that I should ask her to change her religion over to my belief?

E: My answer is no.

S: Well, no. Well this has me stymied. Well I honestly feel that I have been brought up in a certain way and I believe that she has too, and I feel pretty strong about the way I believe. *Not that I am completely orthodox or anything* but of course *there is always family pressure* and things like that. And I am quite sure that she feels, *unfortunately I have never seen a family with a split in religion that really has been able to make a success of it. So I don't know. I think that I would be tempted to ask her to change.* I don't think I would be able to really. I am ready for number seven. Do you feel that it would be a better situation if we were to get married and neither one of us were willing to talk about the religious differences or to give in on either one side, that we bring our children up in a neutral religion other than the two that we believe in?

The subject uses institutionalized features of the collectivity to produce the sense of the advice. There are two specific social structures mentioned by the subject and then used as a scheme of interpretation: orthodox Judaism and "a family with a split in religion."

The finding that the subjects assumed that they knew the social structures in common with the advisor is a reference to the use of the *reciprocity of perspectives.* This assumption on the part of Garfinkel's subjects involves the use of the interchangeability of standpoints as well as congruency of relevance. Garfinkel's practice also directly suggests the interpretive procedure of *descriptive vocabularies as indexical expressions.* The subject is using the institutionalized features of the collectivity as a context for making sense of the "psychoanalyst's" indexical answers. The use of this interpretive procedure directly describes the use of *normal forms:* Part of Cicourel's definition of normal forms includes the assumption of a common body of knowledge, or "what everyone knows." Thus, when Garfinkel's subjects assumed that structures were known in common with the psychoanalyst, they were using normal forms.

Fourth, Garfinkel found that deciding the "truth" of the advice consisted of assigning to the advice "the values of typicality, likelihood, comparability, causal texture, technical efficiency, and moral requiredness" (Garfinkel, 1967:94). In addition, Garfinkel found that these properties were "not so much 'assigned' as managed" through such practices as "searching for and determining pattern, by treating the advisor's answers as motivated by the question, by waiting for later answers to clarify the sense of previous ones, and by finding answers to questions" (Garfinkel, 1967:94). In the example below, the experimenter "answers" the subject's seventh question (see previous example). The subject's assessment of the "advice" is an example of his use of the documentary method to manage the "truth" of the "advice."

E: 1 My answer is yes.
S: 2 Well perhaps that would be a solu-
    3 tion. If we could find a religion
    4 that would incorporate our two
    5 beliefs to a certain extent. I
    6 realize that perhaps this might
    7 be literally impossible to do.
    8 Perhaps in a sense this neutral
    9 religion might be something almost
   10 made up by ourselves because I
   11 honestly feel that religious
   12 training no matter which belief it
   13 is if not carried to extremes
   14 is good, for everyone should have
   15 a certain amount of religious
   16 training along these lines. Per-
   17 haps this might be a solution to
   18 the problem. I guess I should
   19 follow this a little bit further
   20 and see exactly what happens.

Managing the truthfulness or facticity of the advice is accomplished through the use of the following practices of the documentary method. First, there is the use of assigning the advice a scenic source (lines 2–3). Second, the subject uses institutionalized features of the collectivity (a neutral religion) as a scheme of interpretation (lines 3–12). Third, the subject uses the practice of retrospective-prospective review to form the next question (lines 16–20). These practices are used to manage the perceivedly normal values of what was advised. First, the subject uses a neutral religion as a schema of interpretation to manage and assess the technical efficiency of the advice ("I realize that this might be literally impossible to do"). Second, this same practice is used to assess the advice in terms of its moral requiredness ("because I honestly feel that religious training no matter which belief it is, if not carried to extremes, is good") and the likelihood or probable outcome ("perhaps this might be a solution to the problem"). With these findings, Garfinkel strongly suggests that the practices of the documentary method produced the member's sense of social structure. Garfinkel is proposing that the perceivedly normal (factual) character of the advice was created by using the practices of the documentary method.

Accounting Practices and
the Sense of Social Structure

Most ethnomethodologists seek to describe the accounting practices used to create and sustain the factual character of social reality. Typically they present the reader with a phenomenal description of the practice as used rather than labeling certain activities as practices. Ethnomethodologists provide the reader with descriptions of accounting practices without labeling them as such and without linking them to other practices described in the literature. The reader is thus left to recognize these situated descriptions as versions of the documentary method of interpretation. For the reader encountering ethnomethodology for the first time, it is little wonder that it has remained a mysterious enterprise. One way of remedying this unfortunate situation is to examine some of the key pieces of research with the purpose of rendering the accounting practices observable. What follows, then, is an account which seeks to do what all other accounts do: make observable features of social behavior

—the accounting practices described in ethnomethodological research.

Don H. Zimmerman (1974:128–143) studied the record-keeping process in a public welfare agency. Through observation, he noted the ways in which case workers maintained the factual status of records dealing with people applying for public assistance. The documents were accorded the status of "plain fact." That is to say, the information in the documents was treated as being a set of intersubjective facts that are independent of any one person's action or perception and that could not be done away with (or faked) at will (see Chapter IV). The "plain fact" character of the documents was produced through a set of verbal accounts routinely given in the agency and which were reflexively tied to the setting. To quote Zimmerman:

> Accounts of the "plain fact" character of documents are done by members of the organization for members of the organization; they are integral features of the situations they make observable and hence organize. By means of these accounts the documents passing through the hands of agency personnel are seen as documents of the orderly process of society and as produced by them (1974:134).

The social workers' accounts produce the factual features of the setting (in this case, the facticity of the documents) while being part of the public welfare agency. The accounts consist of assembling ethnographic particulars that point to the production of a document in our society. These document-producing activities are then consulted by the case worker to provide the document with its factual character. The "plain fact" character of documents, then, is the product of linking the document to an ethnographic context. The assembly and linkage of these ethnographic particulars to the document is accomplished through the use of accounting practices.

"Using bureaucratic features as schemes of interpretation" was one such accounting practice described by Zimmerman. Organizational features of bureaucracies were invoked as perceptual aids by the case workers to explain the existence or absence of a document that should have been visible if the mechanism of "general bureaucracy" had been set into motion by an action claimed by the client. For example, a client who is seeking unemployment compensation must present the case worker with a list of places where he has sought employment in order to qualify for compensation. The case worker checks the entries by calling the names on the list to establish their facticity. Garfinkel would call this practice "assigning the words a scenic source." Zimmerman reports a case where the case worker did not receive confirmation of the client's application. The case worker then constructed the following account:

> Two places had no record. It may be that if they just weren't hiring anyone so that it would be pointless to make an application (Zimmerman, 1974:138).

Through this account, the facticity of the record and the client's claim are preserved. By invoking the organizational particulars of "if they just weren't hiring anyone so that it would be pointless to make an application," the case worker shows (explains) how the client could have applied but produced no record of having done so. When the case worker reported to his supervisor, he used the same practice to produce the following account, which also produces the "plain fact" character of the document:

> I am trying to verify his search for employment. I've had no luck (referring to form) no record . . . no record . . . will call back. This one they don't know definitely but the person said they have no record of it. *But he might have gone down to another department or something* (Zimmerman, 1974:138).

The last two lines of this example show the case worker using the practice of "using bureaucratic features as a scheme of interpretation." The organization of bureaucracies into departments that do not know what the others are doing is used to explain the lack of a record, thereby preserving the facticity of record and the client's claim. The supervisor's reply is important because it illustrates how the same practice can be used to assemble a different context.

> No record of him even being there even. Well you see a lot of these places . . . have you ever applied at one of these places? They have

a record of you even if you go through the gate to apply. I've walked the streets (looking for work) unfortunately, at a lot of firms in their area and I'm well aware of it. They don't just let you in. For instance if you go to Jordans they won't let you in without taking your name. They have a record of some kind and they keep it for a certain length of time and then they destroy it (Zimmerman, 1974:138).

The accounts of the case worker and the supervisor preserve the facticity of the verification process and the document it produces. The accounting practice used to accomplish this is the use of bureaucratic features as the scheme of interpretation. This practice is used to assemble a set of ethnographic particulars which, in turn, serve as a context for explaining and interpreting the record. Zimmerman's description of this practice has three important implications. First, it can be used to assemble more than one context. The case worker and the supervisor use the same practice to assemble different ethnographic contexts. Thus, the practice is context-free. It is a method that is independent of the contexts it produces.

Second, although Zimmerman does not use the term *indexicality*, he nevertheless describes it. He shows how the same accounting practice can generate two different interpretations of an event by assembling different ethnographic particulars to form the contexts. The ethnographic particulars assembled affect the sense of the record; change them, and the meaning of the record changes. That is what indexicality is all about. An event obtains its meaning from the context in which it is embedded. Without saying so, Zimmerman has also provided us with a description of one of the practices of the documentary method of interpretation: the use of institutionalized features of the collectivity as a scheme of interpretation. In this case, the institutionalized features are features of bureaucracies, which are assumed to be known in common and are used as aids to perception.

The second practice used by the case worker was "conceiving of the applicant as a course of action." Briefly, a person's identity (specifically, his occupation) is used to generate a set of investigatable items—actions which should produce a document. For example:

ABA is a contractor? An independent contractor (yes)? Did you look at his income tax? (no) I'd like to see how he rates himself on an income tax declaration. I really would before I'd make a decision. . . . Does he have a license on all of this? What's his equipment valued at? You would need to know all of this. What kind of contractor is he, cement? I think the only thing you can do probably is one grocery order while you carry out your investigation and check out everything as fast as you can in checking the value of his personal business equipment. I would like to look at his income tax form last year and why if he's a landscape gardener—this just doesn't make sense, that he couldn't get a job this time of year (Zimmerman, 1974:140).

In the above account, the client's occupation is used to generate a set of document-producing activities. The activities, in turn, are used to locate documents to help evaluate the client's claim of eligibility. Using the client's occupation in this manner constitutes the accounting practice of "conceiving of the applicant as a course of action." This practice is similar to "assigning the words a scenic source" and "using institutionalized features of the collectively as a scheme of interpretation. Both are practices of the documentary method of interpretation. The case worker actually used his role as a perceptual aid to produce a set of activities and circumstances that would produce a document if the client was indeed what he claimed to be. By assuming a psychiatrist to be on the other side of the wall, Garfinkel's subjects saw "yes" and "no" as "answers to their questions"; hence, the similarity between the practice as Garfinkel describes it and Zimmerman's finding.

Zimmerman's study of how the plain fact character of a document is established illustrates the ethnomethodological practice of describing the phenomenon rather than coding it. Rather than label the practices of the documentary method, Zimmerman describes their use. The plain fact character of documents is the member's sense of social structure, as seen by the fact that it refers to the unproblematic, taken-for-granted facticity of documents. The social case worker treats the facticity of documents as given in the same way that the man in the street accepts the facticity of the social world as a natural fact of life. The factual character of the documents is established through accounts which are reflexively tied to the setting in which they occur. When Zimmerman describes the way accounts are part of the social order they produce, he is describing their reflexive properties. In short, accounts of the plain fact character of documents are not detached from the setting; the accounts make features of a setting observable while being part of the setting. It is through accounts that investigatable matters are made observable and organized for investigation. The accounting practices Zimmerman describes are situated descriptions of the use of the documentary method of interpretation. They are situated versions of using institutionalized features of the collectivity as schemes of interpretation. Features of bureaucratic organizations and the client's occupation were used by the case worker (1) as interpretive schemes for interpreting the client's claim of having applied for a job when there was no record of his application and (2) to generate courses of action that should produce documents to be used to verify the client's claims.

Deviant behavior is another area that illustrates how the sense of social structure is produced through the use of accounting practices. Ethnomethodology and symbolic interactionism converge to form the labeling perspective in deviance. From this perspective, the objective quality of deviance is viewed as a product of members' accounting practices. It is through members' accounting practices that a deviant population with objective features is produced. Behavior is deviant *only* when defined as such. Hence, the process by which people come to be defined as deviant is viewed as the topic of study.

There have been several studies of labeling using the ethnomethodological perspective. Cicourel's (1968) *Social Organization of Juvenile Justice* is a study of police interrogation and reporting practices. Cicourel shows how interpretive procedures are used by the police to recognize individuals and situations as requiring the application of particular interrogation practices. They are also used to construct a "delinquent career" from truncated official records which are vague, ambiguous, and do not recover the interrogation practices that led to an entry. David Sudnow's (1965) study of "normal crimes" illustrates how interpretive procedures and social typifications (normal crimes) are used in plea bargaining. This study will be discussed later in Chapter VII. Robert Emerson's study (1969) *Judging Delinquents* shows the use of social types and ethnographic particulars to define juvenile delinquents in court as well as the practices used by juveniles to alter delinquent definitions.

A study by John Kitsuse (1969) provides us with an example of the use of the documentary method of interpretation to define people as homosexuals. Homosexuality was chosen because, according to the literature, "homosexual behavior is uniformly defined, interpreted and negatively sanctioned" (Kitsuse, 1969:593). To test this notion and to show the accounting practices used to define someone as homosexual, Kitsuse designed an open-ended interview schedule and administered it to about seven hundred students. His aim was to document the behaviors used to label and interpret an individual as deviant and to describe the process of interpretation.

Kitsuse found that his subjects used three kinds of evidence to point to the existence of homosexuality. The first kind of evidence consisted of indirect evidence: rumor, accounts by other people about experiences with the individual in question, and general information about a person's reputation and sexual preferences. The second kind of evidence was direct observation by the subjects. It should be noted, however, that the behaviors included in the "direct observations" varied widely and were often vague with regard to their connection with homosexuality. That is to say, the behaviors were indexical; they did not, by themselves, constitute homosexuality across different contexts. Homosexuality was imputed to people on the basis of "what everyone knows." For example:

I: Then this lieutenant was a homosexual?
S: Yes.
I: How did you find out about it?
S: The guy he approached told me. After that I watched him. Our company was small and we had a bar for both enlisted men and officers. He would come in and try to be friendly with one or two of the guys.

I: Weren't the other officers friendly?

S: Sure, they would come in for an occasional drink; some of them have been with the company for three years and they would sometimes slap you on the back but he tried to get over friendly.

I: What do you mean "over friendly?"

S: He had only been there a week. He would try to push himself on a couple of guys—he spent more time with the enlisted personnel than is expected from an officer.

I: Weren't the officers friendly?

S: Sure, etc. (Kitsuse, 1969:595).

The third type of evidence used by Kitsuse's subjects was behaviors interpreted by the subjects as overt sexual propositions. The behaviors described ranged from what the subjects considered unmistakable evidence to vague, ambiguous gestures. A common theme in Kitsuse's data is that the behavior used as evidence is indexical. It is behavior which gets its deviant status from being interpreted as such rather than from being inherently deviant. Thus, being defined as homosexual is contingent on the interpretations of this indexical behavior. Kitsuse makes this point to suggest that the critical element in the process is the interpretation of any given behavior. Summing up his findings, Kitsuse shows that his subjects used the documentary method of interpretation to impute homosexuality to people.

A general pattern revealed by the subject's response to this section of the interview schedule is that when a person's sexual "normality" is called into question by whatever form of evidence the imputation of homosexuality is documented by retrospective interpretation of the deviant's behavior, a process by which the subject reinterprets the individual's past behavior in light of the new information concerning his sexual deviance. . . . The subjects indicate that they reviewed their past interactions with the individuals in question searching for subtle cues and nuances of behavior which might give further evidence of the alleged deviance. This retrospective reading generally provided the subjects with just such evidence to support the conclusion that this is what was going on all the time (1969: 598).

Although Kitsuse does not refer to the documentary method, his summary is a description of its use. What Kitsuse describes as "retrospective interpretation" is the interpretive "retrospective-prospective sense of occurrence." Like Garfinkel's subjects, Kitsuse's would wait for further clarification and use later information to reinterpret the individual's past behavior. Kitsuse describes the mutual elaboration between the observed appearances and the underlying pattern when he notes that the label "homosexuality" is used to make the individual's behavior intelligible. Afterward, the behaviors are used to point to an individual's homosexuality.

Kitsuse's study illustrates the role of accounts in creating and sustaining a sense of social structure. The sense of social structure in this case refers to homosexuality as a factual feature of a person's identity. The facticity of an individual's identity was shown to be a practical accomplishment due to the equivocal character of the behavior used to label a person homosexual. That is, due to its indexical property, the homosexual nature of the behavior was a product of interpretation rather than an inherent feature of the behavior itself. The process used to determine the sense of the behavior and the facticity of the individual's identity was the documentary method of interpretation. It was through the use of this method that Kitsuse's subjects fashioned verbal accounts which, in turn, displayed the factual character of the individual's identity. The homosexual identity of the individual was made observable through the respondent's verbal account as constructed through the use of the documentary method of interpretation.

SUMMARY

The ethnomethodological version of the problem of social order turns verbal accounts into a sociological phenomenon. Verbal accounts are no longer mere rationalizations; they are the vehicle through which the features of settings, along with their factual properties, are made observable. This involves more than pointing out that people rationalize their past experiences, present circumstances, and future prospects. Accounts or rationalizations "contribute to the maintenance of stable routines of everyday life . . ." (Garfinkel, 1967:185). The performance of everyday activities is dependent upon maintaining a sense of social structure in spite of the potential equivocality of behavior. Hence, accounts or rationalizations are not products of idle curiosity but are integral to the creation and maintenance of social reality. The ethnomethodological version of the problem of social order directs the ethnomethodologist to locate and describe the practices used in the construction of everyday accounts, thus turning a residual category into the central topic of study.

Accounting practices seem to be of two types: situated practices and fundamental practices that are context-free. Using routine activities of the classroom as schemes of interpretation, using bureaucratic features as schemes of interpretation, and conceiving of the client as a course of action are all situated accounting practices that involve the use of the documentary method of interpretation and its constitutive practices the interpretive procedures. Admittedly the research on this is sparse, but confirmation is suggested by the descriptions of the situated practices presented thus far. In the sections that follow, rules and social interaction are examined from within the framework provided by the ethnomethodological version of the problem of social order.

VII

Topics in Ethnomethodology: The Study of Rules and Social Interaction

We now turn our attention to ethnomethodological versions of some conventional sociological topics that turn out to be topics of ethnomethodological study as well: rules and social interaction. In turning our attention to rule use and social interaction we will not really be leaving accounts and accounting practices. We will be moving their study to different levels. Readers encountering ethnomethodology for the first time get the impression that ethnomethodology does not study rules at all and that rules have no place within the perspective. The same can also be said about the study of social interaction: The study of accounting practices seems far removed from social interaction in that it deals with the understanding of social interaction rather than its social construction. This is not the case. Rule use and social interaction are indeed topics of study within the ethnomethodological perspective. However, the study of rules and social interaction undergoes a shift in perspective when studied from within our particular version of the problem of social order.

Where Have All the Rules Gone?

The theoretical and empirical status of norms, motives, and social types has confused readers of the ethnomethodological literature. Part of the confusion comes from Garfinkel's (1967) study policy that ethnomethodologists should not view behavior as caused by rules but study instead how people *use* rules. One of his early papers on trust (Garfinkel, 1957) used the term *background expectation,* which readers took as a rule. Cicourel's (1973:43–60) distinction between surface rules (norms and values) and deep rules (interpretive procedures) does not clarify the matter. In fact, it has left some readers with the interpretation that ethnomethodology is nothing more than the study of meta-rules. An example of this interpretation is Norman Denzin's (1970:259–284) comparison of symbolic interaction with ethnomethodology. Using Garfinkel's (1967) notion of background expectations, Denzin proposes that ethnomethodology deals with the problem of social order as defined by Parsons (1937) in *The Structure of Social Action.* He states that ethnomethodology seeks a solution to the Parsonian version by describing the norms, rules, and meanings that people use. Denzin's characterization of ethnomethodology is built upon treating Garfinkel's background expectations as a set of meta-rules, which they were in the earlier paper (Garfinkel, 1957) but not in Garfinkel's current work, where the term no longer appears. Denzin's characterization of ethnomethodology reflects the confusion concerning the theoretical status of norms, rules, motives, and social typifications. Denzin does not describe the ethnomethodological version of the problem of social order. Furthermore, his characterization gives norms and rules a causal status not found in ethnomethodology.

This misrepresentation can be corrected by reviewing the following features of the ethnomethodological version of the problem of social order. It should be noted that this version does not seek to provide causal explanations for the patterning of social action. It does not seek to answer the question, Why do men behave the way they do?. The patterned, typical, repetitive, causal texture of social life is viewed as a property of behavior that members of society are continually recognizing and making observable to each other. With this as the ethnomethodological problem of social order, it should be noted that "social order" has a different meaning for ethnomethodologists. It refers to the factual character of social reality as a social product of members' interpretive procedures.

It follows from this version that norms, motives, and rules do not have causal status. The solution to the ethnomethodological version of the problem of social order does not lie in societal members' motivated compliance with rules or internalized motives. Rather, it lies in describing the interpretive work, the accounting practices people use to report (and through the reporting, create) the orderliness, the patterned and recurrent character of social life. Norms, rules, motives, and social types are involved in this reporting, but not as causal agents. They are glosses, devices that people use to render the factual character of social sense and actions observable as such. They are aids to perception used to convert raw behavior into social action and to portray that social action as factual to oneself and to others.

Rules, norms, and motives enter ethnomethodological inquiry as methods for describing and observing the orderly and factual features of behavior and everyday scenes. Seen this way, the theoretical status of these elements of sociological explanation undergoes a change. They are no longer formal and informal elements of social structure that push and pull people into patterned behavior. Instead, they are tools societal members use to create a sense of social structure. Instead of being followed or complied with, they are used as sense-making aids to report and observe people's behavior. In other words, while the sociologist uses norms, rules, and typical motives to make sense of people's behavior, members of society use them in the same manner.

Ethnomethodology is neither the first nor the only perspective to make this observation. Peter Winch makes a similar point in *The Idea of a Social Science* (1958). He proposes that rules are context-dependent and can only be used as aids to perception to make sense of behavior. Herbert Blumer (1969:78–89) states that social structural elements like norms, values, roles, and statuses do not cause behavior: rather, they are tools people use to construct their behavior through interpretation. Ralph Turner (1962:20–40) views role as an interpretive device used to make sense of a person's behavior. Perhaps the best statement outside the ethnomethodological perspective is found in the work of Kenneth Burke (1962) and C. Wright Mills (1940). Burke and Mills view motives as words people use to describe why they (or others) behave in a certain manner. From this perspective, motives are not inside people, pulling them this way and that, but a set of words used to create meaningful action from behavior. In short, rules (motives) are "language events whereby societal members interpret their colleagues' actions and whereby they announce the meaning of their own actions for others ..." (Wieder, 1974:130).

A language event people perform to create and sustain a sense of social structure is a long way from being a causal agent. It is as if the sociological form of causal explanation turned out to be a method used by laymen for depicting the factual character of social reality. True, this version of rules and motives is not unique to ethnomethodology. What is unique is that ethnomethodology has provided an empirical basis for such a perspective and then used it to examine *how* people use rules.

The empirical basis for viewing rules as sense-making devices and language events is found in studies by Leiter (1969), Zimmerman (1970), and Wieder (1974). All of these studies show that rules and motives are used as schemes of interpretation. They also spell out some of the properties of their use. The first study by Zimmerman (1970) concerns rule use in a public welfare agency. Zimmerman studies the assignment of applicants to intake workers by a rule that treated applicants on a first come, first served basis. A routine feature of talk in the agency was for case workers to use the idea of "action according to the rule" to make visible the orderly flow of the applicants. Members of the agency were overheard depicting the sequential flow of people as the result of following the first come, first served rule. As Zimmerman writes:

> . . . the notion of action in accord with a rule is not a matter of compliance or non-compliance per se but of the various ways in which persons satisfy themselves and others concerning what is or is not "reasonable" compliance in particular situations. Reference to rules might then be seen as a common sense method of accounting for or making available for talk the orderly features of everyday activities, thereby *making out* these activities as orderly in some fashion (1970:233).

Zimmerman also found that the sense of the rules was discovered over the course of applying them rather than existing independent of context. Not only was the notion of "action according to the rule" used to locate and describe the orderly flow of people, but also the flow of people was consulted to see what the rule meant. The intent of the rule—its meaning—was formulated by using particulars of existing situations as a context. "In other words, what the rule is intended to provide for is discovered in the course of employing it over a series of actual situations" (Zimmerman, 1970:232). Rather than being a set of prescriptions which operate independent of context, Zimmerman found that the meaning of the rules is located by consulting contexts of its use. Furthermore, the rule and the situation mutually elaborate each other. The rule is used to give meaning to the behavior, and the behavior, in turn, is used to provide the meaning of the role.

These findings are more clearly illustrated in Wieder's (1974) study of the convict code. His is really a study within a study. Wieder uses the conduct of inquiry to show how members of society create social reality. In the first part of his study, Wieder describes the regular patterns of deviant behavior he observed at a halfway house for paroled narcotics addicts. He also describes how a set of rules called the convict code provides a traditional explanation for the deviant behavior. In the second half, Wieder describes how that social reality was created by the residents, the staff, and himself.

The accounting practice used to create the social reality of the halfway house as noted in Chapter VI, was telling the convict code. Residents and staff used the convict code, along with the notion of behavior as a product of following rules, as a device for making sense of residents' behavior. Below are some examples of residents and staff telling the code. In the first example, a staff member uses two maxims of the code ("don't snitch" and "don't mess with other residents' interests") to explain residents' behavior without referring to them as such.

PA: You know, they're in a very peculiar position; I don't know if it's a position that can be justified, but I'd probably justify it. They really can't take responsibility for the fact that this house is clean or dirty, because there is always going to be that sometime when they are going to get into trouble again and have to

face these people [other residents of the house] in prison. I
know enough about parole that it's a very precarious thing,
depends on the whim of the parole agent, the supervisor, the
tempo of the times. So, therefore, that could conceivably happen
[going back to prison]. So they can't take responsibility for
keeping this place clean.

W: It sounds like they told you that's why they can't do anything
about other guys' using.

PA: Yeah, that's what they told me, you know, and I'm saying I
bought it, but I'm not very comfortable with it.

W: So, therefore, they couldn't snitch, for instance, or do anything
about trying to stop another guy from using?

PA: Therefore, they couldn't snitch or the rest, right. (1974:153–154)

In the next example, a resident tells the code to explain his conduct:

On a number of other occasions, the code was employed to explain
concrete episodes of behavior. An example is provided by an incident
which occurred when several parole agents wanted to go out for a
beer after the committee meetings. The agents invited the aide and
me to come along. They suggested several places that we might go,
but the aide said, "No, I don't want to go there," until they started
listing bars outside the immediate neighborhood. The next day I
asked him why he was so hesitant about going to neighborhood
bars. He told me that it was not that he didn't want to go to those
bars, but that he did not want to go to them with the agents. He
did not think they should go to those bars, because it would make
the customers uncomfortable, and he did not want to be seen in that
situation with them, because people (residents and other types)
would think he was "sucking up to the fuzz" and could not be
trusted. By explaining why he had acted in the fashion that he did,
he also identified and defined what he had been doing—namely,
showing his loyalty to the residents. Although he did not concretely
mention the code, the language and the relevancies in his explanation were understood by me as "drawn from" it. In another case, a
resident more concretely used the code to describe a "hassle" between a staff member and himself (1974:144).

Both of these examples show that the staff and residents used
the code as a scheme of interpretation. When describing residents'

behavior, staff and residents used the convict code as a set of motives to explain why an individual behaved the way he did. A resident's conduct was viewed as a product of following the convict code. Using the convict code in this manner (as a scheme of interpretation) not only made a resident's behavior meaningful, it also endowed that behavior with its sense of being typical, regular, patterned, and independent of the particular person observing or performing it. Telling the convict code is a method for constructing social reality and its factual character. Using rules as schemes of interpretation is a member's method for sustaining a sense of social structure.

The documentary method of interpretation is the underlying process whereby telling the code is accomplished. To show this and the properties of telling the code, Wieder uses his own ethnographic activity as data. As a sociologist, he is engaging in the same process of constructing social reality, but with a difference—his construction becomes a topic of study rather than an undisclosed resource. A description of how he found both the code and the patterns of deviant behavior is quoted again because of its importance.

THE DOCUMENTARY METHOD OF INTERPRETATION

Equipped with what I understood to be a preliminary and partial version of the residents' definition of their situation (which was contained in the title, "The Code," and several maxims), I saw that other pronouncements of residents were untitled extensions of this same line of talk. I used whatever "pieces" of the code I had collected at that point as a scheme for interpreting further talk as extensions of what I had heard "up to now." Garfinkel (1967:78), following Mannheim, calls this kind of procedure "the documentary method of interpretation," describing it in the following terms:

The method consists of treating an actual appearance as "the document of," as "pointing to," as "standing on behalf of" a presupposed underlying pattern. Not only is the underlying pattern derived from its individual documentary evidences, but the individual documentary evidences, in their turn, are interpreted on the basis of "what is known" about the underlying pattern. Each is used to elaborate the other.

An example of the use of this method is provided by the interpretation of a remark I overheard during my first week at halfway house. I passed a resident who was wandering through the halls after the committee meetings on Wednesday night. He said to staff and all others within hearing, "Where can I find that meeting where I can get an overnight pass?" On the basis of what I had already learned, I understood him to be saying, "I'm not going to that meeting because I'm interested in participating in the program of halfway house. I'm going to that meeting just because I would like to collect the reward of an overnight pass and for no other reason. I'm not a kiss-ass. Everyone who is in hearing distance should understand that I'm not kissing up to staff. My behavior really is in conformity with the code, though without hearing this (reference to an overnight pass), you might think otherwise." I thereby collected another "piece" of talk which, when put together with utterances I had heard up to that point (which permitted me to see the "sense" of this remark) and used with utterances I had yet to collect, was employed by me to formulate the general maxim, "Show your loyalty to the residents."

The scope of the maxim concerning loyalty was further elaborated a month or so later, when I attended a Monday night group. A resident had suggested that a baseball team be formed. He was then asked by the group leader (the program director) to organize the team himself. He answered, "You know I can't organize a baseball team." The program director nodded, and the matter was settled. Using my ethnography of the code as a scheme of interpretation, I heard him say, "You know that the code forbids me to participate in your program in that way, and you know that I'm not going to violate the code. So why ask me?"

In this fashion, I employed my collection of "pieces" as a self-elaborating schema. Each newly encountered "piece" of talk was simultaneously rendered sensible by interpreting it in terms of the developing relevancies of the code and was, at the same time, more evidence of the existence of that code. Furthermore, the interpreted "piece" then functioned as part of the elaborated schema itself and was used in the interpretation of still further "pieces" of talk.

At each step, the interpretation was based on what was known thus far. If I had not had the general idea of the code as an interpretive device for translating utterances into maxims of a moral order, I could not have collected those utterances together as expressions of the same underlying pattern. Seeing an utterance as an expression of an underlying moral order depended on knowing *some* of the particulars of that underlying order to begin with. In the case of the convict code, having the title, "The Code," as supplied by residents and a statement of several maxims, also supplied by residents, provided enough material to initially formulate a tentative schema. This tentative schema "elaborated itself" as I used it to identify and elaborate the sense of objects and events in the setting. The selfsame perceptual-analytic procedure simultaneously elaborated the code and the setting as the code was employed by me as a schema. Since the use-of-the-code-as-a-schema *was* the procedure, the code was self- and setting-elaborative. In this sense, it is much more appropriate to think of the code as a continuous, ongoing process, rather than as a set of stable elements of culture which endure through time. In Zimmerman and Pollner's (1970) terms, the code is an *occasioned corpus* of "cultural elements," rather than a *stable set* of itemizable elements which reoccur in, or endure through, a collection of successive occasions (1974:184–186).

Wieder's account shows that telling the convict code is accomplished through the use of the documentary method of interpretation. It further shows that the sense of the rules and the sense or meaning of the patterns of behavior are mutually elaborative. The code furnishes meaning for the behavior, which, in turn, supplies the meaning of the code. This has empirical consequences for the use of rules as causal elements by sociologists. As Wilson (1970) and Zimmerman and Wieder (1970) point out, the reflexivity between the code, the behavior, and the setting makes it impossible for the code to satisfy the deductive requirements of a causal agent. To be a causal agent, the code must be capable of being defined and recognized independent of the situation and of dependent variables. The code must be capable of being defined and recognized independent of context. That is to say, changes in context should not alter its recognition as the convict code.

Wieder empirically shows that the convict code fails to meet these requirements of deductive explanation. In the first place, he shows that the code and the deviant behavior patterns mutually elaborate each other. A change in the meaning of one results in a change in the meaning of the other. Wieder demonstrates this point by proposing that if we impute the rules of "strict economic rationality and maximization of democratically organized therapy," the meaning and classification of the behaviors are altered.

> Under the schema of the therapy "game" and the rule of economic rationality, behavior that had been depicted as slouching, facially displayed inattentiveness, and extremely casual dress might well be seen and portrayed as appropriate therapeutic permissiveness, comfort, and relaxation that is sometimes recounted as essential to therapeutic contemplation. Being unresponsive to staff talk (from "disinterest and disrespect") and being unresponsive to staff pleas for volunteers (from "passive compliance"), as well as showing up for only those activities that were required, would be organized under a title which indicated that residents would negatively sanction forms of therapy that they did not think beneficial (and they did, in fact, argue that much of what staff did in group could not be beneficial, because it supposed that as a group they would attempt to control each other's behavior, rather than each member's being singly responsible for his own acts).
>
> It would also be the case that some behaviors would simply go by unnoticed under this hypothetical schema, e.g., eating in group might be such a "non-event." Thus, how the behaviors are seen as motivated conduct is dependent on some supposed motivational scheme (in cases like this, one supplied by rule) which is itself dependent for its determinacy on hearing talk (1974:194).

This example shows that once the content of the rules changes, so does the patterning of behavior. Wieder could not have grouped the residents' behavior into the patterns of doing distance, doing disrespect, and doing passive compliance if he did not have access to the code via talk. And conversely, he could not have recognized the code without the residents' behavior. This is because the code, the behavior, and the talk through which they are reflexively organized are context-dependent. They are all indexical particulars which depend on supplying a context to decide their specific sense.

If that context is changed, so is their meaning. Wieder provides the following example:

> If the remark, "You know I can't organize the baseball team," had been uttered by one staff member vis-a-vis another staff member, I would have heard the remark as something else entirely. Depending on *which* staff member was talking and *which* staff member was listening, the remark could have been heard as, "You know that it is your job, since you are on the recreation committee and I am not." Had it been a case-carrying parole agent who was on the recreation committee speaking to the program director, I would have heard (and presume that the program director would have heard) the remark as, "You know that I am already putting more time into the program than I can afford as it is; I couldn't possibly do more" (Wieder, 1974:187).

The code, as a deductive causal agent, is context-dependent. It cannot be described independent of context because, as Wieder has shown, it is indexical and changes its meaning with changes in context. As a result, it becomes difficult to separate cause from effect. Thus, their exists a dependence between the variables necessary for deductive causal analysis (Nagle, 1961; Wieder and Zimmerman, 1978; Wilson, 1970). Thus, Wieder's study provides an empirical basis for viewing rules as interpretive devices rather than as causal agents. His work also stands as evidence for another order of phenomena: accounts of social action and their accounting practices. The use of rules as interpretive aids turns out to be another instance of accounting. The meaning of behavior and social objects is created by using rules in the manner described by Wieder. Wieder's topic is *how* the meaningful behavior of residents was created, not in particular meanings.

MOTIVES AND SOCIAL TYPES

In addition to rules, societal members also use motives and social typifications to render behavior intelligible. Like rules, they are used as schemes of interpretation or aids to perception, to make sense of someone's behavior. Social typifications or social types are categories of people, behaviors, and reasons for behaving in a certain way. They are labels for people. For example, "snitch," "gorilla," "mature child," and "independent worker" are some of the social types used by prisoners and teachers to identify fellow prisoners and students, respectively.

These labels have a pragmatic basis. They are created to recognize types of people and behaviors deemed important to the functioning of the group (Klapp, 1962; Strong, 1934). For example, "independent worker" is a social type used by elementary school teachers to refer to students who can work with little or no supervision. The pragmatic basis for this social type is the fact that such students free the teacher to work with other students, as the following account suggests:

> They really should know how to work independently by the time they leave kindergarten because during activity time they're all choosing independent activities and some of them are out on the patio working with blocks without direct supervision and Mrs. —— and I will take groups off to the side so they will be completely on their own. So in this way we're hoping they will be independent (Leiter, 1974:56–57).

Recognizing independent workers is critical for a classroom organization in which two teachers give reading and math lessons to two groups while two other groups do activities. If students cannot work independently, the classroom organization with its activity groups cannot function. If the behavior labeled by the social type "independent worker" is not recognized and created, the nature of the classroom organization would change.

Wieder (1974) illustrates this same point more dramatically. The staff in the halfway house used the following social types to label residents "manipulative," "hostile to authority," "dependent," and "rule breaker." Residents who were "manipulative" were always playing one staff member off against another by saying that a staff member gave them permission to miss a meeting. Residents who were "dependent" were always asking for a lot of goods and services, such as food and blankets. Residents who chronically came in after curfew or didn't do chores were labeled "rule breakers." Residents who refused to do things, like apply for a driver's license because of red tape, or who had to be pushed to look for a job were labeled "hostile to authority" or just "hostile." If the behaviors described by these social types were to go unnoticed, the halfway house would collapse; the staff would be constantly bickering with each other; no one would come in at night (no parolees, no halfway house); chores to keep the house livable would not get done; resources like food, blankets, and time would disappear; and no one would go out and get a job. These examples show that social types are a set of categories created to recognize behaviors that are of practical interest to societal members. The definitions of social types are social characteristics created and used by members of society rather than inherent properties (Strong, 1936; Klapp, 1962; Leiter, 1974; Wieder, 1974).

Motives are particular kinds of social types. They refer to the reasons behind a person's behavior. Motives are words societal members use to make sense of their behavior and the behavior of others (Mills, 1940; Schutz, 1962). Because we cannot get inside a person's head to discover the causes of his behavior, we impute typical reasons. Motives are the typical reasons we impute to others or avow ourselves. Without the imputation of motives, the behavior of other people would be meaningless.

> In all the other forms of social relationship (and even in the relationship among consociates as far as the unrevealed aspects of the other's self are concerned) the fellow man's self can merely be grasped by a "contribution of imagination of hypothetical meaning presentation" . . . that is, by forming a construct of a typical way of behavior, a typical pattern of underlying motives, of typical attitudes of a personality type . . . (Schutz, 1962:17).

The typical motives, typical attitudes, and typical behavior patterns act as a context for understanding the behavior of the other person. Using this context as a background, we are able to give meaning to an individual's behavior and to our own. For example, the following account from a teacher illustrates how the imputation of particular motives alters the meaning of the same behavior. The teacher is answering the question "What do you learn from conferences with parents?"

T:
1　And also interesting things
2　come out like one little boy
3　who was always wiggling
4　around and never paying
5　attention, you know. I set him
6　my favorite place for wigglers
7　or people who talk is the back
8　corner of the rug 'cuz it only
9　puts one person on the side of
10　them and sometimes I'll put
11　them in the middle straight ac-
12　ross from me where I can watch
13　'em and this little boy was always
14　wiggling away from me.
15　wiggling never looking where he's
16　supposed to. And so I mentioned
17　this to the mother and she said
18　"O.K. you know he can't see out
19　of one of his eyes." I guess he has
20　double vision or something. I
21　don't understand exactly. She said
22　he's going in for eye surgery in a
23　couple of months. So right then
24　I knew to move the poor little boy
25　right up close to me where he
26　could see and he was just perfect
27　from then on when he could see
28　and I would hold everything up.
29　And he had to look at everything
30　like this (T turns her head to side)
31　and that's why he was always
32　wiggling around.

In lines 1–4 and 13–16 the teacher imputes the motive of "never paying attention" to the child. Then, after the mother tells her that the student has a vision problem (lines 17–23), the teacher imputes a different set of motives (lines 29–32). This second motive has the result of altering the wiggling from deviant to nondeviant behavior; the wiggling becomes a sign that the student was paying attention (lines 31–32). In this way the motive imputed renders the behavior intelligible.

Social types and social motives are part of the Gestalt-like context against which the meaningful character of a person's behavior is produced. Like all commonsense constructs, the relation between social types and behavior is reflexive. Social types are used to interpret the behavior of others, which, in turn, is used to interpret the meaning of social types. Social types do not, therefore, constitute a set of precise, logical categories the meaning of which is independent of the situation. Social types are pragmatically and reflexively tied to the occasions of their use.

A good deal of ethnomethodological research centers on the use of commonsense constructs. Leiter (1974) shows how kindergarten teachers use social types to promote students. In one of the schools he studied, the students were placed into the first grade by matching the social type of the student (bright students, average students, slow students, immature students, independent workers, and behavior problems) with the social type of the first grade teachers (academically strong, new teacher, and mother type). Below is an example of this practice:

I: 1 What is your impression of her?

T: 2 Of her now?

I: 3 Yes.

T: 4 I think she's a very slow worker and I think she needs
    5 individual help in order to get the concept of what I'm
    6 giving. And that's a lot of time I say. Do you understand?
    7 I think that she's just slow and needs a lot of help. She's
    8 a large child. Now here's a case where even though she
       would
    9 not be ready for first grade—she's ready for a low first
   10 grade—but even if she were not ready in other ways, I would
   11 pass her on to a first grade because that girl another year

12   in kindergarten—look how big she'd be before she went into the

13   first grade! See so we would pass her on.

I: 14   What kind of ahh. Have you had any other contact
15   with her mother and father?

T: 16   Ahh no. The mother just brought her in just this one time
17   an' the mother brought in just when we were starting to have
18   parent conferences and I never had a conference with her
19   mother. Amm I have been meaning to call and talk with her
20   mother about Ro and then I think it really does no purpose
21   because Ro will go on to first grade. And she will be placed
22   in a—where she will be comfortable. I believe I placed her
23   with, I have to look on the chart up there, but as I recall
24   I placed her with Mrs. Wa where she will be more, moth-
      erly, mothered and slower. (1974:63–64)

The basis for promoting the student into the first grade is the social type "behavior problem." When the teacher makes references to how big the student is and how large she will be in first grade (lines 10–13), she is saying that one reason for promoting this student is to prevent her from becoming a behavior problem. One of the characteristics used by teachers to identify behavior problems is size relative to the rest of the group. Students who are disproportionately larger than the rest of the class either become bullies or are teased by the other students. In a second interview, I questioned the teacher about this section of the transcript. She explained that if Ro was kept in kindergarten, her size would lead to teasing by the other students, which might cause her to become either uncommunicative or physically aggressive toward her peers. The social type ("behavior problem") and the typical behaviors associated with it serve as the major factor in the student's placement. Placing the student in a particular first grade class is also accomplished by using the social types "slow student" and "mother teacher." In lines 21–24 the teacher accomplishes this placement by linking the two social types together. The basis for the linkage is a theory of educational compatability: "she will be placed in a—where she will be comfortable."

Other ethnomethodologists have studied the use of social types. Cicourel and Kitsuse's (1963) study of high school tracking (ability grouping) focuses on the social types used by high school counselors to place students in college preparatory and noncollege preparatory programs. They found that the social types used by counselors create different interpretations of the same behavior. Mundane problems like cutting classes, poor grades, and tardiness become "deep-seated problems" of a psychodynamic nature through the use of social types from clinical psychology. A comparison of teacher-counselors with professional counselors produced the finding that teacher-counselors described academic problems in terms of social types used by the man in the street, while professional counselors used social types from clinical psychology. As a result, the same problems came to have different meanings, and different procedures are used to deal with them.

Zimmerman's (1970) study of "plain fact" illustrates how case workers use social types as perceptual aids. One of the practices whereby the plain fact character of documents was established was "viewing the applicant as a course of action." This practice amounts to using the social identity of the client to generate a set of investigatable actions that should have produced a record. The occupation of a client (his role) becomes a scheme of interpretation for locating a set of actions which follow from the social type claimed by the client. These actions, in turn, serve as a basis for investigating the client's claims for eligibility through a search for the official documents they would normally produce.

A more formal study of social types is found in the notion of "membership categorization devices" to describe how social types are used in understanding everyday conversations. Sacks (1965) begins his analysis of social types with the following statement:

The baby cried the mommy picked it up.

Sacks asks: How do we hear this indexical expression? We hear it as saying "The baby cried and the mommy of the baby picked it up." The topic of study for Sacks is, *How* do we hear it this way? His answer is, We understand indexical expressions by supplying categories which are referentially paired through the use of membership categorization devices.

Categories like "baby" and "mommy" are occasional (indexical) expressions. That is to say, they are potentially equivocal, being capable of more than one meaning. "Baby" can refer to "baby" as in "member of a family"; it can also refer to a stage of life (baby, teenager, adult, lover). "Mommy" can also refer to "member of a family" or to a stage of life (single woman, married woman, mommy). "Stage of Life" and "Member of Family" are Membership Categorization Devices (MCDs). They form a context that gives a specific sense to the social types. By using "member of a family" as a context for "baby," we supply a specific sense not only to that category but also to "mommy" as well. Sacks proposes that there is a "consistency rule" that governs the use of membership categorization devices: "If a category from a device is used to categorize a member, that category or others from that same device *may be* used to categorize other members of the population under review" (Sacks, 1965). This rule acts as a "pairing rule" for social types. It locks both social types into a common context as a method of understanding. It is more a method for achieving understanding than a rule that must be obeyed. By using the device "member of a family" to context "baby," we *can* use it to context "mommy." Thus, by applying this context to both categories, we hear the statement "the baby cried the mommy picked it up," as "the baby cried and the mommy of the baby picked it up." MCDs are social types that serve as contexts for other social types and give them their specific sense.

The choice of MCDs is a product of commonsense reasoning. That is to say, it is a product of the use of the documentary method of interpretation and interpretive procedures. The choice of MCDs is necessarily an accomplishment because a social type (category) may be part of more than one device. Thus, in choosing devices, one may start with an MCD for the first category one sees and, upon using it for the second category, find that another device is more appropriate. Upon finding that, one may then revise the sense of the first category by applying another MCD. The "appropriate"

MCD is chosen through the use of descriptive vocabularies as indexical expressions and retrospective-prospective sense of occurrence. Sacks' notion of MCDs, then, is an analysis of how members of society use social types to understand each other through the use of interpretive procedures.*

Two of the best studies that illustrate the dynamics of social type usage are Sudnow's (1965) study of "normal crimes" and Emerson's (1969) study of how delinquent identities are constructed in court. A "normal crime" is a social type that describes the kind of person who typically commits it and where, the typical motives, the typical victim, and the typical means. They are situated social types, for the people who use them (district attorneys and public defenders) recognize that they apply only to crime as it is performed in their jurisdiction. Normal crimes are central to the process of plea bargaining whereby a person charged with a felony (burglary, assault with a deadly weapon), is given a lesser sentence in exchange for pleading guilty to a lesser offense (petty theft, assault, loitering). The process of plea bargaining has a pragmatic basis: Courts are crowded; there is often insufficient evidence from the D.A.'s perspective and D.A.'s priority of cases worthy of trial. Plea bargaining is necessarily an interpretive process because the law does not specify to what lesser crimes a charge can be reduced. As Sudnow puts it:

> To what offense can "drunkenness" be reduced? There is no statutorily designated crime that is necessarily included in the crime of "drunkenness." That is if any of the statutorily required components of drunk behavior (its corpus delecti) are absent, there remains no offense of which the assaultant description is a definition. For drunkenness there is, however, an offense that while not necessarily included (described statutorily) is "typically-situationally-included," i.e., "typically" occurs as a feature of the way drunk persons are seen to behave—"disturbing the peace" (1965:260).

In short, because of the law's open structure, the district attorney and the public defender use normal crimes—a set of social types—

* For a similar analysis of Sacks, see Mehan and Wood's *The Reality of Ethnomethodology* (1975).

to arrive at an appropriate reduction. The social types or normal crimes are used as a scheme of interpretation for locating the social features (i.e., typical features) of a crime. These social features, in turn serve as a basis for locating the lesser change to which the crime can be reduced. The socially defined features of crimes are gathered in the form of social types, which are used to accomplish the reduction. Sudnow further describes how this scheme of interpretation is used.

> As the typical reduction for burglary is petty theft and as petty theft is neither situationally nor necessarily included in burglary, the examination of the instant case is clearly not undertaken to decide whether petty theft is an appropriate statutory description. The concern is to establish the relation between the instant burglary and the normal category "burglaries" and having decided a "sufficient correspondence," to now employ petty theft as the proposed reduction. In scrutinizing the present burglary case, the PD seeks to establish that "this is a burglary just like any other." If that correspondence is not established, regardless of whether or not petty theft in fact was a feature of the way the crime was enacted, the reduction to petty theft would not be proposed. The propriety of proposing petty theft as a reduction does not derive from its in-fact existence in the present case, but is warranted or not by the relation of the present burglary to "burglaries" as normally conceived (Sudnow 1965:166).

In other words, the social types (normal crimes) are not used to see if petty theft is part of the present case. Rather, the reduction depends on how closely the present case fits the crime of burglary, or any other, as it is typically conceived through the social types. The social types, then, are truly used as schemes of interpretation, for they serve to place the entire act in context, not just parts of it. Sudnow's description shows that the open-ended character of laws is resolved by embedding the case in question within a context of commonsense typifications. Furthermore, Sudnow shows us a basic feature of commonsense reasoning: appropriateness by correspondence to a context. Commonsense interpretation does not consist of or demand the in-fact existence of the reduced crime. It demands a correspondence in context. The case in question must match the general context for that kind of crime. The context turns out to be the normal crimes which are social types that portray the social features of crimes (the ways they are performed, who commits them, where they are performed, and the typical victims). The meaning of an act, its sense as a reducible crime, is derived from its membership within a type of crime. Sudnow's study makes a contribution to our understanding of how social types are used. It is a disappointing study insofar as the presentation of data is concerned. Sudnow presents direct quotations of social types, but he does not present data showing their use. We are not shown transcripts of interviews with district attorneys and public defenders, and we are not shown field notes of observations made by the researcher. Sudnow does not afford the reader a good look at his data, which run counter to one of ethnomethodology's basic tenets: Show the reader the bases and contextual particulars used to produce the analysis.

Like other ethnomethodological studies, Emerson's study of delinquents in court examines how the factual character of the social world is created. Emerson views the delinquent identity and the delinquent character of an act as things that are actively created in the courtroom. To quote Emerson:

> Moral character is not passively established. It is the product of interaction and communications work involving the delinquent, his family, enforcers, complaints generally, and the court itself. Specific versions of moral character must be successfully presented if they are to be adopted by others (1969:101).

The "specific versions of moral character" that Emerson refers to are a set of social types use by the court, attorneys, and defendants. The set includes the normal youth, the delinquent youth, and the disturbed youth. In addition, there is a set of normal crimes typically performed by each kind of youth which describes the kind of crime, how it is typically done and the typical motives. Below are some examples of normal crimes as described by probation officers:

> *Boy shoplifters:* "Usually it's a very mild type of boy. There are not many seriously delinquent boys." Generally no previous record.

Often from "well-to-do families" and taking goods "for kicks."
"Usually they're pretty nice children. They give you no trouble."
Seldom in court again. "Usually they're not thieves at heart. They're
in the store and they succumb to a beautiful display or something
that looks good to them."

Handbag snatchers: "These are generally pretty seriously delinquent
boys. They're known to other courts or on parole. . . . They're
either probationers or parolees. Very aggressive delinquent boys."
(Emerson, 1969:107).

The establishment of moral character by police takes place in the
streets (Piliavian and Briar, 1964; Cicourel, 1968; Skolnick, 1968)
and the courtroom. It is created against a background of social
types and practical circumstances. The court has limited time; it
cannot hear every case in which a youth has gotten into trouble.
The court also has limited resources for handling such youths.
Space in correctional institutions, psychiatric clinics, and foster
homes is scarce and expensive. (Consequently, the court must decide such cases carefully.) The court's use of the stock of knowledge
in creating a specific moral character is practical. It is also interpretive, for the creation of moral character involves assembling contexts and ethnographic particulars that point to a specific kind of
moral character.

The decision of the court is not based on applying the rule of law
or upon the merits of a case. As in plea bargaining, the court attempts to establish a correspondence between a youth's moral character and the social types.

Cases are settled against the background of what is the "normal"
disposition for "cases of this kind," i.e., for delinquents of this kind
of moral character (Emerson, 1969:103).

This correspondence is accomplished through two basic presentation strategies: pitches and denunciations. A *pitch* is a presentation
of ethnographic particulars in the direction of lenient disposition;
a *denunciation* strives for a severe disposition. Pitches and denunciations create a youth's moral character in court. Although they are

aimed at creating different moral characters (normal versus delinquent youth), they utilize the same practices. To accomplish either
presentation, the person making it must embed the behavior of the
accused in an ethnographic context.

The moral character of the youth is created by showing that the
youth's behavior belongs to one of the three types of delinquency.
This is accomplished by assembling features of the act, motivation
of the youth, and features of the youth's biography into a context.
This context, in turn, provides the act with its specific sense of being a delinquent act, a normal prank, or a symptom of a disturbed
mind. The ethnographic particulars assembled by the attorneys are
crucial in creating the meaning of the act. Emerson demonstrates
this point with the following case:

> Two older girls who had run away from home and been caught
> shoplifting in a department store claimed they had spent the night
> in a doorway. The judge seemed reluctant to accept this story, and
> asked the arresting officer if the girls had been "clean" when he
> caught them. The policeman said no, and added that the blond girl
> had been wearing eye make-up and had her hair done up.
>
> Here it can be noted that a typical normal runaway by girls in-
> volves staying away from home and living on the streets for a day
> or two following a family argument. *This fades into a more
> criminal-like runaway, where the girls become involved in prostitu-
> tion.* Hence it becomes critical to determine where the runaways
> spent the night, and the court routinely questions runaways about
> this and other topics pertinent to living "on the streets." The answer
> here that the night was spent in a doorway arouses the judge's sus-
> picion. He then attempts to gauge the nature of this runaway epi-
> sode by asking the police officer about the girls' appearance at the
> time of arrest (on the assumption that had they indeed stayed in
> some doorway they could not stay "clean," while if they had been
> in an apartment somewhere they would have). The policeman's
> answer is ambiguous in this respect, since he reports that they were
> clean, but that one girl was heavily made up, a possible indicator
> of prostitution. Nonetheless, *the circumstances of this inquiry clearly
> suggest how one minute aspect of a report may shape the perceived
> nature of a delinquent act* (i.e., determine the class of typical delin-
> quency in which it will be placed) (1969:112).

The ethnographic particulars of the act are critical in creating the criminality or the normalcy of the act and the moral character of its performer. Thus, particulars that point to preparation (map plans of a building), technical equipment (lock picks, bolt cutters, boxes with false bottoms for picking up merchandise), and the technique used to perform the act are used to give criminal meaning to the act. Spontaneity, lack of equipment, and impulsiveness, on the other hand, are particulars used to create a nondelinquent, non-criminal sense to the act. For example, Emerson presents a case where the use of "professional burglar tools" undercuts the defense attorney's attempt to present the offense as a spontaneous event.

A 16-year-old Negro boy was accused of trying to break into a church social center at night. The night watchman there had heard him and called the police, who had caught him on the roof with wirecutters and other tools in his possession. The judge looked these over carefully. The police reported: "He said he had been drinking and did not know how he got up there. . . . He wouldn't say anything."

The judge found the boy delinquent and asked for the probation report. PO noted that the boy had been committed to reform school on a school complaint, had been in trouble several times there, but had been released when he turned 16.

Public defender then made his argument on behalf of the boy. He indicated that the boy had been into no trouble for nearly three years. Probation officer interrupted to say that this was not quite true, since there had been several recent parole violations. Defender continued: "I think this is another case of idle hands where this boy has nothing to do. I—" Judge: "Idle hands? How can you say it's a case of idle hands when he went out buying these tools? These are professional tools. It's not just a kid breaking into a place with a crowbar. These are professional tools . . ." (1969:116–117).

In addition to an ethnographic context, the meaning of the act is created by placing it within a context of a general pattern of behavior. The moral character of the youth and his behavior are created by assembling features of the youth's biography. Such features that are frequently invoked are the youth's prior record of delinquency, trouble in school, and features of his family life that are seen as causing career delinquency. Both pitches and denunciations involve constructing the youths biography using these particulars. Often the same features of a youth's biography are invoked by both sides. When this occurs, the feature is embedded in a context to support the moral character being presented. The same feature thus provides a different meaning by supplying an alternative context. The aim of both pitches and denunciations is to assemble particulars that point to an underlying pattern or process that would produce the type of moral character being created.

Emerson's study clearly illustrates how members use social types in their construction of social reality. The factual properties of the youth's act—its definition as a certain kind of delinquency—and his moral character are established through the use of social types. The social types serve as the focal point for assembling ethnographic particulars of the act and biographical particulars of the youth into a context. The context, in turn, gives meaning to both the act and the actors. The use of the documentary method of interpretation is the central process for assembling such contexts. Emerson shows that the construction of social reality is an ongoing process. The ethnographic particulars making up the context are themselves indexical. The features of the act and the biographical particulars that were used to create the moral character of the youth were ambiguous. The same particulars would be used by both sides but given a different meaning by embedding them in a different context.

The creation of social reality is a practical activity. The court could not accept anyone's definition of a youth who was troublesome. Because its own time, staff, and resources were scarce, the court had to construct its own definition of trouble. These practical circumstances, along with the social types of youths and offenses, constituted the court's stock of knowledge at hand. The facticity of the youth's moral character was determined by constructing a correspondence between the case at hand and the stock of knowledge. Emerson's (1969) account of the process whereby moral character is created and sustained illustrates every aspect of the ethnomethodological perspective: the stock of knowledge, the sense of social structure, indexicality, the use of the documentary method, and the theoretical status of norms, social types, and motives. It is an example of how ethnomethodologists describe the members' methods of creating and sustaining a sense of social structure.

ETHNOMETHODOLOGY/SOCIAL INTERACTION

The previous sections have dealt implicitly with one aspect of social interaction: how it is understood. All of the previous methods are used to understand interaction. Through their use, behavior is converted into social action that is meaningful and that has a sense of inherent meaningfulness. We now turn to how members of society construct face-to-face interaction.

It is safe to say that no single area of ethnomethodology has been more misunderstood than the attempts to deal with face-to-face interaction. Lewis Coser, in his recent (1975) address to the American Sociological Association, characterized the work of the late Harvey Sacks as trivial. In effect, Coser's criticism was that ethnomethodology had become so micro in its approach that there was no relation between the phenomena it described and everyday social order. Coser could not have been more incorrect. The work of Sacks and his associates (Emmanuel Schegaloff, Jo Ann Goldberg, Roy Turner and Matthew Speier) is an attempt to make everyday social interaction describable in sociological terms, or at least in ethnomethodological terms. Sacks' (1975) work is controversial among ethnomethodologists as well. The rule-governed character of his formulations has alienated ethnomethodologists who stress the interpretive side of social behavior. Cicourel (1973) criticizes Sacks for drawing on context-bound particulars without informing the reader. What I am about to propose is a way of reading Sacks and his associates that makes their work compatible with ethnomethodology and its version of the problem of social order.

The sense of social structure applies to conversations as well as to the social order. Conversations must also preserve a sense of social structure. Cicourel (1973) makes this point when he refers to talk itself as being reflexive:

Talk is reflexive to participants because it is seen as fundamental to "normal" scenes. I am not referring to the content of talk but simply its presence during speech and the expectation that particular forms of speech will give a setting, the appearance of something recognizable and intelligible (Cicourel, 1973:55).

Cicourel is saying that the very presence of conversation or talk that is recognized as conversation provides members with a sense of social structure. Sacks takes this point a step further and addresses himself to the methods whereby members create conversations.

This line of inqury begins with the specification of the social structure of conversation. By this I mean a specification of properties of conversation recognized by members of society. The following are *properties*—not rules—of conversation. Talk possessing these properties is recognized and attended by members as a conversation.

1. Speaker change is minimal.

2. One party generally speaks at a time.

3. More than one speaker may speak at one time, but such occurrences are brief.

4. Transitions from one speaker to another occur with little or no gap or overlap.

5. The basic unit of a conversation is the turn, which can vary in length from a single word or phrase to several sentences. Transitions from one turn to another mark the end of a turn. Hence, transition points can be at the end of single words, phrases, and sentences.

6. Conversationalists do not decide the order of turn taking before they begin conversing. The order of turn taking develops over the course of the conversation.

7. Conversationalists do not decide the size of turns before conversing: consequently, turn size varies.

8. Conversationalists do not specify the length of a conversation in advance.

9. What people say or have to say in a conversation is not specified in advance.

10. Conversationalists do not decide in advance who is to get a certain number of turns in the conversation. (Properties 4–9 distinguish conversations from other talking events, such as debates, lectures, and panel discussions and meetings.)

11. The number of parties to a conversation can vary from two to ten or more. Size affects the distribution of turns, for in a two-party conversation the nonspeaker knows that at some point he will become the speaker. In conversations of three or more parties, there is no such guarantee. If one does not select oneself as the next speaker or is not selected by the current speaker, the turn goes to someone else. Also, in conversations consisting of several parties, there can be more than one conversation taking place at the same time.

12. Talk in conversations can be continuous or discontinuous. Continuous talk occurs when it goes on across a transition place with a minimum of gap and overlap. Discontinuous talk occurs when the current speaker stops and no other speaker starts.

13. Conversations have openings and closings. They are social events with beginnings and endings that can be closed off (i.e., an opening can be closed) or reopened.

14. Repair mechanisms exist to deal with turn-taking errors.

The concepts listed above were originally formulated as rules of conversation. However, they have become a set of properties which constitute conversations. There are other speech events, such as debates, lectures, meetings, and panel discussions, which are not conversations because they do not contain these properties. The properties of conversations can be said to be a specification of the social structure of conversations. Speech events with these properties are recognized as conversations by societal members.

This reading of Sacks' work has a rationale. In the first place, Sacks (1974) and Speier (1973) refer to these properties as properties that are recognized by members of society. Speier (1973) refers to them as formal elements of interchange and elements of conversation. Sacks et al. (1974) call for the need to arrive at a set of features of conversation that apply regardless of what is said in any specific conversation. In his most recent paper on turn taking, Sacks et al. (1974) refers to this list as "apparent facts" of conversation. Furthermore, it is proposed that "a model (of conversations) should be capable of accommodating, i.e., either be compatible with or allow the derivation of the following glossy apparent facts" (Sacks, et al., 1974:700). Finally, this reading is consistent with the ethnomethodological perspective. The properties listed by Sacks are the constitutive properties of conversation. Speech events possessing these properties are recognized by societal members as conversations. If these properties are not present in a speech event that is claimed to be a conversation, it is a cause of complaint (Sacks, 1965; Speier, 1973).

Like other ethnomethodologists, Sacks is concerned with describing the methods members use to create the properties of conversation. Conversations are viewed as products of members' methods for creating openings, topic change, turn taking, and closings. The aim of Sacks' research is the construction of a model of conversation that is both context-free and context-bound. That is, his aim is the construction of a model that applies to all conversations regardless of their settings. To quote Sacks and his associates:

> We have found reasons to take seriously the possibility that a characterization of turn-taking organization for conversations could be developed which would be important twin features of being context free and capable of extraordinary context sensitivity (1974:699–700).

Sacks seeks to produce a model which simultaneously maintains the situated character of a conversation and is context-free. Such a model is founded on the fact that conversations take place in a variety of contexts and are capable of "dealing with changes of a situation within a situation" (Sacks et al., 1974:699). Hence, Sacks and his colleagues direct their attention to providing a model that preserves the context-bound properties of conversation while "requiring no reference to any particular context" (Sacks et al., 1974: 700). This program is the same as Cicourel's attempt to locate interpretive procedures which are context-free but which allow the member to produce a variety of context-bound meanings. To quote Cicourel:

To handle the problem of articulating general rules with particular social settings, I have used the notion of interpretive procedures as invariant properties or principles which allow members to assign meaning or sense to substantive rules. . . . The principles outlined above are generative in the sense that they constitute a few (but not exhaustive) procedures interacting together so as to produce instruction for the speaker-hearer for assigning infinitely possible meanings to unfolding social scenes (1973:85–86).

Using turn taking as their starting point, Sacks and his colleagues propose the following model of conversation. It meets the requirements of being context-free while preserving the context-bound character of conversation.

1. At any turn-transition point the following sequence of alternatives can occur:

   a. If the current speaker selects the next speaker, that person has the right and obligation to speak.

   b. If the current speaker does not select the next speaker, then the person who starts first becomes the next speaker. That is, if the current speaker does not select the next speaker, potential speakers select themselves as next speaker.

   c. If the current speaker does not choose someone else to be the next speaker and no one selects himself as the next speaker, then the current speaker may continue to speak although he does not have to continue.

2. The current speaker continuing (in the event he does not choose the next speaker and in the event someone else does not select himself to be the speaker) the turn-taking system begins anew at the next turn-taking transition point in the conversation (Sacks et al., 1974:704).

This turn-taking model has several properties worth mentioning. First, it is both context-free and context-sensitive. It applies to conversations regardless of contexts, while at the same time it provides for context-specific practices of conversational organization. The model itself can be produced using practices that are situation-specific. Second, it preserves the features of conversations. Viewed as a set of basic methods used by societal members, this model produces speech events and conversations possessing the factual properties of conversations.

Third, the model is an interactionist model of conversational turn taking. It consists of a set of options which are contingent upon people paying attention to what each is doing. Each option in the model is contingent upon the parties to the conversation. To quote Sacks and his colleagues:

> The party-administered, local management of turn-order is effected through the rule-set, whose ordered properties provides a cycle of options in which any party's contribution to turn order is contingent on and oriented to the contribution of the other parties (1974:726).

The model essentially puts a set of options at the disposal of the parties to a conversation. What they do with them is interactionally determined. By "interactionally determined" Sacks and his associates do not mean that the speaker determines the form of conversation and the other parties merely recognize it and follow it. They mean instead that a speaker turn is something that parties to a conversation work at together. The ordering, size, and turn transitions are products of the parties to the conversation and are embedded in that particular conversation. Conversations are "recipient designed":

> By "recipient design" we refer to a multitude of respects in which the talk by a party in a conversation is constructed or designed in ways which display an orientation and sensitivity to the particular other(s) who are the co-participants. In our work we have found recipient design to operate with regard to word selection, topic selection, admissibility and ordering of sequences, options and obligations for starting and terminating conversations. . . . Recipient design is a major basis for that variability of actual conversations glossed by the notion "context-sensitive" (1974:727).

In short, *recipient design* means that conversations are tailor-made by the participants for themselves and contexts through collaborating together. Sacks' model for turn taking preserves this feature of conversation by requiring that parties to a conversation pay attention to each other throughout the course of the conversation.

Each part of Sacks' model relies on the participants' awareness of what the other is doing.

Given this model for turn taking, let's examine some of the turn-taking methods used by societal members. Turn-taking methods are divided into two broad classes: methods whereby the current speaker selects the next speaker and methods of self-selection. A method whereby the current speaker selects the next speaker is the use of "adjacency pairs" (Speier, 1973; Sacks et al., 1974). Sequences like greetings, complaints, challenges, and insults are notable for the fact that the initial unit of the sequence sets constraints on what should be said in the next turn. For example, a greeting typically elicits a greeting, a question gets an answer or another question, complaints are followed either by denial or rejection, and insults are followed by a return insult. Sacks and his colleagues provide the following instances:

Complaint/denial

A: Hey yuh took my chair by the way an I don't think that was very nice.

B: I didn't take yer chair, it's my chair.

Complaint/rejection

A: I'm glad I have you for a friend.

B: That's because you don't have any others.

Challenge/rejection

A: It's not break time yet.

B: I finished my box, so shut up. (1974:716)

The current speaker can select the next speaker by using a first-pair part. The party to whom it is addressed is thereby selected as the next speaker by his relationship to the utterance pair. Another method is to end a statement with a "tag question" (Sacks et al., 1974:718), such as "You know?" or "Don't you think so?" A tag question is a method for ending a turn. It can be a "turn exit," whereby the current speaker announces that he is ending his turn. As Sacks and his colleagues explain:

When a current speaker has constructed a turn's talk to a possible transition relevance place without having selected a next, and he finds no other self-selecting (speaker) to be next, he may, employing his option to continue, add a tag question, selecting another as next speaker upon the tag question's completion and thereby exiting from the turn (1974:718).

In the second type of speaker selection method, a person selects himself to be the next speaker. "The first person to speak" is one such method. This does not mean that more than one person jumps in at the same time whenever the current speaker does not select the next speaker. There are occasions when more than one person will begin at the same time; more often, however, after a very brief pause someone will start. A method of self-selecting is to use a springboard technique; the person self-selects by using part of the previous speaker's topic as a place to take his turn. This method involves projecting his utterance to fit the completion of the current speaker's talk. "Oppositional beginnings" ("well," "but," "and," "so") are devices that people use to announce that they have selected themselves as the next speaker. They serve as pre-entry devices, just as tag questions serve notice that the current speaker is about to exit.

Thus far, we have looked at a set of methods that members use to produce the socially recognized properties of conversation. These and other methods are located in conversations. By examining conversations, one can locate the methods used in their construction. The methods of turn taking I have described are not intended as an exhaustive set. The search for additional methods can be accomplished only by examining conversations. To do this, one must treat conversations as interactive events constructed by the participants. Upon examining a conversation, one must ask such questions as, How do the participants jointly construct the beginning of a conversation? How do they accomplish turn taking? What methods are used to introduce, expand, and close topics? How are closings of conversations produced, and how are closed conversations reopened? A constant theme that runs through Sacks' work and that of his associates is the methodical production of conversations by societal members. The model of the actor remains the same: Societal members use certain methods to produce social structure. Furthermore, these methods are found in the very language they use. Garfinkel (1967) and Cicourel (1973) propose that the accounting practices are found in the everyday talk of societal members. Sacks and his colleagues have taken their ideas seriously and have attempted to describe the methods used to construct everyday conversations. Their approach differs from that of Cicourel and Garfinkel in that they pay less attention to how conversations are understood and more to how they are produced. The distinction is primarily an analytical one and has not been articulated in the literature. In fact, the status of Sacks' work within ethnomethodology has been debated.

The position taken here is that in spite of its rule-governed nature, Sacks' formulation remains ethnomethodology. The implicit model of the actor is ethnomethodological. The societal member produces the factual properties of conversation through a set of methods embedded in (i.e., part of) the phenomenon itself. Sacks' methods have the same reflexive relationship to conversations that accounting practices have to accounts. Furthermore, Sacks' model is a solution to the "problem" of indexicality. The members' sense of social structure is an ongoing product because of the indexical properties of behavior and talk. Conversations become especially indexical because societal members often leave the meanings of their utterances unstated but presumably intended. By viewing a conversation as a speech event that is jointly constructed by its participants, Sacks is raising the question of how this is accomplished given the indexicality of speech. Using turn taking as a case in point, this question can be put as follows: How does a current speaker inform other participants that he is about to end his turn without explicitly saying to them, "I am through talking, now it's your turn"? Now, it is clear that speakers and hearers do not produce conversations in this manner. Instead, they provide each other with a set of instructions that are embedded in their talk. By using particular methods embedded in his speech (using adjacency pairs like questions, complete tag questions), a speaker offers other participants an indexical statement of his intention. Sacks' model and turn allocation methods are a set of members' methods for receiving and producing conversational instructions which are embedded in the indexical speech used in conversations. The notion of instruction does not mean that conversations are less than interaction events. The indexical properties of speech require constant interpretation by societal members. Hearing a statement at the conclusion of a turn requires placing a construction upon that set of words. Sacks' model is a set of methods societal members use to convert utterances into turn-transferring devices.

I have not tried to cover Sacks' work in its entirety, but rather to show how it makes a contribution at the interactional level. It is an example of one way ethnomethodologists address the accomplishment of social interaction. The ethnomethodological perspective stresses the methodic character of social interaction; it is a product of members' methods. Social interaction is a negotiated product in its sequencing as well as its understanding. The negotiated or accomplished character of social interaction is due to the indexical properties of talk and behavior. Because of indexicality, both the sequencing and the understanding of interaction are constructed by societal members. The flexibility of social interaction is also due to indexicality, for as we saw earlier, one does not have to use the *same* context in order to achieve an understanding of social interaction (Skinner, 1975).

From the ethnomethodological perspective, social interaction is a thoroughly negotiated accomplishment. The sequencing, as well as the understanding, of social interaction is negotiated through the use of commonsense knowledge and the practices of commonsense reasoning. The ongoing, unending character of this negotiation is the result of the indexical properties of talk and behavior. Because talk is indexical, we embed it in a context made up of who the speaker is, the purposes of the speaker, features of the setting, nonverbal gestures, and so on. Practical reasoning is used to assemble such contexts and to make sense of what is happening. Commonsense methods are also used to create the factual properties of conversations so that they are perceived as such by members of society

(Sacks et al., 1974). Indexicality is an important property precisely because it forms the basis for the continual construction of social interaction. Because of indexicality, interaction is flexible.

These points are illustrated by a study of classroom interaction conducted by Hugh Mehan (1974). It is a study of how the teacher and students produce a classroom lesson. The lesson Mehan studied was an "orientation lesson on the use of prepositions ('under,' 'below,' 'over' and 'above')." The teacher expected the students to use these prepositions in complete sentences ("The sun is above the tree") rather than phrases or proterms. Students were asked to draw objects in relation to others or to place an object next to, below, or above an object on a flannel board and then to report on what they had done using the expected complete sentence. Mehan begins his study by examining the teacher's instructions. Below are some examples:

(1)   T: Yes. Let's take our green crayon and make a line at the bottom of your paper. Just take your green crayon and make a green line at the bottom.

S1:   Like that?

T: Yeah.

S2:   Now what are we going to do?

T: Now take your orange crayon and make an orange worm under the green line. Pretend that's grass. Just a little wiggle. Here let me show you on this one. An orange worm.

S1:   Can you make it on yours?

S2:   Under?

T: No, I'm watching you make yours.

S3:   Over here?

S4:   Under?

T: Listen, I'm going to say it just once. Make an orange worm under the green line.

S1:   Like that?

T: Beautiful. Ok we are going to pretend that green line is the grass ok. Can you pretend that with me? Alright, where is the orange worm Do?

(2)   S1:   It has to be away in the corner.

       S2:   One of these.

        T: It doesn't matter. You choose something and put it above the green line.

       S1:   There, that's the sun. I moved it.

       S1:   That's the number. That's the number one.

        T: Ok. Can you find something and put it above the green line?

       S1:   That's the numeral one.

       S2:   That's the stoplight ya see.

       S1:   Hold it down over there.

        T: Choose quickly.

       S1:   Hurry up you are taking our time.

        T: Ok. All right. Can you tell us about what you did? What did you do? (1974:130; 136)

The teacher's instructions are vague and incomplete. They do not recover what she expects of the children. In the first example, the teacher's instructions do not contain the reason for drawing the "grass" and the "worm." That is, they do not explain the nature of the task, nor do they tell one what will stand as a correct answer. In the second example, the teacher's instructions do not inform the students what they are to report on or how. The information needed to carry out the instructions is not found in the instructions themselves because they are indexical expressions. Even when the teacher attempts to remedy the indexical instructions by contexting them, they remain incomplete and vague, as the following examples illustrate:

(1)   T: What' under the tree? Tell me the flower . . .

       S: The flower . . . the flower is under the tree.

       T: Where is the red flower Ri?

     Ri: Under the tree.

       T: Can you tell me in a sentence?

(2)   T: Yes, the flower is by the tree. What can we say about it when we talk about the flower and the tree? Where is the red flower

in relationship to the grass? What can we say when we talk
about the flower and the grass? Do you know what? (1974:
132–133)

In the first example, the teacher attempts to remedy the indexical
character of her instruction by giving the student a sample sentence
to complete. This "complete the blank" technique is still indexical,
for it does not recover the underlying principle. It is not clear from
the teacher's statement or from her response to Ro that the "fill-in"
is an example of how it's to be done all the time. Even when the
teacher asks the next student to use a sentence, she does not give
instructions on how to do it. Thus, not only are the teacher's instructions indexical, but Mehan shows that even her remedies ex-
hibit the same property.

Having shown the indexical properties of the teacher's instructions, Mehan discusses how the students make sense of them. They
assemble contexts using a set of practices we will discuss shortly.

Pointing out the indexical properties of the teacher's instructions
is not an attempt to debunk her teaching. The point is not that the
teacher "thinks" she's doing a good job but in reality is not. The
teacher attempts to change her instructions only to find that the
remedy exhibits the same property. The indexicality of the teacher's
instructions forces us to conceive of the lesson in terms other than
a mini experiment in which the teacher is providing a stimulus,
and the student responding and being uniformly rewarded by the
teacher. Our view holds that the students and teacher are continually negotiating the lesson through their production of meaning
using interpretive practices. Our topic consists of describing those
practices.

The students Mehan studied were not limited to the instructions
as the only source of meaning. They assembled contexts made up
of elements of the setting, the teacher's tone of voice, what happened previously, and so on. These contexts were assembled by
using the following practices: imitation, cohort production, and
searching. The first practice, *imitation,* consists of copying verbal
and nonverbal examples provided by the teacher and fellow students. The following example shows that the students Ri and Je

produce their answers by imitating the teacher's example and by imitating a student's answer and the sequence.

> T: . . . Ri where is the little seed? Where is the seed?
> Ri: Under the grass.
> T: Can you say that in a sentence: the seed is under the grass?
> Ri: The seed is under the grass seed.
> T: Where is the worm Je?
> Je: Under the grass.
> T: Can you tell me in a sentence?
> Je: The worm is under the grass. (1974:115)

The first student (Ri) uses the teacher's example to produce a correct answer. The second student, Je, not only has the teacher's example to imitate but also Ri's answer, as well as the teacher's tacit acknowledgment of a correct response.

Cohort production of answers is the second practice Mehan describes. The student doesn't always have access to perfectly performed examples to imitate. More often than not, the student has access to answer fragments which are provided by the teacher and students during an interchange. These fragments are assembled into a correct answer by the student. Cohort production is the assembling of answer fragments into a correct answer across an interaction sequence. Below is an example of this practice:

> SW: Fine. Now, can you look around the room and see what you can see and tell me about something that is under something else?
> Pa: Under?
> SW: Raise your hand when you see something that is under and tell me. Ok, good, you are thinking. Stay here Je. Stay here.
> Pa: I know what's under.
> SW: Sit down at the chair. Sit down. Ok, Ro
> Ro: The rug.
> SW: Ok, tell me about it. The rug is . . .

Ro: On the floor.

Pa: Under.

SW: Under what? What is the rug under?

Pa: Under the floor

SW: The rug is under the . . .

Ro: Floor.

Ri: I'm finished Mrs. Wa.

SW: Is it under the floor?

Pa: Under the ground.

Ri: I'm finished Mrs. Wa.

SW: Is the rug under the ground?

Ri: I'm finished Mrs. Wa.

Pa: On the ground.

SW: Not now Ri. The rug is under it's on the floor. Is it under the floor? My hand is under the table. Is the rug under the floor? What is the rug under?

Je: On the floor.

Ro: It's on the floor.

SW: It's on the floor and we could also say it's above the floor couldn't we? But the rug is under something too. In some places I can see it's under the—.

Ro: Cabinet.

SW: Right, tell us now, Ro, the rug is . . .

Ro: Under the cabinet.

SW: Ok say it all by yourself now.

Ro: The rug is under the cabinet and the TV. (1974:116–117)

The third practice is *searching*. Searching is an alteration of the traditional question-answer form of questioning to produce additional information used to form an answer. Mehan points out that the traditional format of interrogation is Q-A. In searching, the student, instead of answering the teacher's question, asks a question. The teacher answers, and the student then answers the teacher's original question. The student's question results in additional cues from the teacher, cues which are used in providing a correct response.

1:1 SW: Yes. Let's take our green crayon and make a line at the bottom of your paper. Just take your green crayon and make a green line at the bottom.

2 Ci: Like that?

3 SW: Yeah.

4 Di: Now what are we going to do?

5 SW: Now take your orange crayon and make an orange worm under the green line. Pretend that's grass. Just a little wiggle. Here let me show you on this one. An orange worm.

6 Di: Hey, can you make it on yours? Yours?
  Je: <u>Under?</u>

7 SW: No, I'm watching you make yours.

8 Je: <u>Over here?</u>

9 Ci: <u>Under?</u>

10 SW: Listen, I'm going to say it just once. Make an orange worm under the green line.

12 SW: Beautiful. (1974:122)

11 Di: Like that?

The underlined sections show searching.

Imitation, cohort production of answers, and searching are practices students use to produce answers. Their use shows that the student is not confined to the teacher's stimulus-question-instruction in order to produce an answer. Imitation, cohort production, and searching are situated practices of context assembly. Through their use, ethnographic particulars like nonverbal actions of the teacher, the physical props used in the lesson, clarifications, answer fragments, other students' answers, and the teacher's explicit and tacit responses are formed into contexts for producing correct answers. Although these practices, along with the teacher's use of indexical instruction expressions, are situated practices, they tacitly rely upon the use of interpretive procedures. Imitation involves the use of the reciprocity of perspectives. Cohort production of answers involves the retrospective-prospective sense of occurrence, for in order to assemble the answer fragments, one must wait for further clarification. Searching involves the use of the retrospective-prospective sense of occurrence: The student's question results in a cue that is used to make sense of the teacher's original question. The teacher uses the Et Cetera assumption when she gives her instructions. She assumes that the students will use *more* than just the question to arrive at an answer. This assumption is borne out by the fact that she surrounds the students with contextual particulars: visual aids, other students, use of more than verbal cues, and the fact that students can consult each other and her. Unlike the question-booth format or the testing format of "do your own work, eyes on your own paper," the student is permitted to use a variety of contextual particulars to form his answer. The student-teacher practices are examples of context-specific procedures which involve the use of interpretation. Imitation, cohort production, searching, and the teacher's use of instructions rest on the kinds of processes described as the interpretive procedures. As Mehan wrote in his dissertation:

> Because the member of society must choose among the various aspects of a potentially changing cultural knowledge, it is necessary to ascribe to him a set of instructions which enables the member to invoke required aspects of cultural knowledge for the production and understanding of objects and action in his environment (1972:2).

Mehan's work is another example of how ethnomethodologists view social interaction. Social interaction, like all behavior, has indexical properties which necessitate interpretation. The interpretive process is not merely an intervening variable. It is the central process whereby social interaction is constituted (Garfinkel, 1967; Cicourel, 1968; 1973; Blumer, 1969; Wilson, 1970). I use the term *constituted* because it is through the use of interpretive procedures that social interaction as a social object is recognized by accomplished societal members. The understanding of social interaction is a product of members' interpretive methods. Through the use of the documentary method and its constitutive practices—the interpretive procedures, social types, social motives, rules, imitation, cohort production, searching, and other context-assembling practices—the substantive understanding of social interaction is accomplished

(Schutz, 1964; Garfinkel, 1967; Sudnow, 1968; Mehan, 1974; Wieder, 1974; Cicourel, 1975). The work of Sacks (1974) and his associates (Schegaloff, 1970; Schenkeln, 1972; Speier, 1973; Goldberg, 1975) shows that the sequencing of social interaction and the construction of openings, closings, and topic flow are produced through the use of members' methods. Their early work also showed that understanding was a product of members' practices. Sacks' (1968) work on "membership categorization devices is directed toward locating and describing members' methods of understanding. Thus, from one ethnomethodological perspective, every facet of social interaction (its understanding, the perception of its factual character, the perception of conversations as interaction events, and the participation in interaction) is viewed as an ongoing accomplishment (product) through the use of members' methods of interpretation. The aim of ethnomethodological research is the location and description of these methods as they are used by members of society in everyday life. All of the studies cited in this section represent the commitment to describe the use of these practices not analytically but in everyday situations.

VIII

Conclusion:
The Implications
of Ethnomethodology

The emphasis in the previous chapters was on the research topics suggested by the ethnomethodological perspective and on describing the interpretive procedures that form the phenomena of interest. In this chapter the focus is on the implications of that research. The ethnomethodological perspective is more than just a perspective from which to criticize contemporary sociology. It offers an understanding of social behavior which is too often missed.

From an autobiographical standpoint, a major implication of this perspective is that it allows one to talk about how people use rules and other elements of culture. My first introduction to ethnomethodology was via the problem of relevance: How do people decide the meaning and appropriateness of rules? Sociological theory raised the question, but instead of going on to study the interpretive work of using rules, it studied social causation instead. With the sole exceptions of Blumer's (1969) version of symbolic interactionism and early versions of labeling theory (Becker, 1963), ethnomethodology was the only perspective to make the interpretive work of using rules an explicit topic of study. My study of discretion and interpretive procedures began by having subjects verbally code transcripts of Peter McHugh's (1968) replication of Garfinkel's documentary method experiment. I described (Leiter, 1969) the coding practices used to apply the coding rules to the transcripts, which were similar to those used by Garfinkel and McHugh's subjects. I have since studied the discretionary practices of kindergarten teachers to place students into ability groups and into the next grade (Leiter 1974:17–76). I am currently studying the methods used by district attorneys to assemble a case for court. As indicated by the studies in Chapter VII, I am not the only ethnomethodologist with such an interest.

In addition to describing the practices of rule use, these studies contain some important implications for that process. The meaning of rules cannot be regarded as stable. It is constantly shifting. Rather than being independent of its context, the meaning of a rule is obtained from it (Wittgenstein, 1953:80–81). That is to say, people consult the situations in which a rule is used to discover its meaning. This is as true for lawyers working with Durkheim's ultimate social facts—formal laws—as for laymen in other everyday settings. As situations change, so does the meaning of the rule. This means that the social rules found in everyday life are not the same as those found in formal logic. The meaning of the latter is context-free, while the meaning of the former is context-dependent. Upon empirical examination of how people use rules, ethnomethodological research has shown that social rules do not have the properties of formal logical rules attributed to them by sociological theory. People make rules work through the interpretive procedures used to decide the meaning, the applicability, and the objective sense of rules.

Just as the situation is consulted to construct the meaning of a rule, the rules are used to define the meaning of a situation. In other words, rules and settings mutually elaborate each other. Studies by Zimmerman (1970:232–233) and Wieder (1974:167–214) show that depicting someone as following a set of rules is a method that people use to construct the meaning as well as the patterning of social conduct. The sociological solution to the problem of social order is a method people use to create and sustain their sense of social structure and to turn behavior into social action. This lay use of sociological explanations is not unfamiliar to sociologists. Stein and Vitisch (1968) in *Sociology on Trial,* mention it as one of the distinguishing features of social science. Using the ethnomethodological perspective, this phenomenon becomes an integral part of social behavior. We also look beyond the use of sociological concepts and their lay versions to the process of doing folk sociology.

Norms, values, and social types are not eliminated by ethnomethodology, but their status is changed. They are no longer viewed as causes of social behavior. Using the ethnomethodological perspective, they have become interpretive devices people use to make sense of other's behavior and to render their own behavior understandable to others. All of the studies on rules show that rules seem to be used less to determine what is to be done in a situation and more in deciding the meaning of what was done in a previous situation. Put another way, people seem to use rules to construct the meaningful character of behavior. Ethnomethodologists were not the first to notice this feature of rule use. Winch, in his book *The Idea of a Social Science* (1958), and Blumer in his paper "Society as Symbolic Interaction" (1969:78–90), describe this feature of rules. Ethnomethodology has extended these formulations by treating them empirically and by examining the interpretive procedures (the documentary method of interpretation) people use to employ rules in this manner. The studies of Zimmerman, Wieder, Sudnow, Emerson, and Leiter empirically describe the process of using rules as schemes of interpretation. They also link this process to the construction of social reality by showing that using rules as schemes of interpretation is a method for recognizing and portraying the patterned character of the social world.

Ethnomethodological studies of rule use are also studies of socialization. New members of a group or society must acquire a sense of social structure and the interpretive procedures to be able to locate the rules of the group (Cicourel, 1973). Wieder's (1974) study of how he "found" the convict code is a description of the interpretive work used to locate and use an oral tradition. Just as the code was told to Wieder in bits and pieces that were not connected to behavior, new members of society encounter rules in bits and pieces and must perform interpretive work to understand them. No one sits down and tells them all the rules of the game in one sitting. Furthermore, when people do describe such rules, it is usually after something has happened. The person must use the documentary method to use the bits and pieces of rules in order to locate additional rules and to decide their appropriateness.

The studies in the previous chapter also point to the pragmatic basis of rules and social types. They are grounded in the pragmatic circumstances and interests of the people who use them. Embedded in the social types used to interpret students' behavior are the practical circumstances of the teacher. The same is true of social types used in a halfway house for paroled narcotics addicts. In both settings, the social types are used to recognize situations which would alter the nature of the setting from the members' perspectives. In a sense, social types and rules are "invented" schemes used to identify such behavior. Society and its rules are reflexive products. They are created by people and endowed with the sense of being objectively real while being experienced as forces that affect people's lives.

To study rule use, ethnomethodologists must examine rules as they exist in and through people's talk. Talk has furnished sociologists with data for a long time. Through talk in interviews and experiments, people have provided sociologists with descriptions of the social world in which they live as well as their attitudes toward it. Features of the social world revealed in that talk are used by sociologists to indicate social processes and social forces. Talk, from the ethnomethodological perspective, becomes data. Now our subject becomes *how* people depict the social world. The work of describing social reality, of making it observable through talk and behavior, is the topic. As a result, talk is no longer used to convey features of the social world; rather, the work of conveying is the topic of study. Thus, ethnomethodology takes a longtime resource of social science—people's ability to depict the social world—and turns it into sociological phenomena (Zimmerman and Pollner, 1970:90–92).

A consequence of studying the construction of social reality is reexamination of the "social" of social life. In the push for scientific status, sociologists of the normative approach have by and large taken the social for granted. One of the implications of ethnomethodology is that the intersubjective or social nature of sociological phenomena (indeed, of the social world) can be viewed as a social product. Further, the methods whereby it is accomplished can be studied. Indeed, ethnomethodology goes back to examine how the social nature of social reality is created. This has a payoff for the study of social forces. In the first place, ethnomethodology is the study of an important source of the coercive power of social facts. Social facts have this power, in part, because they have the sense of being an objective reality for people. The study of how people create the factual character of the social world, then, is the study of the social basis of social facts and their coercive power. In the second place, such a study becomes a description of how social forces work in and through social interaction. Ethnomethodological studies of interpretive procedures, the use of the stock of knowledge, and the construction of social reality provide the sociologist with descriptions of how social forces operate at the level of everyday life. These studies will not help in prediction because they are context-dependent, but they do show how social phenomena touch peoples' lives and how people affect social phenomena in turn.

Ethnomethodology is also the study of social interaction. It examines social interaction at two levels: how people understand each other and how social interaction is constructed. Many of the studies of accounting practices also analyze how understanding is accomplished. For example, the study of teachers' accounts also shows how students' behavior is rendered understandable over time. Kitsuse's investigation of homosexuality and Emerson's analysis of delinquent identities in court are more than just studies in labeling deviant behavior. They are studies of how people make behavior recognizable and intelligible. In fact, such studies provide a deeper relevance for labeling theory. From the ethnomethodological perspective, labeling is not restricted to recognizing deviant behavior; it applies to all behavior. The process used to recognize and label behavior as deviant is the same process used to render behavior into social action and to perceive its patterned character.

Furthermore, ethnomethodology offers an alternative theory of social meaning. The studies reported and analyzed in this text suggest that we can understand behavior by embedding it in a context rather than by linking it to a set of referential rules. Ethnosemantics leaves out the judgmental work of the person and, like other normative theories, creates a judgmental dope. Ethnomethodological studies by Skinner, Mehan, Zimmerman, and others show that meaning is constructed by assembling a context. The context is not another version of rule-governed meaning because contexts are also subject to indefinite elaboration. Thus, contexts cannot be viewed as another set of rules; unlike rules, their meaning is not a bounded set. Meaning by context also suggests that interpretive procedures are used to decide what kind of talk is being attended to. To hear talk as a metaphor, *double entendre,* or a statement of fact, we must assemble a context through the use of interpretive procedures. Thus, when ethnomethodology refers to understanding as a practical accomplishment, the reference includes deciding the type of talk as well as its content.

The construction of face-to-face interaction forms the second level of studying social interaction from within the ethnomethodological perspective. Here the topic is the practices people use to construct everyday conversations as well as the patterned sense of conversations. The work of Harvey Sacks addresses this topic. Sacks conceives of conversations as joint products of the participants, and he examines the methods whereby people collaborate with each other to produce a conversation. Conversations are tailor-made by the participants using methods that apply to a variety of conversations. Thus, Sacks' conversational methods have the same theoretical status as interpretive procedures: They are a set of context-free methods that produce context-dependent phenomena. The properties of everyday conversations constitute a sense of social structure, for they are a description of people's experience of conversations as patterned, orderly phenomena. As such, they constitute the sense of social structure; the orderly presence of talk is used by people to assure themselves that the other person is talking about an intersubjective social world and not some private world within his head. Thus, Sacks' work is a solution to the ethnomethodological version of the problem of social order at the level of everyday conversations.

The relationship between ethnomethodology and sociological research should be discussed. The ethnomethodological perspective has been viewed as proposing a new set of methods for improving sociological research. George Homans (1977) has challenged ethnomethodologists to come forth with their new research methods. It should be clear, from reading this introduction, that ethnomethodology offers no new methods. One way of looking at ethnomethodology is to view it as the study of the research methods people use to objectify social reality. If we include sociologists as subjects of this study, then the very work of social research becomes a valuable source of data about social behavior. Social science methods rely on social behavior to work. Therefore, the practical enterprise of social research constitutes a setting for studying the use of interpretive procedures and the stock of knowledge to understand people and to construct social reality. This is not mere programmatics. Leiter (1969) took the mundane research activity of coding and turned it into a setting for studying the interpretive practices of rule use. Crowle (1971) used the postexperimental interviews of an experiment on person perception to study the reality construction in the experiment. Cicourel (1974) replicated a fertility study using survey and ethnographic methods. His study of the research project shows how interpretive procedures and the stock of knowledge are essential for making sense of survey interviews and their tabular results. Thus, the practical activity of conducting social science research is a site for studying the basic "stuff" of which social interaction is produced.

Ethnomethodology recasts not only our look at research methods but also one of our favorite concepts: the social situation. Sociologists usually refer to the social situation and situational variables to account for the variances in social conduct. Ethnomethodological research gives additional meaning to the phrase "it depends on the situation." First, the concreteness of the situation and of social forces becomes a product of people's sense making. Second, the situation, as an open-ended set of contextual particulars, becomes something that is assembled and reassembled to provide meaning to social conduct as well as to the setting in which that conduct takes place. One of the implications of reflexivity is that the setting and the behavior are mutually elaborative of each other. This sets up an unending dynamic wherein the situation truly becomes a dynamic process in social interaction. The dynamic character of the situation, according to this view, does not lie in our ability to predict which meanings will be given or what conduct will take place. When conceived of as an open-ended context of shifting particulars that are continually assembled to form a setting for social interaction, the situation truly becomes a dynamic element in social situations. The process of social interaction becomes one of continual costruction because of the dynamic nature of the background against which its meaningful character is created.

I think ethnomethodologists would agree that there is a crisis in contemporary sociology, but that the crisis lies in the fact that sociology is increasingly turning to secondary data analysis and to formalized theory construction. Both of these developments take sociology further away from the study of social interaction. Ironically it is ethnomethodology, with its subjectivistic philosophical basis and its proposal that current research problems are problems of theory and not of method, that is arguing for a return to "the field." Ethnomethodology is not armchair sociology (Filmer et al., 1972). It has an empirical bias: The only place to find the sense-making methods used to create a sense of social structure is in people's talk and behavior. There are few specifications of what those methods are, apart from some research. Zimmerman and Pollner's (1970:93–103) method of viewing the social world as an occasioned corpus does not specify what practices one will find. It is up to the researcher using this method to locate and describe the sense-making practices and to render them observable as a topic. In other words, an implicit instruction of the method is to study social interaction in everyday settings. Furthermore, this empirical bias does not involve substituting "scientific" knowledge for commonsense knowledge. Instead, the aim of ethnomethodology is to study the use of commonsense reality and the methods used to create and sustain it rather than replace it.

Bibliography

Armstrong, Edward. 1977. "Phenomenologiphobia." Presented at the American Sociological Association Meetings, Chicago.

Austin, J. L. 1961. Philosophical Papers. London: Clarendon Press.

Bales, Robert F. 1950. Interaction Process Analysis. Cambridge: Addison-Wesley.

Bar-Hillel, Jehoshua. 1954. "Indexical Expressions." Mind 63:359–379.

Becker, Howard. 1963. Outsiders. Glencoe: Free Press. 1970. Sociological Work. Chicago: Aldine.

Bernstein, Basil. 1972. "A critique of the concept of compensatory education." Pp. 135–151 in Courtney Cazden, Vera John, and Dell Hymes (eds.), Functions of Language in the Classroom. New York: Teachers College Press.

Bittner, Egon. 1967. "The police on skid row." American Sociological Review 32:699–715.

Blumer, Herbert. 1969. Symbolic Interactionism. Englewood Cliffs: Prentice-Hall.

Boese, Robert J. 1971. "Native sign language and the problem of meaning." Unpublished Ph.D. dissertation, University of California, Santa Barbara.

Briggs, Jean. 1970. Never in Anger. Cambridge: Harvard University Press.

Brown, Roger and Ursella Bellugi. 1964. "Three processes in the child's acquisition of syntax." Pp. 131–161 in Eric Lenneberg (ed.), New Directions in the Study of Linguistics. Cambridge: MIT Press.

Bruner, Jerome, Jacqueline Goodnow, and George Austin. 1956. A Study of Thinking. New York: Wiley.

Burke, Kenneth. 1962. Rhetoric of Motives. Berkeley: University of California Press.

Casteneda, Carlos. 1970. A Separate Reality. New York: Simon and Schuster. 1971. Journey to Ixlan. New York: Simon and Schuster.

Chomsky, Noam. 1965. Aspects of the Theory of Syntax. Cambridge: MIT Press.

Cicourel, Aaron V. 1964. Method and Measurement in Sociology. New York: Free Press. 1968. The Social Organization of Juvenile Justice.

New York: Wiley. 1973. Cognitive Sociology. London: Penguin. 1974. Theory and Method in a Study of Argentine Fertility. New York: Wiley.

Cicourel, Aaron and John Kitsuse. 1963. Educational Decision Makers. Indianapolis: Bobbs-Merrill.

Cohen, Albert. 1955. Delinquent Boys: The Culture of the Gang. New York: Free Press.

Coleman, James. 1968. "Review symposium on Harold Garfinkel's Studies in Ethnomethodology." American Sociological Review 33:126–130.

Coser, Lewis. 1975. "Two methods in search of a substance." American Sociological Review 40:691–700.

Crowle, Anthony. 1971. "Post experimental interviews: An experiment and sociolinguistic analysis." Unpublished Ph.D. dissertation, University of California, Santa Barbara.

Dalton, Melville. 1959. Men Who Manage. New York: Wiley.

Daudistil, Howard, William Sanders, and David Luckenbill. 1978. Criminal Justice: Situations and Decisions. New York: Holt, Rinehart and Winston.

Davis, Kingsley. 1948. Human Society. New York: Macmillan.

De Mauro, Tullio. 1967. Ludwig Wittgenstein: His Place in the Development of Semantics. New York: Humanities Press.

Denzin, Norman. 1970. "Symbolic interactionism and ethnomethodology." Pp. 259–284 in Jack Douglas (ed.), Understanding Everyday Life. Chicago: Aldine. 1974. The Research Act. Chicago: Aldine.

Douglas, Jack. 1970. "Understanding everyday life." Pp. 3–44 in Jack Douglas (ed.), Understanding Everyday Life. Chicago: Aldine.

Durkheim, Emile. 1938. Rules of the Sociological Method. New York: Free Press.

Eglin, Peter. 1974. "Leaving out the interpreter's work: A methodological critique of ethnosemantics based on ethnomethodology." Semiotica 6:23–33.

Elliot, Henry. 1974. "Similarities and differences between science and common sense." Pp. 21–26 in Roy Turner (ed.), Ethnomethodology. London: Penguin.

Emerson, Robert. 1969. Judgir ʒ Delinquents. Chicago: Aldine.

Filmer, Paul, Michael Phillipson, David Silverman, and David Walsh. 1972. New Directions in Sociological Theory. Cambridge: MIT Press.

Frideman, Neil. 1967. The Social Nature of Psychological Research: The Psychological Experiment as a Social Interaction. New York: Basic Books.

Garfinkel, Harold. 1952. "The perception of the other: A study in the problem of social order." Unpublished Ph.D. dissertation. Harvard

University, Cambridge. 1957. "Some experiments on trust." Pp. 187–238 in O. J. Harvey (ed.), Motivation and Social Interaction. New York: Ronald Press. 1967. Studies in Ethnomethodology. Englewood Cliffs: Prentice-Hall.

Garfinkel, Harold and Harvey Sacks. 1970. "On formal structures of practical activities." Pp. 338–366 in Edward Tiryakian and John McKinney (eds.), Theoretical Sociology. New York: Appleton-Century-Crofts.

Glaser, Barney and Anselm Strauss. 1966. Awareness of Dying. Chicago: Aldine.

Goffman, Erving. 1959. Presentation of Self in Everyday Life. New York: Doubleday.

Goldberg, Jo Ann. 1975. "A system for the transmission of instructions." Semiotica 14:3.

Goldthorpe, John. 1974. "A rejoinder to Benson." Sociology 8:131–133.

Goode, William and Paul Hatt. 1952. Methods in Social Research. New York: McGraw-Hill.

Gordon, Chad. 1974. Lectures on Sociological Theory. Rice University, Houston.

Goslin, David. 1966. The Search for Ability. New York: Wiley.

Gouldner, Alvin. 1963. "About the functions of bureaucratic rules." Pp. 386–396 in Joseph Litterer (ed.), Organizations: Structures and Behaviors. New York: Wiley.

Gubrium, Jaber and David Buckholdt. 1977. Toward Maturity. San Francisco: Jossey-Bass.

Gumperz, John and Jan-Petter Blom. 1971. "Social meaning in linguistic structures: Code switching in Norway." In John Gumperz and Dell Hymes (eds.), Directions in Sociolinguistics. New York: Holt, Rinehart and Winston.

Gumperz, John and Eduardo Hernandez-Chavez. 1972. "Bilingualism, bidialectalism and classroom interaction." Pp. 84–108 in Courtney Cazden, Vera John, and Dell Hymes (eds.), Functions of Language in the Classroom. New York: Appleton-Century-Crofts.

Gurwitsch, Aaron. 1964. The Field of Consciousness. Pittsburgh: Duquesne University Press.

Handel, Judith. 1972. "Learning to categorize." Unpublished Ph.D. dissertation, University of California, Santa Barbara.

Hebb, D. O. 1946. "Emotion in man and animal: An analysis of the intuitive process of recognition." Psychological Review 53:88–106.

Hill, Richard, Kathleen Crittenden, and Kathleen Stones. 1968. The Proceedings of the Purdue Symposium on Ethnomethodology. Lafayette, Indiana: Purdue Research Foundation.

Homans, George Casper. 1961. Social Behavior: Its Elementary Forms.

New York: Harcourt, Brace and World. 1977. "The myth of a value-free social science." Address to the Southwestern Sociological Association, Dallas.

Husserl, Edmund. 1960. Cartesian Meditations. The Hague: Martinus Nijhoff. 1965. Phenomenology and the Crisis of Philosophy. New York: Harper. 1969. Formal and Transcendental Logic. The Hague: Martinus Nijhoff.

Hyman, Herbert, William Cobb, Jacob Feldman, Clyde Hart, and Charles Stember. 1954. Interviewing in Social Research. Chicago: University of Chicago Press.

Inkles, Alex. 1964. What Is Sociology? Englewood Cliffs: Prentice-Hall. 1968. "Personality and social structure." Pp. 3–18 in Talcott Parsons (ed.), American Sociology. New York: Basic Books.

Jennings, Kenneth H. 1970. "Using context to decide the meaning of dictionary entries." Unpublished seminar paper, University of California, Santa Barbara.

Jennings, Kenneth and Sybillyn H. M. Jennings. 1974. "Experiments with children." Pp. 248–299 in Cicourel, et al., Language Use and School Performance. New York: Academic Press.

Kitsuse, John. 1969. "Societal reactions to deviant behavior: Problems of theory and method." Pp. 590–602 in Donald Cressey and David Ward, Delinquency, Crime and Social Process. New York: Harper. Reprinted from Social Problems, 9:247–256.

Klapp, Orin. 1962. Heroes, Villains and Fools. Englewood Cliffs: Prentice-Hall.

Labov, William. 1972. Language in the Inner City. Philadelphia: University of Pennsylvania Press.

Leiter, Kenneth C. W. 1969. "Getting it done: An ethnography of coding." Unpublished Masters thesis, University of California, Santa Barbara. 1971. "Telling it like it is: A study of teachers' accounts." Unpublished Ph.D. dissertation, University of California, Santa Barbara. 1974. "Adhocing in the schools: A study of placement practices in the kindergartens of two schools." Pp. 17–75 in Cicourel et al., Language Use and School Performance. New York: Academic Press. 1976. "Teachers' use of background knowledge to interpret test scores." Sociology of Education Journal 49:59–65.

McHugh, Peter. 1968. Defining the Situation. Indianapolis: Bobbs-Merrill.

MacKay, Robert. 1974. "Standardized testing: Objective and objectified measures of competence." Pp. 218–247 in Cicourel et al. Language Use and School Performance. New York: Academic Press.

Mannheim, Karl. 1936. Ideology and Utopia. New York: Harvest. 1952. Essays on the Sociology of Knowledge. London: Routledge and Kegan Paul.

Mead, George Herbert. 1934. Mind, Self and Society. Chicago: University of Chicago Press.

Mehan, Hugh B. 1972. "Social interaction and the problem of meaning." Unpublished Ph.D. dissertation, University of California, Santa Barbara. 1974. "Accomplishing classroom lessons." Pp. 76–142 in Cicourel et al., Language Use and School Performance. New York: Academic Press.

Mehan, Hugh B. and H. Lawrence Wood. 1975. The Reality of Ethnomethodology. New York: Wiley.

Merton, Robert K. 1967. On Theoretical Sociology. New York: Free Press.

Mills, C. Wright. 1940. "Situated actions and vocabularies of motive." American Sociological Review 5:904–913.

Mishler, Elliot. 1972. "Implications of teacher strategies for language and cognition: Observations in first-grade classrooms." Pp. 267–298 in Courtney Cazden, Vera John, and Dell Hymes (eds.), Functions of Language in the Classroom. New York: Teachers' College Press.

Nagel, E. 1961. The Structure of Science. New York: Harcourt, Brace and World.

Parsons, Talcott. 1937. The Structure of Social Action. New York: Free Press. 1951. The Social System. New York: Free Press.

Phillips, Derek. 1971. Knowledge from What. New York: Rand McNally.

Piliavian, Irving and Scott Briar. 1964. "Police encounters with juveniles." American Journal of Sociology 70:206–214.

Pollner, Melvin. 1970. "On the foundations of mundane reason." Unpublished Ph.D. dissertation, University of California, Santa Barbara.

Rosenthal, Robert and Leonore Jacobson. 1968. Pygmalion in the Classroom. New York: Holt, Rinehart and Winston.

Roth, David. 1972. "Intelligence testing as a social activity." Pp. 260–341 in Cicourel et al., Report to Department of Health, Education, and Welfare. 1974. "Intelligence testing as a social activity." Pp. 143–217 in Cicourel et al., Language Use and School Performance. New York: Academic Press.

Sacks, Harvey. 1965. Unpublished lectures at University of California, Berkeley.

Sacks, Harvey, Emmanuel Schegloff, and Gail Jefferson. 1974. "A simplest systematics for the analysis of turn taking in conversations." Language 50:696–735.

Schegaloff, Emmanuel. 1968. "Counting." Unpublished paper.

Schenkein, Jim. 1972. "Toward an analysis of natural conversation and the sense of hehh. Semiotica 6:344–377.

Scott, Marvin and Stanford Lyman. 1968. "Accounts." American Sociological Review 33:46–62.

Schutz, Alfred. 1962. Collected Papers I: The Problem of Social Reality. The Hague: Martinus Nijhoff. 1964. Collected Papers II: Studies in Social Theory. The Hague: Martinus Nijhoff. 1967. The Phenomenology of the Social World. F. Lehnert (trans.) Evanston: Northwestern University Press.

Selltiz, Clare, Lawrence Wrightsman, and Stuart Cook. 1976. Research Methods in Human Relations. New York: Holt, Rinehart and Winston.

Skinner, Thelma-Jean. 1975. "The processes of understanding in doctor-patient interaction." Unpublished Ph.D. dissertation, Rice University, Houston.

Skolnick, Jerome. 1968. Justice Without Trial. New York: Wiley.

Speier, Mathew. 1973. How to Analyze Everyday Conversations. Pacific Palisades: Goodyear.

Strong, Samuel. 1946. "Negro-white relations as reflected in social types." American Journal of Sociology 52:23–30.

Stark, Rodney, et al. 1973. Sociology Today. Del Mar: CRM Press.

Sudnow, David. 1965. "Normal crimes." Pp. 174–185 in Earl Rubington and Martin Weinberg (eds.), Deviance: The Interactionist Perspective. New York: Macmillan.

Thomas, W. I. 1951. "The four wishes and the definitions of the situation." Pp. 741–744 in Talcott Parsons et al. (eds.), Theories of Society. New York: Free Press.

Tobias, Peter and Kenneth C. W. Leiter. 1975. "Towards a redefinition of rumor." Unpublished paper, Rice University, Houston.

Turner, Ralph. 1962. "Roletaking: Process vs. conformity." Pp. 20–40 in Arnold Rose (ed.), Human Behavior and Social Processes. Boston: Houghton Mifflin.

Turner, Roy. 1972. "Some formal properties of therapy talk." Pp. 367–396 in David Sudnow (ed.), Studies in Interaction. New York: Free Press.

Vidich, Arthur and Lou Stein. 1968. Sociology on Trial. New York: Harper.

Walsh, David. 1972. "Sociology and the social world." Pp. 15–36 in Paul Filmer et al. (eds.), New Directions in Sociological Theory. Cambridge: MIT Press.

Weber, Max. 1947. The Theory of Social and Economic Organization. Glencoe: Free Press.

Whyte, William F. 1955. Street Corner Society. Chicago: University of Chicago Press.

Wieder, D. Lawrence. 1968. Lectures: Introduction to social psychology, University of California, Santa Barbara. 1969. Lectures: Introduction to social psychology, University of California, Santa Barbara. 1970.

"On meaning by rule." Pp. 107–135 in Jack Douglas (ed.), Understanding Everyday Life. Chicago: Aldine. 1974. Language and Social Reality: The Case of Telling the Convict. The Hague: Mouton. 1976. "Phenomenology and ethnomethodology." Unpublished paper, Austin.

Wieder, D. Lawrence and Don H. Zimmerman. 1976. "Regeln im Erkärungsprozess. Wissenschafllinche und Ethnowissenschafliche Soziologie." Pp. 105–129 in Elnar Weingarten, Fritz Sack, and Jim Schenkein (eds.), Ethnomethodologie Fr Bei Träge zu Einer Soziologie des Alltagshandlens. Berlin: Suhrkamp. (Rewritten version of "The recognizability of social action.")

Winch, Peter. 1958. The Idea of a Social Science. New York: Humanities Press.

Wittgenstein, Ludwig. 1953. Philosophical Investigations. New York: Macmillan.

Wootton, Anthony. 1975. Dilemmas of Discourse. New York: Meir.

Zimmerman, Don H. 1970. "The practicalities of rule use." Pp. 221–238 in Jack Douglas (ed.), Understanding Everyday Life. Chicago: Aldine. 1971. "Ethnomethodology and the problem of social order." Colloquium talk delivered at University of Southern California. 1974. "Fact as a practical accomplishment." Pp. 128–143 in Roy Turner (ed.), Ethnomethodology. London: Penguin.

Zimmerman, Don H. and Melvin Pollner. 1969. "Making sense of making sense: Explorations of members' methods for sustaining a sense of social order." Unpublished paper, University of California, Santa Barbara. 1970. "The everyday world as a phenomenon." Pp. 80–103 in Jack Douglas (ed.), Understanding Everyday Life. Chicago: Aldine.

Zimmerman, Don H. and Candace West. 1975. "Sex roles, interruptions and silence." Pp. 105–129 in B. Thorne and N. Henley (eds.), Language and Sex Difference and Domination. Rowley, Mass.: Newbury House.

Zimmerman, Don H. and D. Lawrence Wieder. 1970. "Ethnomethodology and the problem of social order: Comment to Denzin." Pp. 285–295 in Jack Douglas (ed.), Understanding Everyday Life. Chicago: Aldine.

Zimmerman, Don H. and Thomas P. Wilson. 1974. "Prospects for experimental studies of meaning structures." Paper presented at the American Sociological Association meetings.

Index